1986

POLITICAL LEADERSHIP IN AFRICA

J. CARTWRIGHT

CROOM HELM
London & Canberra

ST. MARTIN'S PRESS
New York

© 1983 J. Cartwright
Croom Helm Ltd, Provident House, Burrell Row,
Beckenham, Kent BR3 1AT

British Library Cataloguing in Publication Data

Cartwright, J.
   Political leadership in Africa.
   1. Leadership 2. Africa — Politics
  and government
   I. Title
   306'2'0960   JO3121.A56A/
   ISBN 0-7099-0751-6

All rights reserved. For information write:
St. Martin's Press, Inc., 175 Fifth Avenue, New York, N.Y. 10010
Printed in Great Britain
First published in the United States of America in 1983

ISBN 0-312-62314-3

Printed and bound in Great Britain by
Biddles Ltd, Guildford and King's Lynn

CONTENTS

TABLES

ACKNOWLEDGEMENTS

     Although the actual writing of a book is a
solitary occupation, few scholars can complete their
work without drawing on a wide range of colleagues,
friends, acquaintances and others for help in the
form of critiques, technical aid, and above all,
inspiration and encouragement. In preparing this
work, I received encouragement, ideas, constructive
criticism and personal hospitality from many aca-
demics and other individuals, including: Kwabena
Bame, Emil Baran, Barry Bartmann, Dick Conlin, Linda
Freeman, Mark Graesser, Ronnie Gruhn, Owen Kalinga,
Rob Martin, Esrom Maryogo, Gordon Means, Gelase
Mutahaba, Cran Pratt, Mary Hrabik Samal, Richard
Sandbrook, Ozzie and Sharon Schmidt, Richard Stanley,
Christine Troughton and Richard Vernon, to all of
whom I express my thanks, and the usual exoneration
from any responsibility for the interpretations or
errors herein.
     I also wish to thank the Social Science and
Humanities Research Council of Canada for funding a
major trip to Africa in 1978 to allow me to see for
the first time some of the countries I wished to use
for my case studies, and the University of Western
Ontario for providing additional research support
whenever I needed it.
     Special thanks are due to our Departmental
typists, and especially Janet Horowitz and Jo Clark
for meeting the demanding challenge of preparing the
final camera-ready copy. Above all, I wish publicly
to thank Rosemary for her meticulous and critical
editing of my final drafts and for her constant
support and encouragement, all leavened with patience,
humour and love.
                                   London, Ontario

A NOTE ON CURRENCIES

Throughout this book I have used the U.S. dollar as the unit of currency, since it seemed desirable to standardize units for comparative purposes, and the dollar was generally used in international financial statistical sources. For each country, I have given the name of the currency and its official rate of exchange with the U.S. dollar as cited in the IMF International Financial Statistics monthly issues. However, it should be borne in mind that official rates of exchange sometimes bore little relationship to the (black) market value of the currencies, as was most clearly illustrated by the Ghanaian cedi after 1965 and the Uganda shilling in the 1970s.

The currencies and their values in relation to the U.S. dollar, for the periods I have dealt with, are:

Ghana: Ghanaian pound to 1965, = $2.80; thereafter, cedi = $1.17 to 1967.

Ivory Coast, Senegal (and Guinea to 1960): CFA franc = $0.00571 to 1956, $0.00408 to 1965, and thereafter fluctuating from $0.0036 in 1969 to $0.00498 in 1979.

Tanzania: Tanzanian shilling = $0.1399 to 1974, and thereafter in the range $0.1201 to $0.1222.

Uganda: Uganda shilling = $0.1399 to 1972. Official rate of exchange then ranged from $0.1449 in 1973 to $0.1203 in 1976.

Ethiopia: Birr, or Ethiopian dollar = $0.40 to 1970, and $0.48 from 1971 to 1979.

INTRODUCTION

In January 1964 some 2,000 men of the
Tanganyikan Army mutinied for higher pay. For five
days, until British troops intervened at the
Tanganyika government's request and disarmed the
mutineers, Julius Nyerere and his Cabinet were
powerless in the face of this threat, while the
thousands of members of his TANU party, along with
the rest of the civilian population, simply stood by
and watched. Nine years later, the same Julius
Nyerere told a TANU conference that all of
Tanzania's rural population should be moved into
villages, and in the next four years, some 11
million people were uprooted from their ancestral
homesteads and settled on new village sites. Although some force was used, Nyerere rightly observed
that "11 million people could not have been moved by
force in Tanzania; we do not have the capacity for
such forced movement."[1]
        In 1950 Kwame Nkrumah called for Positive
Action in the form of a general strike against the
Gold Coast colonial government, and work in Accra
and other cities came to a halt, despite the government's declaration of a state of emergency and its
arrest of all the CPP and trade union leaders. In
1961, a new tax levy imposed by Kwame Nkrumah's
government led to a strike by the railway union and
other workers in Sekondi-Takoradi and the railway
workers stayed out despite a direct promise by
Nkrumah himself to negotiate grievances. It was
only when the President threatened the massive use of
force against the strikers that they returned to work.
        These four episodes show dramatically how much
a leader's influence can expand or contract according to time and circumstances, and how at its peak
this influence can have a considerable effect on
what happens to a state. Suppose, for example that

1

Nkrumah had not been able to rally popular support for his movement in 1950, and the CPP had subsequently faded from the scene? Or at the same time the French repression next door in the Ivory Coast had so embittered Felix Houphouet-Boigny that he had organized armed resistance to French rule? Or if in Tanzania in 1973-1976 villagization had engendered sufficient anger to produce a civil war and a military coup? These and countless other events in recent African history illustrate the main argument of this book, that an individual political leader can have a substantial effect in shaping the evolution of almost any African state.

The very fact of most African states' newness, and the consequent fluidity of their political systems, has given great scope for leaders to take them in a wide variety of directions. Their fragile institutions and weak civic culture have paradoxically both limited what a leader can do and at the same time enhanced his power. They limit a leader in that with few institutions or common values, the contact between a leader and his people is restricted to a limited range of channels, and is often infrequent or non-existent. Yet at the same time this lack of strong institutions and of widely shared values affecting the new polity gives a leader some scope, if he so wishes, to persuade people to accept new institutions and values that he favours. Thus we see attempts at instilling a variety of new attitudes, from the strong commitment to personal acquisition of Felix Houphouet-Boigny or Hasting Kamuzu Banda to the cooperative and egalitarian goals of Julius Nyerere or Samora Machel. By the same token, a leader can try to shape political institutions in ways consonant with his own political philosophy. If he can establish sufficient popular support, he has a chance of persuading people to accept both new values and new political structures which will outlast his own rule. It can still be argued, in fact, that the best hope for African political institutions to acquire enduring strength is through a widely respected leader diffusing his own personal popularity over them.[2]

However, if we look across the states of Africa two decades after the "independence explosion," it is very clear that most rulers do not have this popular support, nor do most of them even try to rule in the interests of the people of their state. The predominant form of rule today in Africa has aptly been called "personal rule," a system whereby the head of state and his immediate hangers-on pursue only their own private good, while ignoring the interests and concerns of the great mass of the population.[3] Quite a number of rulers have managed to use such systems to keep themselves in power for long periods of time, at least so long as they can keep their armed forces loyal. Rule by force, or at least rule with no real consent given by the governed, has established itself firmly as the prevailing pattern.

Why then concern ourselves about leadership, about persuading others to do one's bidding willingly rather than coercing them into obedience? My central contention is that to achieve any lasting improvement in the polity, whether it be economic development, a sense of nationhood, or an equitable society, a leader must obtain popular support for his goals, and to do this requires leadership. The superiority of persuasion over coercion is indicated in a number of areas. For example, in the economic field, there have been countless cases both under colonial regimes and in independent states, where attempts to force farmers to produce particular crops have been thwarted by mass passive resistance, whereas when incentives have been offered that make growing the crop beneficial to the farmers, they have given a strong positive response. In the political sphere we find considerable evidence that regimes which incorporate divergent interests in their ruling elites, and which show a degree of responsiveness to popular attitudes in the selection of leaders and the pursuit of policies, have been more stable than ones which suppressed all criticism.[4] The trend to "departicipation" that had been pronounced in the decade after independence in most states has begun to reverse itself, as regimes learn that the costs and the risks of continuing coercion may outweigh the effort required for persuasion.

Nevertheless, to provide leadership in contemporary Africa is not easy. Any African leader pursuing goals that will benefit his countrymen faces a daunting array of obstacles imposed by nature, by social formations and attitudes within his state, and by other states. Furthermore, the leader's very desire to achieve specific goals can tempt him to short-circuit leadership in favour of force.

It is when a leader first comes to power, before he has disillusioned his followers by compromise or by coercion, that he has the greatest opportunity to persuade them to support him voluntarily. I will argue that the best chance for new

leaders to exercise leadership in recent African
history came during the period of peaceful decolonization, when leaders could establish credentials as
champions of all the people of their territory, yet
not have to cope either with the animosities
stirred by a violent struggle, or with a bankrupt
economy. Occasionally other governments collapsed
in circumstances that allowed new leaders some
scope to try persuasion, as for example in Congo-
Leopoldville in 1965, in Nigeria in 1966, or in
Ethiopia in 1974, but in the post-independence
period there was rarely the overwhelming consensus
behind a new leader that had marked the period of
decolonization. I therefore am focussing largely
upon leaders who emerged during the period of decolonization, and am seeking to answer three questions.
First, at what stage in their careers could they be
said to be exercising leadership? Second, how did
they maintain their appeal over the years, or more
commonly, at what point and through what actions
did it begin to fade? Third, what kind of long-
term effects did these leaders have upon their
countries, and to what extent could these effects be
attributed to leadership?

In exploring these questions of how much effect
African leaders have had upon their states and the
extent to which they have exercised leadership, I
will look first at Africa in general terms and
second at a series of specific leaders. Chapters 1
to 4 examine the nature and role of leadership in
African states before and after independence.
Chapter 1 considers in broad terms the constraints
faced by African leaders at independence: the
economic ties, the popular aspirations and the political structures that they inherited. Chapter 2
explores the nature of leadership and its relationship to coercion, and examines systematically the
range of constraints that limit the choices open to
a leader. Chapter 3 looks at the pattern by which
African leaders emerged during the movement toward
independence, particularly the ease with which
Britain and France granted independence and the
exclusive concentration upon this goal, while
Chapter 4 considers the alternative strategies for
economic development pursued since independence, the
weakness of governments' control, and the lack of
constraints against leaders relying on coercion to
keep themselves in power.

The specific case studies I have chosen are
Ghana under Nkrumah, the Ivory Coast, Senegal,
Tanzania, Guinea, Uganda under both Obote and Amin,

4

and Ethiopia under both the Emperor Haile Selassie and Major Mengistu. In selecting these particular case studies, I have been guided by several considerations. First, I wanted cases in which one individual clearly dominated the polity. Second, I wanted cases where there were enough sources available that I could make reasonably well-informed judgments on the significance of a leader's actions, which meant that most episodes considered had to be several years back in time. This combination of requirements eliminated some interesting cases, such as Mozambique since independence, or the role of General Lamizana in Upper Volta. A shortage of information was also a major consideration in eliminating two other military leaders who had replaced discredited regimes and subsequently produced major transformations in their countries, General Siad Barre of Somalia and Col. Muammar Gaddafi of Libya. Finally, I wanted a balance among the range of different goals pursued by leaders, and among the routes different leaders took to power. My case studies thus include four accommodationist leaders (Houphouet-Boigny, Senghor, Haile Selassie and Obote), four who attempted radical transformation (Nkrumah, Touré, Nyerere and Mengistu) and one who defies classification (Amin). Five of these leaders came to power with a heroic stature gained during the anti-colonial struggle, one (Haile Selassie) had enjoyed an almost sacral status as a monarch, two (Amin and Mengistu) came to power through military coups which made them heroes among some sectors of the populace, and one (Obote) came to power largely by default. No doubt other scholars would have picked other leaders for examination, but this group does serve to cover a wide range of traits and degrees of success.

Lastly, in a concluding chapter I try to draw out some common threads from the successes and failures of these leaders, and to argue that while the opportunities for a leader to exercise persuasion successfully are likely to remain severely restricted for the foreseeable future, there is nevertheless some limited scope for such leaders to emerge. It is hard to be optimistic about Africa's propects today, given the structure of the world's political economy, the ecological constraints, the tendency for costly unforeseen consequences to arise even from what seem to be sound choices of policy, and the likelihood that without effective domestic constraints, a leader will probably pursue personal interests that are detrimental to his polity. Nevertheless, there does seem to be at least a slight possibility for some

African states to improve their situations, and the leadership of an astute and dedicated leader may be the best means of bringing a state through these hazards.

NOTES

1. Julius K. Nyerere, The Arusha Declaration Ten Years After (Government of Tanzania, Dar es Salaam, 1977), p. 42.

2. This argument was first put forward by David Apter in The Gold Coast in Transition (Princeton University Press, Princeton, N.J. 1955). Although Apter's contention that Nkrumah's "charismatic legitimacy" would legitimate Parliamentary institutions in Ghana proved ill-founded, his general point could be supported by looking at cases such as Kenya under Jomo Kenyatta and the Ivory Coast under Felix Houphouet-Boigny.

3. The patterns of "personal rule" have very recently been analysed in detail in Robert H. Jackson and Carl Rosberg, Personal Rule in Black Africa: Prince, Autocrat, Prophet, Tyrant (University of California Press, Berkeley, Los Angeles and London, 1982).

4. See Ruth B. Collier, "Parties, coups and authoritarian rule: patterns of political change in tropical Africa", Comparative Political Studies, 11, 1 (April 1978), pp. 62-93, and Naomi Chazan, "The New Politics of Participation in Tropical Africa", Comparative Politics, 14, 2 (January 1982), pp. 169-90.

Chapter One

THE ENVIRONMENT FOR LEADERS: COLONIAL LIMITS
AND OPPORTUNITIES

        Most African leaders of the past two decades
have ruled territories which had been colonies of
European states for the previous sixty years. This
colonial period set the major limits - and also
created the basis for major opportunities - within
which present-day leaders can pursue their goals.
I shall look in this chapter at the key limits and
opportunities arising out of Africa's natural
features, its pre-colonial societies, and the
economic, social and political aspects of colonial
rule.
        First, we should note those basic natural
features that provide a permanent setting within
which any human activity must take place. Africa
is the second largest continent, and also the
second driest, with the Sahara Desert in the north
and the Kalahari in the south, while between the
deserts lies a horseshoe of sparsely treed savanna,
running through West Africa, down through Kenya and
Tanzania and back across Angola. The only "jungle",
in the sense of heavy rain forest, covers a relatively narrow belt along the west coast and down into
Zaire. Whether one is flying over Senegal or
Tanzania, Nigeria or Zambia, one is struck by how
much of Africa is grassland rather than forest.
These dry areas are susceptible to drought and
cannot produce much of an agricultural surplus, thus
limiting the possibility of a substantial non-
agricultural population.
        Though it was the cradle of human life, Africa
has always been sparsely populated; there have been
few areas suffering from severe shortages of land
outside the colonies of white settlement, Kenya
and Rhodesia, where Africans were excluded from
large tracts. Some areas, such as eastern Nigeria
and Ruanda-Burundi, seem always to have had high

populations and others have become crowded in recent decades as infant mortality rates fell; but there is nothing comparable to the population densities of south and east Asia. One historical implication of this lack of crowding was that pre-colonial rulers or dominant classes could not exercise power based on land-holding; the conditions which created feudalism in Europe did not exist.[1] The ability to move away from an overly oppressive rule, coupled with a fairly egalitarian weapons technology (spears and bows could be made and distributed more widely than muskets or rifles) kept rulers from building too powerful a system of control over their subjects, though we should not infer from this that Africa was made up of egalitarian, classless societies. This situation did serve, however, to put a limit on the size and permanence of states.

The pre-colonial states of Africa nevertheless varied greatly. They ranged in size from the nomadic bands of Bushmen and Tuareg and the autonomous villages of the Kikuyu, to the great Sahelian empires of Mali and Songhai, or the later kingdoms of Ashanti and the Kongo. Political control could be scattered among all the adult menfolk, as in the Ibo, or concentrated in the hands of a single divinely-anointed ruler, as among the Hausa. Usually, however, people enjoyed some checks on the power of their ruler. It might be the power to move away, as noted above, or it might include the right to remove him from office if he broke the generally understood rules of conduct. Most political systems were fairly conservative, in that they usually justified their practices by appeals to generations of tradition, but states were constantly splitting, re-combining, and launching out as new entities, according to the fortunes of migration, trade and war. Compared to most of Europe and Asia, there was little basis for Africans to develop a strong identification with any large political unit. The problem of "national integration" facing post-independence African leaders was a more fundamental one than that of changing peoples' commitments from one large "nation" to another; it involved getting people to shift their basic allegiance from a town-sized to a country-sized political unit.

The colonial era was brief; in the 1960s, most African leaders or their fathers had been born before the Europeans first imposed their formal rule. However, the impact of colonial rule in Africa permanently changed all the continent's major political, economic and social patterns. More than any other part of the Third World, Africans had to adjust to the pressures imposed by alien rule. Unlike the Latin American Indians, they did not fuse with European colonists to form a new cultural synthesis; they retained most of their own social organizations and identities as distinct peoples. But far more than in southern or eastern Asia, they accepted the denigration of their own cultures and the Europeans' assumption of superiority.

Two factors were particularly important in producing such a thorough-going colonization of Africa: the slave trade, and the imposition of colonial rule at the height of European technological advantage over the rest of the world. The slave trade was not, as some critics have argued, a fatal or even severely debilitating haemorrhage of Africa's able-bodied, productive workers.[2] But it did slow down indigenous economic development, and at the same time it helped to create in both European and African minds an attitude that Europeans were in some critical way superior to Africans, thus providing a justification for the latter to be "saved" through colonialism. In the years after ending the slave trade, the Europeans perfected a number of civilizing instruments - the missionary, the rifle, the rocket (very effective against flammable grass roofs) and the Maxim gun. The overwhelming power they were able to display, and their perceived readiness to use it, greatly facilitated their conquest of Africa with a startlingly small number of troops, and allowed them a subsequent half century of political control with little in the way of physical resistance.

The colonial period had major impacts upon the economic, social and political patterns of African societies. The most persistent economic impact was the way in which Africans were drawn into the money economy through exchanging a limited number of raw materials for the European's manufactured goods. Europeans opened up a number of mines and some plantations, obtaining African labour partly by the lure of cash wages to buy trade goods, partly by requiring that Africans pay their taxes in cash, and when all else failed, by conscripting Africans for forced labour in their enterprises. African entrepreneurs themselves grew most of the agricultural products for export; Ghana's cocoa farmers, who began bringing cocoa beans for sale before the British were even aware they had planted cocoa trees, provide the most famous success story, but in

9

most of West Africa and some parts of East Africa as well, many small farmers grew cash crops as well as their own food supplies, thus accustoming themselves to the largely imported manufactures that a cash income allowed them to buy.

The expansion of bulk trade stimulated the growth of ports and other urban centres, and these soon began to exert a strong attraction on the younger men who chafed under their elders' restrictions in the rural milieu. A wide range of jobs opened up, even for the unskilled and illiterate: dockworkers and others to move goods, construction workers for buildings and roads, street cleaners and sanitation workers - the list seemed endless. Higher in prestige were those jobs requiring some degree of skill or literacy: taxi-drivers, messengers, tally clerks, and various record-keepers. Then there were the opportunities for self-employed traders, selling food, small goods, and personal services. Not everyone who went to the city could find a job, however; some lived by petty thievery, while most of the unemployed sponged as long as they could off relatives and friends. Yet even for those who could not find work, there was still the excitement, the sense of adventure, of something always happening.[3] By independence, all African leaders had to cope with the fact that the goal of many young people was to get away from farming to the greater opportunities perceived in the cities, even though these "opportunities" already were becoming an illusion.

The growth of this support economy also produced an incentive to spread European-style education throughout Africa. Traditional African education for both men and women had been a matter of inculcating practical skills for village living and an appreciation of traditional beliefs. The Europeans, even the missionaries whose primary objective was to win converts, offered the more broadening skills of literacy and numeracy, which the student could use in diverse situations and build upon later in life. To ambitious young Africans, European education seemed to hold the key to explaining how Europeans enjoyed so much power over them. The most powerful Europeans were the administrators who seemed to spend their time writing memos to each other, so not surprisingly most Africans sought the kind of training that would qualify them for white-collar jobs. When European educators tried to provide a more technical education or to relate the curriculum more to African conditions, they were frequently criticized for trying to foist "inferior" education on their charges. To many Africans, the only worthwhile education was that copied exactly from the metropolitan curriculum.

The desire of Africans for an education was indicated by the fact that even in the 1930s, there were approximately 2.4 million children in school in all the colonies, out of a total population of 84 million. Even more striking as an indicator of Africans' desire for schooling is the fact that 1.4 million of these children were attending schools which received no support from the colonial governments.4 What calibre of education they were receiving in these schools was uncertain; often the African teachers' own grasp of their materials was very shaky, with the result that a great deal of rote memorization took place. Nevertheless, an impressive list of intellectuals managed to emerge from the colonial-era schools. Dr. Kenneth Dike, the Nigerian historian, Leopold Senghor, who was a poet of renown in French before he began his Senegalese political career, and Dr. Kofi Busia, who first gained fame as a sociologist, illustrated the fact that great talent could arise from this system, despite its limitations.

By the late 1950s, the numbers of children receiving some schooling had increased sharply. The Economic Commission for Africa found that no less than 12 of 34 sub-Saharan African territories claimed at least 50% of their children were in primary schools, while only eight (all in the poverty-stricken Sahelian belt) claimed less than 20% enrolment. However, the figure dropped dramatically for secondary schooling, with only two countries claiming as much as two percent.5 Clearly many children were dropping out of school before they had attained functional literacy or other skills, but having had this minimal exposure to schooling, they often considered themselves fit for a life better than the farming that still was the occupation for most of their compatriots. Like the cities, education created expectations among youth that were almost impossible to meet. Yet somehow post-independence leaders would have to try to meet or deflect these expectations by providing the youth with opportunities commensurate with their perceived entitlement, or face their anger and disillusionment.

Education also played a more direct role in bringing about the political upheaval of the nationalist movement. In the British and French territories, those who struggled up to the higher levels of education (and in British West Africa by 1939 those who had been abroad for training in professions, such as the law, that offered good opportunities for Africans, numbered in the hundreds) were exposed to the incongruity between the colonial powers' professed belief in democratic participation, and the arbitrary and authoritarian nature of the colonial regimes. Education provided a whetstone on which nationalists could sharpen their claim that Africans ought to control their own destiny.

The material out of which the claim was forged, however, came from a number of levels of African society. For the educated minority, racial discrimination, the refusal by the colonial authorities to let them enjoy the jobs, salaries, housing and other privileges to which they felt their educational attainments entitled them, was the most directly infuriating aspect of colonial rule. For the would-be businessman, the authorities' tendency to favour large metropolitan firms for all types of licencing, access to labour, and other aids available through the political system, was galling. But it was the ordinary farmer in the bush who suffered most from the arbitrary nature of colonial administration, sometimes at the hands of European administrators but far more often at the hands of his own chief, his erstwhile "father" and protector, who now was compelled to carry out the Europeans' orders on pain of losing his post. Sometimes the farmer would be ordered, "for his own good", to cultivate a particular crop, or till his field in a particular way, even though he knew from experience that some other crop or method was better for him. Always he would find new taxes being levied on him, and sometimes the chief or the tax collector would build a fine new house shortly afterwards; but if he dared complain to the European district officer, he might find himself jailed as a "trouble-maker" and certainly would find his chief taking revenge on him. Sometimes, too, he might be seized and taken away to do roadwork or labour on Europeans' plantations, usually under very harsh conditions; here again it was well to keep on the good side of his chief, since the chief could generally decide who among his people would be singled out for forced labour.

All these actions under colonial rule, and

12

the fact that colonial authorities had so much more
power than previous rulers to enforce their edicts,
left a legacy of deep suspicion and distrust of
"the Government." The prudent man lay low when
government officials appeared; even an innocent
census question about one's children or cattle or
crops might be the prelude to a new tax. For their
part, government officials tended to build up the
view that most rural dwellers were obtuse or
evasive, and responded much better to the threat of
force than to persuasion.[6] Despite the overlay of
representative institutions which was attached to
each colony during the period of decolonization,
the reality of government for most Africans was
authoritarian power wielded in an unpredictable
and capricious manner.

For any African leader seeking to use government as the instrument through which to induce
people to change their way of life, this attitude
of suspicion and distrust toward government was a
major obstacle. For leaders who saw government's
role as a minimal one of keeping the peace while development proceeded through private initiatives,
popular suspicion of government was not a severe
handicap. But since most development involving a
major transformation of society or a substantial
role for Africans rather than foreigners would
inevitably require government action, this legacy
posed a problem for any African leader who sought
major changes involving African control.

The world economic boom after World War II
brought a marked increase in prosperity to most
African territories. Growing world demand for
edible oils helped Senegal's peanuts and Dahomey's
palm oil, coffee drinkers enriched the planters
of the Ivory Coast and Uganda, smokers and tea
drinkers bought Nyasaland's tobacco and tea crops.
The fact that each colony typically relied on one
or two main export crops, and thus was very vulnerable not only to fluctuations in world demand but
also to competition from other growers and from
substitutes, was not as yet an obvious problem.
Nor had the fact that most products left the
colonies in unprocessed form, and thus took with
them to the industrialized countries all the jobs
in weaving cotton cloth, making chocolate bars and
soaps, or transforming iron ore, bauxite and
copper into countless manufactured products, as
yet begun to concern many would-be leaders. The
colonial governments stepped up their encouragement
to "progressive" African farmers, built more roads

and harbours, and increased school and health
facilities at the same time as they undertook constitutional changes. The prosperity from export
sales created some prospects for local light manufacturing in the richer colonies, such as Nigeria,
the Gold Coast, the Ivory Coast, Senegal and Kenya,
and the long-established expatriate firms began to
move into this area.[7]

    But Africa remained overwhelmingly agricultural.
Even a state such as Zambia, which depended almost
entirely upon copper mining for its export earnings,
still employed in 1968 only 50,000 men in mining
against 800,000 in agriculture.[8] For all of Africa
in 1960, the World Bank noted that every country
except South Africa had more than 50% of its labour
force engaged in agriculture, and 27 of 38 had more
than 75% so engaged. (By contrast, only one of 22
Latin American and Caribbean countries, and only 10
of 22 South and East Asian counties, had more than
75% of their labour force in agriculture.)[9] The
Economic Commission for Africa estimated that in
the early 1960's, "well over half" of all agricultural production was for personal subsistence
rather than cash sales.[11]

    The continent also was poor. The majority of
states had per capita Gross National Products of
less than $100 (US) by independence and outside of
South Africa, only Libya, Tunisia, Ghana and Senegal
had as much as $200 per capita in the early 1960s.[11]
Some of the dry land-locked states such as Upper
Volta, Niger and Chad simply did not have any
mineral or agricultural products the rest of the
world was willing to pay much for. Niger, for
example, had total annual exports of about $12
million, or less than $5.00 per capita, in the early
1960s; the Ivory Coast, by contrast, had about $178
million worth of exports, or $52.00 per capita.[12]
But even comparatively rich states like the Ivory
Coast and Ghana still were far from either the
export diversification or the base of human skills
that could allow them to expand their prosperity.

    Many Africans' perspectives were also limited
by the fact that they still lived in what has aptly
been termed the "pedestrian society," a society in
which the horizon of their personal experience was
set by the furthest village they could walk to and
back from in a single day.[13] To be sure, the opening of new roads which allowed lorries to penetrate
much of "the bush," the wage labour in the mines
and cities, and even forced labour and wartime conscription into the army, had all allowed growing

14

numbers of individuals to see for themselves what other parts of their territory were like, and what problems they shared with other people. The roads also helped the flow of information along the "bush telegraph," the news from urban centres and other areas carried by lorry drivers and other travellers to the most remote villages. Despite the scarcity of newspapers, and of a literate audience for them even before the cheap transistor radio brought mass communication in the early 1960s, word of mouth had disseminated a good deal of information about what colonial governments were doing, though not necessarily with the interpretation they would have approved. Nevertheless, until people were ready to see their own experiences in a broader perspective their concerns tended to be concentrated upon their own village and its immediate surroundings.

The growth of cities and increased movement of people throughout the colonial territory had the further effect of stimulating the political problem of "tribalism," which was to force most post-independence leaders into very delicate balancing acts in allocating jobs, resources and other benefits. New arrivals in the city generally would seek out established residents who shared their language and customs, and even long-time residents looked to "tribal" associations to provide loans, unemployment insurance and contacts with the government. All of this helped forge a "tribal" identity, bringing together all those who saw advantages in emphasizing a shared common language and common customs. But because there were never enough jobs, loans and other benefits, and later because vote-seekers looked for easy ways of assembling blocks of support, many conflicts came to run along "tribal" lines.

In rural areas, people were less conscious of such an abstract and large-scale entity as "tribe," but there too ethnic competition could develop. As people travelled from their homes to other parts of the colony, they could see areas that were much richer than theirs, and could come to wonder whether they were getting a fair share of goods from the central government. Such benefits as civil service jobs were primarily of concern to the upwardly mobile educated elites, but they could arouse their fellow tribesmen to support them by pointing to disparities in the numbers of schools, miles of roads and other benefits which could go to one or another area. A further force creating ethnic conflict arose when one group perceived another group as threatening its fundamental cultural and religious values, or even its physical survival. Nigeria's long and tragic history of ethnic conflict gained its major impetus when Yoruba leaders managed in preparation for the 1951 elections to rouse their people to the alleged threat of "Ibo domination" posed by the National Council of Nigeria and the Cameroons, and Hausa-Fulani leaders in the north campaigned against control by "infidel" southerners. While some ethnic conflicts, such as that between Tutsi and Hutu in Rwanda and Burundi, had been going on long before the colonial era, most were unleashed by the urbanization and economic development that occurred under colonial rule.

The colonial powers' superior force could hold ethnic conflicts in check most of the time, and most Africans could subordinate their ethnic differences to the shared goal of getting rid of the colonial ruler. But once the end of colonial rule was in sight, keeping ethnic conflicts from erupting became a major concern in most states, adding a very substantial complication to the problem of allocating resources effectively.

In summary, then, any would-be inheritors of the colonial mantle faced several major constraints. They faced, first of all, a lack of wealth in their territories, and a shortage of the skills necessary to create this wealth. Yet at the same time they had to cope with many demands for more wealth, including the desire of elites for imported consumer goods, and also the more widespread desire to escape the bush and enjoy the excitement and affluence of the cities. This kind of problem, how to reconcile the means available for development with popular desires, was not unique to Africa, to be sure. But further more specifically African constraints converged to complicate the task of leaders. The lack of any strong sense of national community, which forced leaders to engage in a careful balancing act in allocating those few resources they possessed, stemmed from three main roots. First, the fact that most pre-colonial political units had been small meant that there was rarely a unifying pre-colonial tradition to which leaders could appeal. Second, the suspicion of government as alien and arbitrary made it very difficult for any leader to mobilize popular enthusiasm for a government-led developmental effort. Third, the growth of ethnic awareness as a result of increased

communication and unevenly distributed development
meant that leaders had to devote special attention
to balancing different groups' claims.

These problems however, did not stop the movement toward independence which the colonial powers
had unintentionally begun. By developing the mines,
getting Africans to grow crops, and training them
in a range of activities intended to benefit the
Europeans economically, the European powers
developed the Africans' ability to operate modern
economic and political structures. As they came to
understand the basis of the Europeans' power, and
to realize how much benefit the Europeans were getting for themselves compared to the Africans' share,
the Africans began to demand changes. However,
they did disagree among themselves on how the
system should be changed. Some groups, such as
white-collar workers, realized their privileged
position depended on continuing the kinds of jobs
the Europeans had introduced, while others wished a
return to a less monetized economy. Some vulnerable
minorities, and some inhabitants of poorer regions,
feared they might even be worse off under the rule
of other Africans. These conflicts needed to be
contained by any would-be leader. But before looking at how leaders emerged, and what they could do
in the African context, I should clarify what I
mean by "leaders" and "leadership" and consider how
we can most effectively examine the relationship
between a leader and the people of his country.

NOTES

    1. See Jack Goody, Technology, Tradition and
the State in Africa, (Oxford University Press,
London, 1971), pp. 29-31.
    2. Two well-known presentations of the argu-
ment that slavery drained Africa of needed man-
power are Basil Davidson, Black Mother, (Gollancz,
London, 1961) and Walter Rodney, How Europe
Underdeveloped Africa (Bogle-L'Overture, London,
1972), pp. 103-112. For data suggesting that the
drain was not so severe, see Philip Curtin, The
Atlantic Slave Trade: A Census (University of
Wisconsin Press, Madison, Wisc., 1969). A
restrained summary indicating how little we really
know of the effects is contained in a pamphlet by
P.E.H. Hair, The Atlantic Slave Trade and Black
Africa (The Historical Society, London, 1978), pp.
25-32.
    3. An excellent overview is in Thomas Hodgkin,

Nationalism in Colonial Africa (New York University Press, New York, 1957), pp. 63-83. The flavour of city life in this period is captured in the novels of Cyprian Ekwensi, such as People of the City and Jagua Nana.

4. Figures from Lord Hailey, An African Survey (Oxford University Press, London, 1938), table opp. p. 1308.

5. Melville Herskovits and Mitchell Harwitz, Economic Transition in Africa (Routledge and Kegan Paul, London, 1964), p. 273, Table 12.5.

6. On this uneasy relationship between rural dwellers and officials, see John Dunn and A.F. Robertson, Dependence and Opportunity: Political Change in Ahafo (Cambridge University Press, London, 1973), esp. pp. 157-73.

7. Anthony Hopkins, An Economic History of West Africa (Longmans, London, 1973), p. 276.

8. Richard Sklar, Corporate Power in an African State (University of California Press, Berkeley, 1975), p. 127. However, there were an additional 270,000 wage workers in other non-agricultural occupations.

9. Calculated from World Development Indicators (World Bank, Washington, 1978), Table 14. The World Bank data excludes countries with populations of less than one million.

10. Economic Commission for Africa, Survey of Economic Conditions in Africa (United Nations, 1968), p. 58.

11. Andrew Kamarck, The Economics of African Development, Praeger, New York, 1967), p. 251.

12. Africa Report (November 1963), pp. 25, 32.

13. See Norman H. Miller, "Political Mobility and the Pedestrian Society", in Canadian Journal of African Studies, 4,1 (Winter 1970), pp. 17-31.

Chapter Two

THE NATURE OF LEADERSHIP

"Leadership" is a phenomenon which we all think we can recognize, but which becomes elusive and changeable when we try to analyse it. The essence of leadership is the ability to persuade others to comply voluntarily with one's wishes. When we try to determine what creates this ability to persuade, however, we enter a nebulous region in which subjective attitudes toward a personality and toward symbols, perceptions of effectiveness, and other elements equally hard to pin down, play major roles. The study of leadership has been largely neglected by modern social scientists, who for both methodological and ideological reasons have tended to concentrate on mass movements and other more easily measured phenomena. No one has yet developed a general theory of leadership.[1] Yet today there is a growing recognition that an individual leader's actions, or his failure to act, can significantly affect the course his country follows.

LEADERS AND LEADERSHIP

When we speak of "leadership" what comes to mind most frequently is the activity of the larger-than-life individual who draws his people to pursue goals that he has already committed himself to. Winston Churchill expressing Britain's determination to continue to fight in 1940, Charles de Gaulle imposing his vision of a strong executive Presidency to overcome the paralysis of the Fourth French Republic in 1958, Mahatma Gandhi transforming the Indian Congress Party into a mass movement to drive out the British through non-violent resistance, are well-known examples. In Africa, Kwame Nkrumah's and Sékou Touré's appeals to Ghanaians and Guineans to struggle for their freedom from colonial rule offer further illustrations of the phenomenon. On the darker side Adolf Hitler won a widespread following from Germans through his attacks on the iniquities of Versailles and the treachery of "aliens" within the Aryan state. At this extreme, then, we can say that leadership involves a deep commitment by the leader to a mission, and that followers accept that commitment.

But leadership need not always fall in this "heroic" mould. It can also involve pulling together some coherent compromise out of a diversity of conflicting interests. Franklin Roosevelt groping toward his New Deal program in the United States, or later Lyndon Johnson piloting the most massive civil rights program in American history through the U.S. Congress, are classic illustrations of this ability to lead by finding an acceptable middle ground. Similarly, Mackenzie King's ability to avert a French-English split in Canada over conscription during World War II, or Yakabu Gowon's skill in reconciling Ibos to a restored Nigeria after the civil war, show the importance as well as the creative possibilities inherent in compromise.

It is no accident that all these illustrations of "leadership" do share in common the ability of a leader to act, rather than being the passive beneficiary of events. "Leadership" clearly involves the leader doing something, something that wins support from followers. Yet not all leaders exercise "leadership." We should therefore distinguish between these two terms. If we are approached by a visiting Martian with the request "Take me to your leader," we normally have little difficulty deciding who it is the Martian should meet. In almost all states there are one or more institutions comprising the "government," with their hierarchies of role-holders, topped by a particular office whose occupant is entitled to take most major actions in the name of the state, subject to varying degrees of consultation and ratification by other officials. The "leader," in short, is the head of the dominant hierarchy in the government. There are some problems here, to be sure. A role may be accorded the deference and symbols of the head of a hierarchy, but the role-holder's power to take major actions may be far less than that of a nominally subordinate individual; the Queen in the British parliamentary system is an obvious example. Or there may be someone right outside the institutions of government who is able to override the top government office-

holder; the Ayatollah Khomeini's demonstrations of
his power to reverse decisions by the official
Iranian Head of State show this clearly. But
generally speaking, the person holding the formal
position of leader can have the final say on what
course of action shall be followed by the state on
major issues. He can manage this in part because
we tend to accept that a person in the role of
leader has the right to make these decisions and
to be obeyed, but this is aided by the more practical consideration that the role provides him with
the power and the resources to reward or punish
people according to how well they obey him.

But a person enjoying the powers inherent in
the role of "leader" may not necessarily be exercising "leadership," nor is "leadership" necessarily
confined to the occupants of such roles. President
Carter of the United States, President d'Estaing of
France, and other heads of government clearly occupied the role of "leader" in their countries, yet
were continuously assailed for failing to provide
"leadership." On the other side of the ledger,
individuals such as Mao Tse-tung and Kwame Nkrumah
built up the Chinese Communist Party and the
Convention Peoples Party of Ghana from scratch without access to any major resources beyond their own
personalities, and used the support of others
through these parties to gain access to the role of
leader of the state. Leadership is a relationship
between individuals, in which one person manages to
get others to do what he wishes. But not all such
relationships involve "leadership"; few of us would
consider leadership to be involved, for example,
when a hijacker using a gun forces a plane crew to
fly him to his chosen destination. Leadership
involves voluntary compliance by those over whom it
is exercised. Burns has captured its essence most
satisfactorily, in my view, in describing it as a
special subset of a more general power relationship
in which "leaders induc[e] followers to act for
certain goals that represent the values and the
motivations--the wants and needs, the values and
aspirations--of both leaders and followers"
[emphasis in original].[2] Leadership, then, is the
ability to obtain non-coerced, voluntary compliance
which enables followers to attain goals which they
share with the leader.

While separate, the two concepts of "leader"
and "leadership" are closely linked. It is quite
possible for a leader to obtain some compliance
with his wishes through force rather than

21

leadership; in fact, as we shall see in a moment, there is a tendency inherent in the role of leader which favours coercion over persuasion. But to obtain compliance for many actions or for any length of time, a leader must be able to exercise leadership over some other individuals. It is simply not possibly for him to coerce everybody all of the time. Even the most tyrannical leader must have some individuals around him whom he can trust to apply coercion to others even when he cannot supervise them personally; Idi Amin, for example, could not possibly have forced his State Research Bureau and military units to kill thousands of Ugandans unless they had been willing to do so. At the same time, the leader must be able to keep his followers motivated to give this compliance. This motivation can come from a supra-rational commitment, such as the religious zeal being manifested in Iran by the Ayatollah Khomeini's followers. But usually some more material reward is needed, and the resources to provide such rewards are most readily obtained through control of the machinery of the state.

Despite this link, there is also an inherent tension between the role of leader and the exercise of leadership, because a leader can use force as well as persuasion to get his way. As David Kipnis has pointed out,[3] it is much easier for a power-holder to see a subject as obeying in response to coercion rather than in response to persuasion, and thus the power-holder is likely to receive more gratification from coercion than from persuasion. But using coercion against others is self-reinforcing; to justify its use the leader devalues his subjects, and distances himself from them, thus reducing his inhibitions against using still more coercion. As he comes more and more to impose his own values on others regardless of their wishes, his erstwhile followers cease to give voluntary obedience, requiring still more force, until we reach the end result of a regime resting solely upon bayonets, an uncomfortable posture to maintain for any length of time.

Not all leaders fall into this force-contempt-more force spiral. A few will be checked by their own moral code and other inhibitions. More will be stopped by checks within the political system, such as the constitution and active political opponents, or by pressure from groups beyond their control within the society. But these are all <u>restraints</u>: when they are weak or absent, the leader can

22

easily slide into using force.

A central dilemma, then, faces every leader, and especially one who seeks changes in his society. To ensure that his wishes are carried out even without his direct supervision, he needs to be able to persuade people to support him voluntarily. But because his resources in the role of leader include the means of coercing others, and because other people may not share perfectly his vision of what he wants, or may not be ready to pursue it at the pace he wishes, he is constantly tempted to use force rather than persuasion. How severely he feels this dilemma depends upon the interaction of two factors: the extent to which the goals he is trying to pursue require him to control the behaviour of other individuals and the extent to which other actors put limits on his ability to achieve such control. I should like now to turn to the question of who (or what) imposes limits on the leader, what kinds of limits they impose, and how this affects the kinds of goals a leader may pursue.

CONSTRAINTS ON A LEADER

We can view the range of choices open to a leader as a vast field, with its farthest horizons set by his imagination and conscience. But in the foreground, looming in on him from every direction, are a series of barriers. Specifically, these limits to his free choice can be grouped into the following categories:

1. Limits imposed by actors beyond the leader's own state: (a) the power and interests of other states, and (b) trans-national organizations, which while lacking the political and military power of states, can impose other forms of sanctions.

2. Limits within his own state: (a) environ-mental and physical resource limitations; (b) common or dominant values within the society; (c) the perceived self-interest of various social grouping and functional groups; and (d) the political institutions, above all the basic or "constitutional" rules of conduct, developed out of the society's constellation of values and interests.

3. The leader's own personal limitations,

such as ability and time available.

The limits imposed on a leader by other states are a function of a complex of factors, including the other state's power to provide benefits or impose sanctions on the leader's state, his power to do the same to the other state, and the willingness and power of third parties to intervene. This last factor can be particularly important when the military power of two adversary states is grossly disproportionate, as in the case of the United States and Cuba. Sanctions, of course, can be far more subtle than the use or threat of military force; they can include such actions as reducing flows of aid or purchases of goods, tightening customs inspections, or loss of interest in joint cultural or sporting events. The more broadly two states are inter-dependent, the more readily each can limit the choices of the other.

While only states exercise political and military sanctions against each other, they sometimes can be persuaded to exercise these sanctions on behalf of other organizations, most notably today multi-national corporations. The range of retaliatory responses, including suspension of aid and credit facilities, and support for domestic opponents, orchestrated against Chile in the early 1970s after Allende completed the nationalization of two American-owned copper mining companies, amply illustrates this.[4] Corporations also have their own bargaining leverage. Just as in an earlier age the leading transnational organization, the Catholic Church, could deny communion to unfriendly leaders, so today multinational corporations can deny credit and investment funds to states they consider undesirable. And once again, the effectiveness of this sanction depends upon how badly the leader perceives himself as needing the corporation's investment.

Within his own state, the leader's situation is more complex. There are, first of all, certain fixed "natural" features to any state, such as its climate, its supply of fresh water, and its mineral and agricultural resources, although clearly these resources have to be judged in terms of their potential development at varying levels of technology as well as their existing levels of use. For example, a desert country may be able to transform its agriculture through applying deep drilling techniques to obtain subterranean water supplies or a state may be able to exploit a mineral resource after it learns deep mining or concentrating techniques.

The social boundaries to what a leader can do are somewhat more malleable, but also impose limits. Every society has some generally agreed notion of what constitutes equitable treatment for its members, and of what constitutes appropriate conduct for a leader. For example, North Americans generally believe that everyone should have a chance to pursue their own self-interest by being given an equal start through education, but also that political leaders should foreswear some aspects of this pursuit of self-interest by refraining from taking bribes while in office. To the extent that a society is self-governing and that all its members are able to participate in its political affairs, these values will be expressed in the political rules under which its government operates, and these rules will include some method of stopping a leader from transgressing the society's shared values.

There are, to be sure, some differences within most societies about just how values are interpreted, with the most significant of these differences arising out of individuals' different situations in the society. We can distinguish here two types of situational placing in society for individuals: the broad social groupings such as class, ethnic and religious affiliations, and the more specific functional groups such as occupations and other shared interests.

At the extreme, a broad social grouping can constitute a society in itself, with its own distinctive institutions and values. This is particularly likely with ethnic groups, which can provide an all-embracing sense of identity for their members, although it is also possible in some cases for a group based on religious affinity to set itself apart similarly. Other groupings such as social classes are necessarily more integrated as parts of a larger whole, although even here a social class can develop its own values at variance with those of other sectors of society. Finding a course of action that does not conflict with the differing value systems of various social groupings is often one of the most difficult challenges facing a leader.

Functional groups, by contrast, generally base their claims upon some more widely-shared values, although their interpretations of, and the conclusions they draw from those values, may not be generally accepted. Functional groups' strength varies as their own cohesiveness and numbers, the strategic position they occupy in the society, and the extent to which they can act free from the threat of government sanctions. Strong autonomous groups occupying key positions in the society (for example, medical doctors) can exercise a great deal of pressure on a government, although they lack the power to withdraw from the state or (with the exception of the military) to take it over. Their pressures are likely to be exerted only in the specific fields that directly concern them, and the influence of one group can often be balanced by calling up an opposing one.

The political institutions themselves set further limits on a leader's power to do what he wishes. Where competitive elections are strongly entrenched, a leader faces a regular test of his public acceptability. Then too, there are frequently constitutional limits on what he can do, with autonomous agencies such as the courts to enforce them. These limitations, however, are only effective insofar as they have some basis of public support. Where the rules are imposed from outside, or where a significant section of the populace feels that they are not deserving of support, then they are likely to be overidden.

A final set of limits on any leader that we should note are those imposed by his own personal capabilities: the time he has available, his own ability, and his interest in ruling. The time a leader has available to consider problems is finite, and with the multitude of problems and the shortage of support staff that faces most Third World leaders, long-range or less urgent problems often get only cursory attention. A leader's own ability to grasp issues also sets limits to the choices he will consider. Finally, a leader may not be willing to invest a great deal of effort in achieving his goals, and if he takes this "passive" approach toward the use of power[5] he will likely rule out those alternatives that require substantial effort, preferring instead to trim his goals.

How do these limits affect African political leaders? Briefly, I will argue that most leaders are in a weak position in their dealings both with other states and with foreign investors, and that they generally find few shared values around which they can rally all the people of their state. At the same time, however, they have to meet only a limited range of domestic demands, and are subject to few checks from within the state on their behaviour. The overall effect of these factors has been to discourage leaders from trying to achieve major developmental transformations of their societies, but to encourage them to seek personal security and self-enrichment, against which widely shared social values and strong political institutions generally act as barriers.

In dealing with forces outside their own state, African leaders have received constant reminders of their lack of power. The 15 years during which less than a quarter million white Rhodesians maintained their pariah regime in the face of nearly all the African states' hostility and demands for sanctions was the most glaring indication of African weakness, but the interventions by European troops and mercenaries in Zaire, the Cubans' and Russians' military roles in Angola and Ethiopia, and the contemptuous way in which the French made and unmade governments in their former colonies, all underlined the inability of African states to prevent outside intervention in their affairs.

In economic matters too the African states generally had only limited power, although here part of their apparent weakness was a lack of bargaining skill, which was gradually remedied as the years went by.[6] Still, in dealing either with other states or with multinational corporations, the fundamental factor was how badly each side wanted what the other side had to offer. Thus in the early 1960s Ghana wanted to develop the Volta River hydroelectric project, and to use its own bauxite in making aluminum from the project. Kaiser Aluminum Company was the only private investor seriously interested, and wanted to use its own existing sources of bauxite, partly as a safeguard against being expropriated. Because Ghana wanted the dam and electricity, whereas Kaiser indicated it could go elsewhere for aluminum smelting capacity, Kaiser got its way. On the other hand, in the 1970s, Botswana, by virtue of having very rich diamond deposits, was able to obtain a comparatively beneficial deal from de Beers, whereby the company paid the cost of developing the Orapa mine, while giving the government initially a 15%, and later a 50%, equity share.[7] Generally, however, any raw material that one African state could offer was also available in several other parts of the world, and at the level of processing or manufacturing, almost no African state could offer enough skilled labour, cheap energy supplies or transportation, or a

sufficiently rich domestic market to tempt corporations to make major investments.

Their own limited technology and heavy dependence upon subsistence agriculture made African
states highly susceptible to physical and environ-
mental constraints. The Sahel drought in the 1970s
dramatized how crucial rainfall was for maintaining
adequate food production, while widespread deforest-
ation for fuel and subsequent erosion of land underlined the limited range of energy sources available
to African states in the wake of soaring oil costs.
The break-up of the Mali Federation in 1960 and
Rhodesia's unilateral declaration of independence in
1965 underlined the precarious access to the outside
world of Mali, Zambia and the other twelve land-
locked African states.

The problem of finding shared values on which
to build a common sense of citizenship was often a
difficult one for African leaders to resolve.
Different ethnic groups frequently held different
perceptions of what constituted acceptable conduct,
or for that matter, what kind of person was an
acceptable leader. Within Nigeria, for example,
Hausa culture favoured leaders born to high status
and supporting a rigidly hierarchical society, while
Ibo culture favoured the "self-made" leader who
would support a more egalitarian, more open society.
A leader acceptable to Hausas, then, would not be
readily accepted by Ibos, and vice versa.

A more serious problem for a leader in his
relations with ethnic groups arose out of the fact
that all shared a common desire for increased
affluence and access to benefits such as education
and jobs. Yet in the process of development under
colonial rule and afterwards, some groups had
inevitably enjoyed more access to these benefits
than had others, with the result that the
"disadvantaged" groups now demanded the opportunity
to catch up, while those who had enjoyed advantages
wanted to keep them. A leader was inevitably caught
in the middle of such conflicts, unless he could
somehow direct both sides away from their perceptions that ethnicity "explained" the differences in
benefits.

Class identities also provided a basis for
conflict, although generally a more muted conflict
than ethnicity. Educated persons who came to realize that they shared many benefits as members of a
new elite and had an interest in maintaining the
structures, such as educational requirements for
jobs, that justified their privileged status, were

usually quite class-conscious, but those who occupied lower-status positions tended to be less so, or at least to acquiesce in the enjoyment of privileges by these new men of power.

The more specific functional groups which make the largest number of demands on a leader in an industrialized, interdependent society were considerably less demanding in African states. Ordinary farmers and fishermen might not even be aware they shared a common interest with farmers in other parts of the country, and even if they did realize this, communicating beyond the village was difficult, government was too powerful and distant to be influenced, and it might even punish them for making demands. Groups such as taxi-drivers, market women, chiefs, local councillors and others who could communicate with each other more readily, as well as teachers, doctors, civil servants and other high-level occupations, were less inhibited from making demands on government, although even here there were some constraints. The government could depose chiefs, refuse licenses to taxi-drivers or market women, post teachers to remote areas, or in other ways make life difficult for a person who pressed demands too hard. These means of limiting groups' power to express their demands could make a leader's conduct appear acceptable to his people, at least insofar as nobody was overtly objecting to his actions.

However, "acceptable" conduct could cover a long continuum of attitudes, ranging from enthusiastic support through resigned acquiescence. The ordinary peasant in the bush can look at the country's leader in a number of ways. He may worship the leader as a superman who succeeded in forcing the colonialists to end forced labour, and therefore can command the peasant's undying loyalty. Or he may give the leader a more calculating support, speaking up for him or working for him because the leader has been able to obtain good coffee prices or brought piped water to the villages. Sliding from support to acquiescence, the peasant may pay his taxes or even come out and cheer when the leader visits his village because he fears trouble from the police if he fails to show this enthusiasm; and he will give just as heartfelt a cheer for the colonel who ousts the leader a few weeks later. At some point, he may even cease acquiescing completely, and take such token steps of resistance as smuggling produce out of the country rather than selling it to the Marketing Board. Finally, his resistance becomes overt when, goaded by the government's failure to pay cash for produce, he joins with his neighbours in burning down the local Marketing Board office.

The level of acceptance a leader needs varies according to what he is trying to do. A leader who is simply trying to gather wealth for himself, or to have development handled by multinational corporations, can manage with the acquiescence of most of the populace, provided he can count on the support of the army and police to put down any hint of resistance. At the other extreme, a leader who is trying to revolutionize rural life by drawing all peasants into new agricultural practices through co-operatives, needs a high level of support, probably of a supra-rational type, since it is unlikely he can produce improved material payoffs immediately. Such a leader is vulnerable to a form of pressure that does not affect the leader requiring only acquiescence, the sanction of non-cooperation. If he wishes, for example, to encourage forest replanting, or to organize farmers into co-operatives, or to get his officials to plan low-cost housing instead of luxury villas for government officers, he has to persuade farmers or officials that they ought to do such things.

The elite groups of Africans possessing technical or administrative skills, and strategically located in the capital, are particularly able to use the lever of non-cooperation. In extreme cases, persons with valuable skills, such as doctors or engineers, may leave the country. More commonly, civil servants will simply re-interpret orders in a way more pleasing to them or will provide information in such a way as to promote their preferences. In these ways they can nullify a good portion of the leader's approach with which they disagree.

Other groups such as urban wage workers or farmers rarely can achieve such effective results through non-cooperation. Workers are generally too easily divided or replaced, while farmers are usually too isolated to form a united front, unless conditions have become intolerably bad. In Guinea in the 1960s, when Guinean francs were useless because there was nothing to buy with them, most farmers did stop producing cash crops and either concentrated on their own subsistence crops or smuggled their surpluses into neighbouring countries. But even here it took a decade of resistance to force the government to change its policies.

The more positive means of limiting a leader's actions, such as removing him at an election, going

on strike or demonstrating, or mustering a coalition
of influential interests to persuade him to change
his ways, have been severely circumscribed in nearly
all African states. The opportunity for citizens to
make any meaningful choice of political representatives has nearly ceased to exist. In most states,
the opportunities to organize for any public political demand, whether by labour, businessmen,
professionals or farmers, have also been largely
removed, and even spontaneous uprisings are as
likely to be met by harsh retaliation as by sympathetic attention. Privileged and powerful sectors
still get private access to most governments, and
some ordinary people can also get access through
family and other personal connections, but generally
the range of demands that can reach governments has
become even more skewed in favour of the rich and
powerful than it is in the industrialized societies,
and even they are not assured of access. Almost the
only effective way in recent years of dealing with a
leader who chose not to listen to popular demands
was to have the military take over the government,
and besides being a rather extreme step, this seldom
produced a great improvement in most people's well-
being.

Non-cooperation then, seemed to be the only
effective political check that a people could impose
on their leader, and even this would work only
against a leader who needed to induce people to
carry out actions. A leader who needed nothing more
than the acquiescence of the bulk of the populace in
his chosen course was largely immune to sanctions,
as long as he could find a few competent people to
take the limited number of actions necessary for the
state to function.

This brings us to a final limit on African
leaders that we should note briefly. Most of the
world's information-gathering systems, whether for
economic, scientific or political intelligence, are
centered in the industrialized states. Furthermore,
to use this information requires a good deal of
screening and filtering, which in turn requires
skilled analysts. Small, poor African states can
rarely afford the analysts necessary to keep their
leaders well informed on what is going on elsewhere
in the world, let alone the intelligence-gathering
network that would allow them to obtain information
relevant to their perspectives. In their international dealings and even in dealing with
foreigners in matters concerning their own states
(for example, crop prospects or mineral deposits)

African leaders simply may not have the information available to them to bargain most effectively, either because they cannot get the information, or because they have insufficient staff available to analyse it.

African leaders, then, have been severely checked in the international arena by their lack of bargaining power, and have been constrained in their domestic developmental goals by physical and human resource shortages within their states. But in the domestic arena they have not been checked by societal values, by organized interests or by political institutions. The lack of shared values in a society meant that a leader had a hard time appealing for popular support, but at the same time it meant that there was no clear consensus on what he could not do. The weakness of organized interests in nearly all African states and the newness and strangeness of political institutions made these both ineffective as constraints upon a leader's behaviour, with the result that within his own country a leader could behave pretty much as he pleased, even though he could not readily achieve developmental goals for his society.

CHOOSING A COURSE OF ACTION

Within the series of limits I have indicated, the leader can make some choices among possible courses of action. Here I will look briefly at what guides him in making these choices, and how, having made his choice, he can seek to implement it.

I should like to emphasize first, however, that choices themselves impose constraints on a leader, in that they foreclose as well as open up other future choices. For example, in the struggle for African independence, a leader who built a network of local party activists independent of the conservative "big men" in each village had an instrument that could later be used to change the social structures of the villages, whereas a leader who worked through the "big men" would find himself limited later to those programmes he could persuade these notables to carry out for him. A leader who brought in large-scale foreign investment reaped a reward of jobs and export earnings for his country, but he also paid a price in the build-up of a powerful privileged lobby for maintaining foreign investment. These consequences could come about through inadvertence as well as through deliberate design; often a

course of action was taken before the leader saw
that a choice was possible, and even when choices
were perceived, not all their consequences were
apparent.

Five factors seem particularly important in
guiding any political leader to select one course of
action rather than another. These five factors are:
(1) the nature of his goals for the society; (2) the
extent to which these goals cohere into a consistent
and comprehensive vision for the society; (3) his
moral code, specifically the kinds of means he is
prepared to use to achieve his ends; (4) the
strength of his commitment to achieving his goals;
and (5) his sense of security and self-confidence in
the role of leader.

Some of these factors call for a few comments.
The first is self-evident. Any person coming into
the role of leader has some goals, even if these are
only to root out the old regime, or to hold onto the
office. Generally, however, a leader will have certain values which he will try to use his power as a
leader to impose on the society, whether the values
are a belief in imposed economic equality, a free
market in labour, or rule by religious tenets.

Whether a leader possesses a comprehensive blue-
print for the kind of society he would like to
create affects his choices in several ways. It
tells him, first, what over-all goals his specific
policies should be promoting, and thus serves to
alert him to the side effects and long-term implications of these policies. It can also serve to
inspire and guide his followers, thus simplifying
the problem of seeing that his wishes are carried
out. At the same time, it can blind him to choices
that might be more beneficial to his people, and it
can encourage him to strive fanatically for a goal
whatever the cost. Without such an ideology, on
the other hand, a leader is more likely to alter
course readily whenever circumstances seem to him
to require this, and he can pursue conflicting policies in different areas in order to conciliate
different interests. This can create problems; without broad goals, a leader can drift along the path of
least resistance until he discovers too late that
the country is trapped in a costly impasse, and he
can justify any kind of action that contributes to
his personal survival or well-being.

A leader's moral code, while seldom completely
inflexible, also will affect the ways in which he
tries to resolve problems. Some leaders, such as
Col. Gaddafi of Libya, seem to have no scruples

against ordering the assassination of critics at home or abroad; other leaders, such as Albert Margai of Sierra Leone, drew the line at jailing prominent opponents. More broadly, the extent to which a leader is prepared to refrain from pursuing ends because the means required violate his moral code will affect the range of "thinkable" choices open to him.

How badly a leader wants to achieve goals will also affect his choice of policies, since some policies call for heavy commitments of the leader's time, energy and other resources, while others are almost self-executing. A leader who has no strong preferences among possible courses of action is likely to choose the one which requires the least effort on his part, whereas the leader with a burning desire to achieve a particular goal will gladly sacrifice much time and energy toward this end.

The extent to which a leader is psychologically secure and self-confident will also affect his choices. The leader who is self-confident can take actions he thinks are right or necessary, even though they involve the risk of mistakes, criticism, or loss of popularity, whereas the leader who is unsure of his own abilities or fears others are plotting to remove him is more likely to hedge and hesitate, or try to remove critics. Sometimes, to be sure, a leader's position within a political system really can be threatened; as Henry Kissinger once observed, "Paranoiacs can have enemies." But those leaders who tend to magnify the threats to their position are likely to be less tolerant of criticism or organized opposition than those who downplay threats or appraise them realistically.

Again, how do these five factors affect African leaders' choices? One feature which we shall discuss further in the next chapter is the fact that the first generation of African leaders came to power with the goal of securing political independence, while most of their successors have made their main goal cleaning up or obliterating the mistakes of their predecessors. These limited goals meant that once independence was achieved, leaders frequently drifted with events rather than trying to shape them.

Those who have evolved a more comprehensive vision have shown both the benefits and dangers of ideology. Felix Houphouet-Boigny, who has always maintained that the development of the Ivory Coast into an African capitalist society is his over-riding concern, can claim that his consistent pursuit of this goal even at the expense of more popular ones such as rapid Africanization has produced the Ivorian "economic miracle." Julius Nyerere's egalitarian vision has induced many Tanzanian senior civil servants to act in far more altruistic ways than their counterparts elsewhere in Africa. On the other hand, Sékou Touré's commitment to building "socialism" in Guinea has brought not only economic disaster but also the purges, executions, and mass flight of dissidents which after twenty years of independence left two-thirds of his original Political Bureau dead or in jail, and an estimated fifth of Guinea's population in exile.[8]

Leaders lacking a comprehensive vision for their society have tended to ignore problems or to enter into deals which promised short-term benefits at the cost of long-term disadvantages. The many states which found themselves burdened with expensive contractor-financed factories and other projects, such as Sierra Leone under Albert Margai, offer evidence of this. Even more dangerous, because of the weakness of the checks on most leaders, is the risk that a leader lacking any ultimate vision for his society will act solely to ensure his own well-being or survival. The rulers who have left their countries in the greatest shambles, such as "Emperor" Jean-Bedel Bokassa and General Idi Amin, had no discernible vision of how they would like to make their countries better places, but only a desire to keep themselves in power.

While the effect of their moral code has not been a conspicuous restraint upon most African leaders, it has affected the behaviour of some. Julius Nyerere clearly has been influenced by moral considerations as well as practical ones in his reluctance to use force to promote developmental programmes, while in a very different context, the two Margais in Sierra Leone both refrained from a number of actions they could have taken to destroy opponents, apparently out of moral scruples.

The degree of commitment shown by different African leaders has also varied. Although to gain the pinnacle of power and to retain it in an African state has invariably taken a good deal of tactical skill, there have been perceptible differences in the amount of time and energy committed by, on the one hand, the driven political visionaries like Sékou Touré or Kwame Nkrumah, and on the other hand, the poet-philosopher Leopold Senghor, who spent several weeks' annual vacation in France, or

Dr. Milton Margai, whose illness sharply reduced
the time he could spend governing Sierra Leone.
There have even been a few figurehead leaders, such
as General Ironsi in Nigeria, who genuinely appeared
to have been thrust into the role rather than seeking it out.

The degree of commitment shown by a leader has
its most important implications in the field of
economic development. As between the two basic
approaches to development, the "accomodation"
approach of letting foreign entrepreneurs expand the
economy through exports of raw materials and some
assembly of manufactured products, and the "transformation" approach of re-organizing the economy to
involve Africans in a range of undertakings geared
to domestic consumption (to be discussed in more
detail later), the latter requires considerably more
effort by the political leader in guiding and inspiring his people's economic activity. A leader who
lacks a strong personal commitment to this approach
is unlikely·to undertake the heavy burden of work
required to bring it to fruition. A leader's lack
of commitment thus builds in a bias toward an
"accommodationist" approach.

Insecurity has plagued many African leaders.
There have been some who have felt fairly confident
of their right to hold the position, most notably
those who either could claim high status in traditional African society or were markedly older than
potential rivals. Houphouet-Boigny and Dr. Milton
Margai could claim both these bases for respect;
Jomo Kenyatta of Kenya and Siaka Stevens of Sierra
Leone could claim superiority on the basis of age;
while Sir Seretse Khama of Botswana and Amadou
Ahidjo of Cameroun could gain assurance from their
family status. Many leaders, however, had no such
basis to bolster their claim to office; their emin-
ence arose from the fact that they had done a better
job of organizing a political party than any rivals,
and had led it to victory in one or two elections.
Compounding their insecurity was the fact that after
independence they rarely could deliver on the promises they had made to their supporters of increased
material prosperity, a weakness that could easily
lead to their overthrow if they held further elections. Even less secure were the military rulers,
who inevitably were aware that just as they had used
their control of key elements of the armed forces
and justified their action on the basis that their
predecessors had failed in office, so other military
men could use the same justification and control of

troops to oust them. The fear of losing power, then, hung as a dark cloud over most leaders, and affected many of their decisions.

To succeed in implementing his goals, and also to survive in office, a leader needs support. He needs, first of all, some measure of general public support, although whether this is active co-operation or mere passive acquiescence depends on how far his goals involve activity by the people as a'whole. Furthermore, whatever the role of the public at large, he always needs some intermediaries who will carry out and interpret his orders.

To win support from the general public, a leader can in part rely upon the impact of policies which are seen to provide benefits. This rational calculation on the part of followers that the leader has provided benefits in the past, and seems likely to continue to provide them, entails an element of consistency in the leader's behaviour, as well as an ability to explain what he is doing. However, this calculating relationship is less important than the intangible, non-rational bond we can call "trust." This trust is essentially a feeling by followers that the leader knows their needs and is trying to meet them, a sense of empathy between leader and follower. The follower believes that the leader stands for something the follower deeply desires, whether or not he has ever managed to articulate this desire. What the leader says can be imprecise or ambiguous, inter- preted in widely divergent ways by different follow- ers, at least until the results of his policies remove ambiguities about what he is doing. The important point is that the leader strikes an emotional response rather than a purely calculating one.

Trust can derive from a number of attributes per- ceived in the leader by his followers: selflessness, age, intellectual ability, militance, or even famil- iarity. Perhaps selflessness, the perception that what the leader is doing is for the good of all and not particularly for his own benefit, comes closest to being a necessary ingredient in creating this bond. It seems to be intertwined with each of the other elements that have allowed leaders to retain the support and affection of their countrymen.

In Africa, respect for age has given a number of leaders a powerful hold over their countrymen. Felix Houphouet-Boigny, "Le Vieux" of the Ivory Coast, Jomo Kenyatta, "Mzee" or the "wise elder" of Kenya, William Tubman, "the Old Man" of Liberia, and Dr. Milton "Pa" Margai of Sierra Leone all enjoyed

wide respect for the presumed wisdom and detachment
that age and experience gave them. Seniority by
itself was not enough to protect a leader against
dissatisfaction over widespread economic hardship,
as the fate of Emperor Haile Selassie of Ethiopia
and King Idris of Libya showed; but it did seem to
give a ruler a reserve of support even after his
performance began to fail.

Other rulers built their bond on quite different
qualities. Kwame Nkrumah, who in forming the
Convention Peoples Party was opposing many of Ghana's
elders, presented himself as a militant, and eventually took the military title of "Osageyfo," the
warrior-redeemer. Julius Nyerere has always cast
himself as "Mwalimu," the teacher, and appears to
have maintained respect in this role of the thought-
ful intellectual. However, other leaders failed to
win widespread respect since their behaviour appeared
at variance with the role they had cast for themselves. Albert Margai of Sierra Leone was never
taken seriously in his self-selected role as a militant
leader against imperialism because he was obviously
too busy enriching himself, while Dr. Kofi Busia,
"The Prof," lost the respect many Ghanaians had held
for his intellectual qualities once he took power in
1969 and began to act in ways that were not only
high-handed but economically hard on people.

In each of these cases, the attributes of age,
militance or intellectual capacity were supposed to
be used for the benefit of the people as a whole,
and those leaders who lost support seem to have done
so because they began to pursue their self-interest
at their people's expense. While a leader does not
lose support by benefitting himself, he does lose it
if he seems to neglect his people. A bond of trust
gives him a reservoir of acceptance that can sustain
him over temporary setbacks and even allow him to
provide psychological rather than material benefits
for a long time. However, it does seem necessary
that in the long run, the leader who wishes to retain
support must be able to give his people some material
benefits.

Beyond this general base of support, a leader
needs support for the specific policies he is pursuing. Clearly the policies themselves partially
determine how he tries to build support: one does
not pursue a policiy of redistributing wealth more
evenly by working through the richest members of the
society. But in shaping the policies, a leader can
choose between two broad approaches to win support.
He can take peoples' attitudes and the line of

division among them as a given, and act as a "broker"
trying to put together a body of supporters by
bargaining among these existing interests. Or he
can try to get people to look at their situation in
a new way which allows them to override their divisions and unite together in support of his goals.

These two styles, the "brokerage" and the
"creative," are effective in different situations.
The "brokerage" approach works best where the range
of demands being made is not too broad, and where
there is no widespread discontent over the existing
balance of forces within the society. A "creative"
approach, by contrast, requires a certain fluidity
of alignments, and perhaps even a degree of restlessness among substantial portions of the society to
enable the leader to call upon hitherto uninvolved
members for support, or to induce its members to
accept new approaches. A leader who is not seeking
major social changes involving widespread participation is thus likely to pursue a "brokerage" style,
whereas a "creative" style is almost obligatory for
a leader seeking major changes. The leader pursuing
a creative style will need also the support of substantial numbers of his countrymen to offset the
likely opposition of those who resist change in the
status quo, whereas the brokerage leader can manage
quite satisfactorily with the acquiescence of most,
provided he manages to offer sufficient benefits to
strategic elites.

In order to implement any kind of policies, a
leader necessarily has to rely upon intermediaries.
The "brokerage" leader can work through what we may
characterize as strong intermediaries, individuals
who owe their primary commitment to their own community and act for the leader primarily because they
perceive his actions as benefitting them and their
community. The "creative" leader, by contrast,
needs to work through loyal intermediaries, persons
who are committed above all to the leader's goals
and will try to win the community to those goals.
The loyal intermediary, however, is unlikely to have
the kind of hold over the local community that the
strong one enjoys. Thus, while he is more likely to
do what the leader wants than is the "strong" intermediary, he is less likely to be able to get the
community to carry out the leader's wishes.

In summary, the leaders of independent African
states have found themselves faced with a constant
temptation to slide from leadership to coercion.
Facilitating this slide has been the lack of
domestic constraints upon their behaviour either

within the political structures or through the
values and organized interests outside the political
system. Then too, those leaders who held a clear
vision of the society they would like to build were
frequently frustrated by the slowness or unwilling-
ness of their countrymen to grasp this vision, while
leaders who lacked any burning vision were frequently haunted by the tenuousness of their claims to
power.

On the other hand, some leaders have relied
largely upon leadership rather than coercion. They
might be restrained by the nature of their goals or
by their own moral code, or they might feel secure
enough that they could accept challenges to either
their goals or their personal position. This sense
of security was enhanced when they could perceive
themselves as enjoying widespread trust from their
people, rather than having to rely solely upon
providing material payoffs. But this ability to
lead was found only among a limited number of
leaders.

NOTES

1.   James MacGregor Burns, "Wellsprings of
Political Leadership", American Political Science
Review, LXXI, 1 (March 1977), p. 266.
2.   Ibid., p. 274.
3.   David Kipnis, The Powerholders (University
of Chicago Press, Chicago, 1976), esp. Chs. 5,6.
4.   See T.H. Moran, "Transnational strategies
of protection and defense by multinational corporations; spreading the risk and raising the cost for
nationalization in natural resources", International
Organization, 27, 2 (Spring 1973), pp. 273-87.
5.   For the dichotomy between "active" and
"passive" leaders, see James D. Barber, The
Presidential Character, 2nd ed., (Prentice-Hall,
Englewood Cliffs, N.J., 1977), pp. 11-13.
7.   For Ghana, see A. Krassowski, Development
and the Debt Trap (Croom Helm for ODI, London, 1974),
pp. 49-53; for Botswana, see David Jones, Aid and
Development in Southern Africa (Croom Helm for ODI,
London, 1977), pp. 80-81.
8.   R.W. Johnson, "Guinea", in John Dunn (ed.),
West African States (Cambridge University Press,
Cambridge, 1978), p. 57; Africa, June 1977, p. 59.

Chapter Three

COLONIALISM AND THE EMERGENCE OF AFRICAN LEADERS

Two developments combined after World War II to
speed the African colonies toward political independence at a pace that no one had anticipated: the
growth of demands by Africans that they should
control their own affairs, and the colonial powers'
loss of their earlier certainty that their own
superiority entitled them to decide what was best
for the Africans. In this chapter I shall emphasize
two points; first, how the diverse demands of
African allowed a wide range of types of leaders to
emerge; and second, how the readiness of the two
largest colonial powers, Britain and France, to
seek an accommodation with the nationalist leaders
brought the African states to political independence
with only a minimal degree of unifying struggle and
working out of post-independence goals.

THE BREADTH AND DEPTH OF AFRICAN DISCONTENT

The bases for a nationalist movement in the
African colonies were many and varied, although at
all levels there was a degree of ambivalence toward
colonial rule. For the ordinary farmer, the "white
man's goods" such as metal cooking pots, attractive
printed cloths, and for the more affluent, watches
and bicycles, offered strong inducements to grow
cash crops as well as one's own subsistence. But
much of the cash was taken by chiefs and the government for taxes or for the chief's own purposes, and
frequently men were compelled to work on the chief's
fields in addition to paying taxes. Protest even
against visible abuses by chiefs was unavailing,
since the European District Commissioner supported
the chief, and behind the DC lay the threat of overwhelming armed force. Nor could one move away, as

in the old days, because the Europeans' control was everywhere. Then too, the prices paid by produce buyers dropped mysteriously, while the goods coming from Europe always were increasing in price. Among ordinary Africans, there was a great reservoir of discontent with the colonial system, a reservoir which could be tapped by anyone promising to end its abuses.

The chiefs and other rural notables fared somewhat better. Often they could turn their traditional right to land and housing into sources of cash income, and provided they did not question the colonial administration's overall control, they would generally be protected against their people by the administration. For those chiefs, most common in French territories, who were upstarts with no claim to support from the people of their area, siding with the administration was a logical course of action. However, a strong traditional chief who valued the respect of his people was in a dilemma. To fight for his people against the administration could lead to his deposition, but to side with the administration against his people would bring him into contempt and shame, as well as leaving him isolated if the colonial power withdrew its support. Many chiefs, therefore, were at least tacit sympathizers with the nationalist movements, and a few even took leading roles in speaking out against colonial rule.

The cities were the main breeding ground for nationalism in Africa. It was in the cities that Africans were most thoroughly exposed to the houses, cars and other symbols of affluence enjoyed by Europeans, and also to the Europeans' power and racial prejudices, as expressed in segregated housing, job discrimination and denial of medical facilities, social clubs and other benefits to Africans. Town-dwelling Africans ranged from illiterate migrants eking out a living from odd jobs, petty crime or sponging on friends, through petty traders, full-time artisans and others with low but secure incomes, to graduates of metropolitan universities working in such professions as the law and medicine. At the lower levels, both the pleasures and pains of colonial rule were fairly diffuse. Men (and some women) came to the cities to get away from the monotony of rural life and the chief's exactions, and to enjoy the cash incomes, consumer goods, and the diversity and excitement of the city. But they also found many frustrations. Incomes were high, but so were living costs. Many

did not find jobs, and those who did found that
their wages were determined in a very arbitrary
manner by European employers or by the government.
The luxury goods they saw around them were unattain-
able, and for those without literacy and some
additional skills, likely to remain so. The gap between dreams and reality was wide enough to create
a simmering discontent, which occasionally erupted
in riots, and could be channelled into a powerful
movement.

The higher level Africans, the lawyers, the
teachers, the larger businessmen and the middle-level
civil servants, had both higher expectations and
sharper frustrations than any other group. Their
education and skills allowed them to aspire to a
"European" standard of living, yet in nearly all
colonies they were denied this by a formal or infor-
mal colour bar which kept them out of the senior
civil service posts and the higher-level jobs with
expatriate private firms. One reason why so many
Africans took up law and so few entered engineering,
in fact, was that they could set up their own
practice as lawyers, whereas engineers and other
technically trained people worked for expatriate
companies which until shortly before independence
discriminated against Africans. These were also the
Africans who were best placed to develop a vision of
their colony as an independent state, with themselves holding down the top positions. Furthermore,
in most colonies they formed a small enough group
for all to know each other and to meet frequently.
All this facilitated their taking the leading role
in organizing nationalist movements. While more
than anyone else they owed their high statuses to
colonial rule, they had the most to gain from ending
it. However, because they stood to inherit the
structures of privilege the Europeans had set up,
they were loath to renounce these aspects of the
colonial legacy. Their attitude toward colonialism
was in fact the most ambivalent of any social group;
they wanted to take the Europeans' place, but few
said much about altering the colonial social strata,
trade relations or economic activities.

Most Africans who expressed their views on the
colonial situation concentrated on ending European
political control. A few, such as Sékou Touré or
Julius Nyerere, had the longer-term goal of building
a socialist society; others, such as Felix Houphouet-
Boigny, envisioned a mature, industrial capitalist
order. But for most, the objective of gaining political control, or at least working out a political

relationship with the colonial power that ended
Africans' subordination, was sufficiently over-
riding to obliterate the need to look at further
goals. The vast array of possibilities opening
after independence could be explored after the
immediate goal was secure.

In the aftermath of World War II, the number
of channels through which discontent could be
expressed increased greatly. In the British and
French territories, the expansion of the franchise
encouraged the growth of political parties. These
in turn built on numerous prior organizations. In
the cities, study groups and professional associations among the intelligentsia, and trade unions,
mutual aid societies and tribal unions among the
working class all began to discuss how changes
might be made and thus heightened peoples' political
consciousness. In the rural areas, co-operatives
and other marketing organizations for farmers filled
a similar role, while lorry drivers travelling
around the countryside carried information about
what was happening in other districts. While nearly
all political parties originated in the towns, word
of their creation spread rapidly around the "bush,"
with the result that local branches often sprang
into being before party organizers ever arrived in
a locality; for example, Convention Peoples Party
branches sprang up spontaneously in the Gold Coast
in 1951, and the Parti Solidaire Africaine in the
Congo in 1960 had rural branches long before organizers had left the cities.[1] Popular discontent
found numerous outlets, and needed only to be given
direction by some spokesman.

Numbers of potential leaders thus appeared in
most territories as the movement toward independence
started. The fact that no one could foresee how
brief the struggle would be, and how painless in
most of Africa, meant that few of the individuals
who challenged the colonial structures through their
own organization saw how decisive getting an early
start would prove to be. It was generally a matter
of luck and timing that one African rather than
another emerged as the leader of the nationalist
movement in a territory. The fact that Kwame Nkrumah
was called back to the Gold Coast to work for the
United Gold Coast Convention in 1947 rather than
staying in England another two or three years, that
Julius Nyerere was back in Tanganyika and available
while potential rivals were abroad or otherwise
committed when the opportunity came to launch the
Tanganyika African National Union, or that

Felix Houphouet-Boigny could muster the largest
ethnic bloc in his bid to become leader of the
African planters in the Ivory Coast, all were
decisive in their becoming national leaders. But
few people at the time saw these events as leading
to control of the state, and thus there was rarely
a major struggle for such positions of potential
power. Once an individual with the training, skill
and courage to challenge the colonial rulers had
gained a position which enabled him to make such a
challenge, his stature was magnified, and he thus
acquired more authority to direct the struggle,
including the opportunity to set up an all-embracing
nationalist party.

There was seldom much debate on the direction
the movement should take beyond the goal of achieving independence. The lieutenants the leader drew
around him, the context within which his organization
struggled against others to gain powers, and the
nature and strength of the established relationships
with the colonial power, all were important in laying
down directions for post-independence policies.
Nevertheless, the leader could choose fairly freely
what interests and identities he would try to stimulate in his audience, the kinds of structures and
the individuals he would use to reach the people,
and the extent to which he would try to involve the
people in the nationalist movement. Later, as he
gained control over the machinery of government, he
could also hasten or retard the changeover from
European to African personnel, and change the
structures and goals of the administrative machine.
While there were pressures on him in all these
choices, the most important factor generally was that
one person rather than another had gained control,
and this, as I have said, was to a large extent the
result of chance.

WHY THE COLONIAL POWERS LOST THE WILL TO RULE

Had the colonial powers still been as convinced
of the rightness of their own rule as they had been
at the turn of the century, they would quickly have
suppressed these emergent movements (as the Portugese,
the Rhodesians and the South Africans, who correctly
perceived their own survival to be at stake, in fact
did). But at least since the germ of self-
determination had been planted at Versailles, the
British, French and Belgians had been considering,
hesitantly and reluctantly, ways of bringing their

African subjects into a more equal relationship some time in the distant future.

A series of factors after World War II combined to make the colonial powers much more responsive to the demands of the African nationalists. Their own domestic economic and social problems of reconstruction made both Britain and France more reluctant to be drawn into costly efforts to retain control of colonies. The view of the British Labour Party, and of the French Communists, Socialists and liberal Catholics that colonial relations were "exploitative" encouraged a search for new forms of relationship in which the economic benefits could be retained while the visible political responsibilities could be relinquished. The new forum of the United Nations, where the United States as well as the Soviet Union criticized other states' colonial rule, provided an international stage on which the iniquities of the colonial powers were exposed.

Finally, events in other colonial territories encouraged the metropolitan powers to speed up their plans for leaving Africa. Britain had brought its major Asian colonies to self-government in 1946 and 1947, with India, Pakistan and Ceylon remaining within the Commonwealth. France was embroiled in an increasingly costly war in Indochina from 1946 until the defeat at Dien Bien Phu in 1954. The success of the British and failure of the French efforts in Asia strongly indicated the advantages of peaceful accomodation with nationalist movements.

Britain had a clear evolutionary model for its African colonies, the route through "responsible" internal government to full self - government within the Commonwealth. In West Africa, the first steps had been taken on this path immediately after the war, with the introduction of "unofficial" and African majorities in the legislative councils of Nigeria, the Gold Coast and Sierra Leone. In East and Central Africa, where white settlers imposed powerful political obstacles to African rule, and where in any case the presence of the white and Asian minorities suggested that parliamentary majority rule might have shortcomings as a solution, no such easy route was apparent. However, until the 1950s the perceived timetable for this evolution was measured in generations rather than years of pre-independence tutelage, and there was thus time to test various constitutional arrangements.

The French had never been able to see how colonies could evolve into sovereign states and yet maintain harmonious relations with France. The logic of their "mission civilatrice" pointed to the eventual assimilation of colonial people into French citizenship, and the electoral system since the beginning of the Third Republic had supported this by giving seats in the French National Assembly to representatives elected from the various colonies by French citizens, European and African alike. However, since there were far more colonial people than Frenchmen, giving French citizenship to all colonials simply was not politically feasible.[2] From 1946, when a kind of second-class "colonial" citizenship was given to all Africans in the French colonies, France struggled to work out some form of association with the colonies before finally accepting the formula of full sovereignty in 1960.

The cost of two major wars in which France tried unsuccessfully to keep a tight hold over colonies was a major factor in forcing her to accept the independence formula. Following their defeat in Indochina, the French became embroiled in 1956 in guerrilla war in Algeria, which precipitated the collapse of the Fourth Republic and de Gaulle's accession to power in 1958. By this time, sufficient economic links had been forged between France and the more important African colonies that even political independence did not fundamentally alter the relationship.

The other colonial powers in Africa had less domestic pressure to contend with, and succumbed eventually to forces from within their colonies. Belgium had managed to insulate its Congolese subjects from nationalist influences in part by sharply restricting the availability of post-secondary education, and its parties of the Left had never concerned themselves much with colonial questions.[3] Nevertheless, when in 1959 riots broke out in Leopoldville, the Belgian government panicked and rushed through plans to bring the Congo to independence by 1960.

The Portuguese and Spanish dictatorships had no overt domestic opposition to contend with, and by a combination of very limited educational opportunities and secret police, had kept African nationalists under fairly tight control. It was not until the 1960s, when they could obtain bases in neighbouring African states, that Africans in the three Portuguese territories began effective guerrilla campaigns, which eventually precipitated a domestic revolution in Portugal in 1974 and led to the territories' independence the following year. Spain meanwhile had quietly washed its hands of its small and not terribly valuable mainland territories, granting independence to Spanish Guinea in 1968.

The major complication in this process of decolonization was the presence of white settlers. The
French "colons" in Algeria were largely responsible
for successive French governments' commitments to
the untenable notion that Algeria was a part of
France, a position strongly enough held that even
Charles de Gaulle was threatened with a military
coup when he abandoned it in 1962. In British East
Africa, the Kenya white settlers held up African
political advance until the Mau Mau rebellion in the
mid-1950s made Britain realize that the old pledges
of African paramountcy must now be redeemed. In
Central Africa, the Rhodesian whites managed to get
Britain to impose the Central African Federation in
1953 over the protests of all representative Africans
in both the Rhodesias and Nyasaland. But in all the
territories under the direct control of a metropolitan power, awareness of the strength of the "winds
of change" eventually led the British, French and
even the Portuguese to hand over control to Africans.
Algeria became independent in 1962. In 1964 Kenya
became independent under a black government headed
by Jomo Kenyatta, whom the British had jailed only a
few years earlier for his alleged part in organizing
the Mau Mau uprising, while in the same year the
Central African Federation was dismembered and the
new African states of Malawi and Zambia emerged from
its wreckage. The Rhodesian whites declared their
own independence in 1965, and with the aid of the
much stronger bastion of white supremacy, South
Africa, fought off a growing guerrilla movement for
15 years. However, by 1980 the guerrillas in combination with international pressures had forced the
white regime to capitulate and allow the election of
a representative black governmnet, leaving South
Africa alone as a white redoubt against the rest of
Africa.

The colonial powers, then, showed a growing
readiness after World War II to seek a new relationship with the African colonies, one which would give
more scope for African self-determination. This did
not mean they were ready to abandon all their ties
with their African colonies; rather, they were yield-
ing in order to protect the benefits they derived
from the colonies. To this end they sought to
encourage "responsible" African successors, men who
would see the benefits to be obtained on both sides
by a continuing link. However, they were not prepared to go to any lengths to secure such successors;
over-riding all other considerations was the fear

that they would be sucked into costly and ultimately
hopeless colonial wars, which the electorate of the
democratic colonial powers would not stand for.

TOO EASY A TRIUMPH?

The fact that the British, French and Belgians
were prepared to yield to the demand for self-
government in most of their African colonies before
the Africans began a "war of national liberation"
had mixed consequences. It spared these colonies
the great loss of life and the destruction of productive farms and factories that was so costly in
"revolutionary" states like Algeria or Mozambique.
It also averted the bitter divisions among Africans
and the desire for revenge among the victors which
seemed inevitable by-products of a long guerrilla
war. It also offered the more mixed blessing that
the new states inherited functioning government
institutions and economic units, along with existing
patterns of privilege and trade links. At the same
time, it meant that most African leaders in the
independence struggle did not have to build strong
political organizations or a strong commitment among
their followers in order to take over the institutions of the new state. While this tempered their
behaviour in certain respects, it also left them
insecure and vulnerable.
In most colonies France and Britain began in
the 1950s to look for an African leader who could
demonstrate that he had wide popular backing and
would not threaten their interests too severely.
Since to win wide popular support a would-be leader
had to be seen to be challenging the colonial power
successfully, there was inevitably some friction
between the African who emerged as the spokesman for
the nationalist movement and the colonial administration. This generally did not go beyond administrative harassment of the nationalist movement, and
sometimes the granting of a martyr's crown to the
leader by jailing him briefly. In two cases the
French succeeded in destroying a nationalist movement
which seemed too dangerously radical; in Cameroun
after 1955 they provoked to violence and then militar-
ily eliminated the Union des Populations du Cameroun[4]
while in 1958 in Niger they replaced Bakary Djibo's
radical Sawaba Party with a more conservative and pro-
French group by the simple expedient of falsifying
the election results. But when a party could show
it had significantly stronger electoral support than

any rival, even the French acquiesced. They had
recognized by 1956 the popular strength of Sékou
Touré's Parti Democratique de Guinée, and in that
year reversed their previous policies in Guinea and
in Mali by allowing fairly conducted elections, which
the PDG and the Union Soudanaise won easily. The
British had had some misgivings over Nkrumah's
victory in Ghana in 1951, and in Tanganyika Governor
Twining tried from 1955 to 1958 to crush Julius
Nyerere's Tanganyika African National Union, but in
both cases they accepted the election victories of
these parties.

In most territories the requirements of the
electoral system limited the opportunities for
radical movements. The need for sufficient education
to allow representatives to take part in legislative
activity effectively confined candidacies to the
privileged strata of Africans, and the elections in
the 1940s and 1950s took place before the lower
strata of Africans had been politicized into seeing
themselves as having different interests from the
elite. Ironically, one of the few cases where a
grass-roots protest against the privileged strata
surfaced was in Northern Nigeria in 1951, when the
Northern Elements Progressive Union candidates
scored a number of first-round triumphs over the
candidates of the traditional ruling class. This
protest, however, was quickly squelched by the ruling
Emirs.[5]

The leaders of nationalist movements, then, had
to arouse enough support to withstand some persecution by the colonial administration, and to organize
this support so that more people would cast ballots
in their party's boxes than into the boxes of other
candidates. This level of support did not entail
any profound commitment to the leader or his party;
it might indicate nothing more than a tepid sympathy
or a feeling that this was the "least worst" choice
presented to the voters. In most territories, while
one party generally emerged as the leading advocate
of independence, it rarely stirred the peoples'
passions enough to get more than a quarter of the
potential electorate registered on the electoral
rolls and then out to vote,[6] even in support of a
goal which could command broader support than almost
any that might subsequently arise. And even among
those who voted for the leading party, there is
little evidence of an understanding of, let alone a
commitment to, the party's goals in any but the most
general terms.

This ability to win independence without deeply

committed mass support was both a danger and an
advantage. It was a danger in that the leaders often
started pursuing their post-independence goals in
a vacuum, with no aroused populace to urge them on
or to call a halt. It was also a danger in that the
persons who emerged as leaders for these negotiations
might not be very dedicated to any goals other than
their own self-interest. On the other hand, negotiated independence could offer some advantages. A
leader who was able to work out a smooth transition
in harmony with the colonial power did not need the
fanatic commitment or the sense of being on the right
side of history that was required of any person leading a successful guerrilla war. He could thus be more
tolerant of opponents than could a leader who had
just defeated his enemies in a bloody struggle. However, the leader who negotiated independence without
mass support was painfully aware of just how vulnerable his position was.
    The handful of states that had to fight for
independence, or had to build new institutions as
part of an attempted revolution, were forced to
develop a more pervasive organization. The Algerians
built the Front de Liberation Nationale into an effective underground cell network before making peace
with the French in 1962, and were able to maintain
the party as an instrument of administration after
independence. The PAIGC in Guiné-Bissau and FRELIMO
in Mozambique set up complete government structures
in the areas abandoned by the Portuguese, and in a
more limited way the MPLA in Angola and ZANU in
Rhodesia did the same. In all these cases, because
of the capacity of the French, the Portuguese and
the Rhodesians for violent retaliation against
suspected nationalist sympathizers, the nationalist
movements had to make themselves very attractive to
potential supporters; it took a very strong sense
of grievance or commitment to the nationalist cause
for a person to risk being murdered or tortured by
the colonial authorities. It was not surprising
that after independence was achieved, the victorious
leaders frequently had to face the problem of how to
keep their own militants from taking revenge on those
who had opposed them.
    For the great majority of African leaders who
had brought their countries peacefully to independence, there were only a few real possibilities mixed
in with the many mirages of choice. Such possibilities as they had arose from the fact that they had
succeeded in overcoming two major barriers in gaining
independence: the resistance of the colonial

administration to their political organization's bid
for power (even though only Kwame Nkrumah, Jomo
Kenyatta, Ahmed Ben Bella and Hastings Banda actually qualified as "Prison Graduates"), and the fear
and fear-induced apathy of their people toward the
independence struggle. Since when they started they
had no coercive force to compel or material rewards
to offer supporters, they had to exercise leadership,
to build trust among their followers. However, the
goal they sought was usually the limited one of
political independence. Questions of how to expand
and distribute the state's potential wealth, how to
determine priorities among various social claims,
and how to establish Africans' sense of their own
worth, all were largely left unexplored, and thus
the hard barriers to attaining these further goals
were not yet perceived. Nor had most leaders built
up an organization which could exhort and inspire
citizens of the new state to try to resolve these
questions. Their leadership skills, in short, had
been harnessed only to the immediate goal of independence, and not yet to the more difficult problems
they must resolve once independence was achieved.

NOTES

        1. For the Gold Coast, see Dennis Austin,
Politics in Ghana, 1946-1960 (Oxford University
Press, London, 1964), p. 114; for the Congo (Zaire)
see Herbert Weiss, Political Protest in the Congo
(Princeton University Press, Princeton, N.J., 1967),
esp. pp. 198-202.
        2. For a good summary of the shifts in French
policy regarding "assimilation," see M.D. Lewis,
"One Hundred Million Frenchmen: The 'Assimilation'
Theory in French Colonial Policy", Comparative
Studies in Society and History, IV (1961-62),
pp. 129-53.
        3. Crawford Young, Politics in the Congo
(Princeton University Press, Princeton, N.J., 1965),
pp. 21-22.
        4. For the rise and fall of the UPC, see
Richard Joseph, Radical Nationalism in Cameroun
(Oxford University Press, London, 1977).
        5. See Richard Sklar, Nigerian Political
Parties, (Princeton University Press, Princeton, N.J.,
1963), pp. 94-97.
        6. Aristide Zolberg, Creating Political Order:
The Party-States of West Africa (Rand-McNally,
Chicago, 1966), pp. 19-33, is particularly emphatic
on the weaknesses of parties as organizations.

Chapter Four

CHOOSING A STRATEGY FOR DEVELOPMENT

          Winning the political kingdom did not automat-
ically resolve all problems for African leaders,
especially the problem of meeting their peoples'
hopes for improved living standards. They still
faced contradictions in their inherited political
structures and attitudes, severe conflicts in the
relations among the several peoples of their new
state, and above all, the dependence of their domestic economy upon one-sided external links with the
Western industrialized states. In their struggle
for political independence, few leaders had tried to
work out comprehensive strategies for dealing with
these problems. Now they had to evolve approaches
that would cope simultaneously with all of them.
          Over the years, some leaders developed compre-
hensive strategies, although most drifted with
events, responding to crises on an ad hoc basis.
The strategies fell into two broad categories, a
basic "accommodation" to the existing capitalist
world order while trying as far as their bargaining
power permitted to extract some benefits for themselves within this framework, or a "transformation"
into a society largely disengaged from the capitalist states and relying as far as possible on its
own resources for its development.[1] However, whether
they consciously pursued an accommodation or a
transformation strategy or just drifted with events,
all African leaders had to deal with a situation
which gave them a vast range of formal powers but
very little effective control over their states.

PRESSURES TOWARD AUTOCRACY

          A wide range of political, social and economic
forces encouraged the new rulers to eliminate rivals
and to close off channels for direct challenges to

their position, but there was little in the situa-
ion after independence to facilitate their building
mass popular support. While the political structures bequeathed by both the British and the French
anticipated electoral competition, they also featur-
ed a concentration of power in the hands of a single
executive, either a parliamentary Prime Minister or
Gaullist-type President. They also included some
pious constitutional declarations about human
rights, but left sufficient loopholes in these to
allow leaders to dispose of political opponents by
perfectly legal means. They also generally bequeathed a "steel frame" of administration and police and
military forces, generally still effectively controlled by expatriates, although most states quickly put
their own citizens into the key policy-making roles.
Inevitably, however, many of the policies that had
been initiated by the colonial power were still
actively advocated by the administration, and the
new governments frequently found themselves defend-
ing policies they had attacked before they took
office.
    A far more serious limitation on the new
rulers' ability to choose their policies, however,
was the sheer pressure of events. Not only did the
small size (and often the inexperience) of the civil
service restrict its ability to generate and process
the information that a ruler would need in order to
canvass effectively a range of policy options, but
the sheer mass of day-to-day demands meant that few
leaders or their lieutenants had the time to take a
long-range look at where they were going. It was
very easy for a leader to take the line of least
resistance in dealing with a specific problem, such
as whether to allow senior civil servants to retain
the salary levels built up by their European predecessors, even though such a decision might preclude
a later attempt to level off incomes. As the difficulties piled up for the first generation of
leaders, most tended to give increasingly high
priority to their own survival, and thus were inclined to bend to whatever seemed the strongest pressures of the moment.
    The ambiguities of the political values instil-
led under colonial rule also facilitated leaders
justifying increasingly authoritarian practices as
being for the good of their people. On the one
hand, the colonial powers' own professed beliefs in
liberty, the right of free expression, popular
participation in government, and making rulers
accountable to the people had been used effectively

against them by the nationalist parties to demand self-government. On the other side, however, was the long record of arbitrary actions by the colonial administration. Administrators generally had done what they thought best, regardless of the wishes of the people, and frequently without even trying to show people why particular actions were necessary. Thus compulsory cutting of diseased cocoa trees in Ghana, ridging of fields to prevent erosion in Tanganyika, or depositions of chiefs in the Ivory Coast, left people with the firm impression that any government was arbitrary and capricious.

The social divisions and economic problems which persisted at independence accentuated the difficulties within the political arena. In West Africa, where no entrenched racial minorities could try to block Africans' move to control over the territories, the question arose very early of which Africans would take control of the new state. In Nigeria, for example, even before the 1951 elections both Yorubas and Northerners felt impelled to form their own political parties to prevent what they saw as an Ibo takeover of the national and regional governments.[2] Sometimes, as in Nigeria or Dahomey, an uneasy balance could be attained; in other cases, such as Burundi and Ruanda, the "tribal" appeals were a convenient way for politicians to consolidate personal support.

In Eastern and Southern Africa, where Europeans and Asians both blocked Africans' advance and served as a target against which Africans could unite, tribalism was a somewhat less severe problem, although even here Kenya and Zambia in particular saw persistent conflicts among major groups. But once the goal of African rule had been conceded, tribal conflicts emerged here too.

The economic situation of most new states at independence led to considerable frustration. They were generally too poor to raise much capital domestically either to establish new plantations, processing plants or other wealth-creating activities, or to set up new school and health facilities which over the long run would also increase national wealth. They thus had to look abroad for new investment, or do without. But because being "under-developed" meant their people lacked technical skills, their domestic markets were small, and their roads, ports and other facilities for export were limited, most ex-colonies did not suddenly become more attractive to private investors at independence.

Furthermore, nearly all exchanged their agricultural crops or minerals for the manufactured
products of the industrialized states. This meant
that the diversity of jobs created by manufacturing
and processing stayed in the hands of the industrial
states, and so did most of the value added as raw
materials were transformed. However, the handling
of their exports and imports had built up a modest
African middle class which owed its jobs and prosperity to its links with the colonial power. Since
this middle class was normally the best-educated
and most articulate segment of African society, it
exercised a disproportionate influence in political
movements and in the administration. Despite the
stultifying effect of colonial economic policies on
economic development, those states which had become
most closely integrated into the industrial states'
economies would find it hardest to break away from
those policies.

One form of check on a government's power,
however, was very weak in Africa. Interest groups
enjoyed little of the independent strength that
could allow them to challenge the government. The
professional men such as lawyers and doctors either
were employed directly by the state, or depended on
it for a good deal of their work. Businessmen
depended on government licences, contracts, import
permits and other benefits which could be withheld
if they failed to co-operate. The trade unions had
rarely been powerful in Africa, and were generally
one of the first groups to be brought directly
under government control after independence. Market
women, lorry drivers and other similar trade groups
were fairly strong and cohesive, but they were not
likely to campaign against a government unless it
directly affected their own interests. The chiefs,
who in older times enjoyed a degree of autonomy
through the loyalty of their own people, were
divided and had frequently been undermined by being
used as agents of the colonial administration.
There were, in short, very few groups capable of
resisting a government which was wiping out electoral competition or any other form of organized
opposition.

The economic problems of most states contributed in yet another way to leaders eliminating opposition. Because they could not hope to meet the hopes
for more material wealth that had been aroused
during the campaign for independence, most leaders
knew they faced a large number of disappointed
supporters, and thus might lose an election. In

this state of insecurity, and with so little to
stop them, it was almost inevitable that leaders
would try to protect their positions first by
preventing opponents challenging them in elections,
and eventually by removing the opponents themselves.
The one-party state, or at least a state in which
opposition parties were unable in practice to contest
elections, became the dominant pattern; five years
after independence, only four states -- Sierra Leone,
Somalia, Gambia and Botswana -- could seriously
consider the possibility of changing their governments through an election.

Despite this apparent consolidation of power,
most leaders were painfully aware just how fragile
their hold was. They could act in high-handed ways
toward their subjects, and could change the rules
of the political game according to their whims.
They could help themselves to a good deal of the
state's wealth, by taking commissions on contracts,
by channelling government funds into private
accounts through loans and similar devices, and in
countless other ways: this legacy, because it
encouraged similar behaviour at lower levels, and
weakened many people's commitment to the state,
proved a particularly costly one. What they could
not do was to find an easy way to fulfil the dreams
and hopes their people had developed in the movement
toward independence. All the ways of attaining
these dreams seemed hard and demanded even more
effort than the independence struggle. But with
independence achieved, the leaders had lost their
main rallying call for bringing all the citizens of
the new state together.

Most African leaders faced a tantalizing situation at independence. To improve the well-being of
their countrymen clearly called for comprehensive
action involving mass participation toward agreed
goals. But the attainment of independence meant
that the consensus on what was to be done had given
way to a diverse clamour of interests, each with its
own ideas on where the ship of state should sail
next. It was also painfully clear to most leaders
that the chances of redeeming the promises they had
made before independence were poor indeed, and that
consequently they would have to face growing disillusionment. The frequency with which crises arose,
and the shortage of personnel with the skills to
deal with them, were often exacerbated by the
shadow of insecurity under which leaders worked, a
shadow which reduced their trust in, and therefore
the amount of responsibility they would delegate to

their lieutenants.

Nor could a leader even impose his own goals arbitrarily, despite the fact that there were few interests strongly enough organized to check him. The structures necessary for implementing new policies -- a party to educate public opinion and an administration capable of working out the technical problems -- scarcely existed. Because most leaders had taken the line of least resistance by not building their parties into anything more than machines capable of winning elections, and then diverting their most capable organizers into government administration once they had gained power, few party workers had either the dedication or the ability to rouse the people to new tasks. Because the civil services were still largely staffed by persons, Africans as well as Europeans, who had been steeped in the colonial era's policies and procedures, they were strongly biassed toward maintaining the status quo.

The economic dilemma reinforced the political one. To increase the opportunities for processing and light industries which would develop technical skills and provide capital for further expansion required a richer domestic market for goods and services. But to enlarge the domestic market required increased productivity, whether through farmers increasing their outputs through fertilizers and machinery, processors turning logs into plywood or cotton into cloth, or manufacturers turning out cooking utensils, door hinges or sandals, all of which would provide more jobs and income to buy further products. To get this increased productivity required investment in new machinery, skilled technical teachers to train Africans how to operate factories, roads and trucks to carry goods around the country. But all these things needed money, the lack of which was why there was not much of a domestic market in the first place.

The leaders' potential choice of strategies, then, was bounded by several considerations. Politically, most leaders had still not fashioned reliable instruments for controlling or guiding their people. Economically, they were still in the circular trap of "underdevelopment", which they had to escape in order to provide the material payoffs needed to maintain their own support as well as to improve their peoples' lives. Socially, they had to ensure an equitable distribution of such benefits as they could extract, to avoid the danger of their state being shattered by ethnic conflict.

WHY ACCOMMODATION WAS FAVOURED

In examining the implications and the degree of success of the "accommodation" and the "transformation" strategies, we should remember that both evolved only gradually as conscious programmes for economic and social development. The accommodation strategy in particular was for most leaders not one that was thought out, but simply the "obvious" path to development of emulating the Western industrial states, relying on private entrepreneurs to furnish capital in their search for profitable activities, and hoping that these activities would provide the jobs, training and further capital accumulation that would eventually lead to full-scale industrialization. Until about the mid-1960s, when the Chinese experience came to be fairly widely known, the only alternative model for development was that provided by the Soviet Union, which had several disadvantages. Like the Western capitalist models, it called for massive industrialization using sophisticated imported technology; and it also called for a detailed plan for the entire economy far beyond the capability of any African government, although this drawback became apparent only with experience. It also had the costly side effect that to profess using it would guarantee the hostility of Western governments, and would probably frighten away Western private investors.

It was only gradually that the emphasis on industrialization was reduced in favour of agriculture, although the Ivory Coast had from the outset emphasized agriculture as its initial engine of growth, though within a very consciously capitalist framework. The first transformation strategies, such as those of Guinea, and Ghana from 1962 to 1966, relied heavily on industrialization, and it was really only with Tanzania's Arusha Declaration in 1967 that this strategy became predominantly one of building upon agriculture and encouraging small-scale industries which could support rural developmental efforts, and which themselves relied as far as possible upon indigenous capabilities.

The success of the "accommodation" approach in improving the living standards of Africans depended first of all upon what resources a country could offer the world, and second, how skillfully it was able to bargain to obtain such benefits as jobs and manufacturing opportunities for its own nationals. Some countries were fortunate in having natural resources in high demand; Nigeria's oil, Botswana's diamonds, and Gabon's oil and timber all lured

foreign investors, whereas countries like Upper
Volta or Chad had almost nothing wanted by the world
market. Generally, however, a country needed to
develop definite economic policies to get benefits
from the accommodation approach. The Ivory Coast,
which alone among African states built a thriving
economy exclusively upon agriculture, accomplished
this largely because the government carefully
encouraged diversification, as well as a fair amount
of processing of crops for export. Botswana struck
hard bargains for the exploitation of its minerals,
and Nigeria eventually did the same with its oil.

Most states, however, were in no position to
strike hard bargains. Sierra Leone's low-grade iron
ore, for example, was eventually abandoned because
it could not compete with the much richer deposits
of Mauretania and Liberia, while Ghana's bauxite
remained unexploited partly because Guinea, Jamaica
and Guyana among others all possessed high-grade
ore. All the forest belt states of West Africa
could grow cocoa and coffee, a fact which contributed to over-production for these essentially static
markets in the 1960s, and a consequent slump in
prices. Manufactured substitutes from the industrialized states also hit primary producers hard.
Tanganyika's sisal was undercut in the 1960s by the
spread of polypropylene rope, while the Sudan and
Uganda saw their cotton markets invaded by polyester
fibres. The over-all effect of accommodation for
most states was that the value of their exports
declined relative to the cost of manufactured
imports, with the result that standards of living
stayed static or even declined.

Even for those states that could obtain
increasing prices for their raw materials, success
could engender its own problems. If a foreign company was allowed to operate in its own enclave,
students and other upwardly aspiring persons tended
to suspect they were not getting a fair chance at
high-level jobs, and their country was not getting
a proper share of the profits. State intervention
in the management and ownership of the foreign corporation was their preferred solution. But governments had to tread a fine line. If they responded
to these "radical" demands, they might drive present
and future foreign investors away. But if they
failed to respond, the radicals might stage demonstrations and riots, which also could frighten away
foreign investors and which might induce the military to stage a coup. How far a government could
go in meeting domestic demands for greater partici-

60

pation depended largely on the economy's intrinsic attractiveness to foreign investors. A rich state like Kenya or Nigeria, with relatively prosperous markets, a large number of skilled workers, and a number of resources worth exploiting, could obtain investment even when it demanded a high level of indigenization of ownership and of management. But a state such as Niger or Burundi could make few such demands.

Who benefitted from the successful accommodation strategy? The main beneficiaries were the upwardly mobile educated elites, the young accountants, engineers, public relations men and others who could take over high-level jobs at "European" salaries. Lower-level wage workers gained something, since foreign corporations tended to be more highly mechanized and thus could afford to pay their few workers more than could indigenous firms which relied more heavily upon labour and less on technology.[3] All urban dwellers generally benefitted from the "urban bias" which was built into the accommodation strategy insofar as it involved responding to the most vociferous demands for amenities from the populace, demands which almost invariably originated in the urban centres.

Rural dwellers generally did not benefit as much from an accommodation strategy as did urbanites. When agricultural crops were profitable, and when the state allowed farmers to reap a substantial share of the world price, as in the Ivory Coast, those who had large farms did fairly well. But even apart from the fact that clean water, dispensaries and schools did not reach the rural areas as readily as they came to the towns, most rural dwellers either had farms too small to get much wealth from them or had to work as labourers at very low wages.

A major effect of the accommodation strategy, then, was to widen disparities between urban and rural dwellers, and between the educated and technically trained elites and the illiterate and unskilled. Some states, such as the Ivory Coast, defended this on the grounds that the over-all level of prosperity was increasing, and that in absolute terms a good deal of wealth was trickling down to the lower levels of society. But in many states, there was not much additional wealth being created in total, and even where some was trickling down, men tended to notice the disparities more than the improvements in their own situation. In any state adopting this strategy, then, there was the potential for an explosion of anger and frustration from

below,[4] although it was questionable whether such
an explosion could bring fundamental change unless
it persuaded the junior officers of the army to
bring their organized force to bear on its behalf.[5]

A successful accommodation strategy involved
more than just drifting with events. A leader would
have to have some over-all vision of the kind of
society he was trying to create, and a shrewd sense
of how much pressure he could put on foreign investors to open up jobs and other opportunities for his
people. This in turn depended on how accurately he
could assess his bargaining hand relative to other
countries pursuing similar strategies. To the
extent that he succeeded in providing benefits for
his own people, he would build up a loyal corps of
well-educated and skilled supporters, and would
probably enhance his appeal to those Africans who
were prepared to enjoy vicariously the sight of
their countrymen occupying powerful economic positions. The accommodation strategy would tend to
lock his state firmly into the world economy, because this cadre of privileged Africans could exert
strong pressure against any moves toward a more
"self-reliant" strategy.

Within the general "accommodationist" framework
there was, however, a possibility of a much more
self-serving role for a leader. If he were primarily concerned to enrich himself, or feared the
threat to his position posed by wealthy indigenous
businessmen or well-educated personnel, he could
simply encourage foreign entrepreneurs to develop
the country's resources as they saw fit, preferably
in isolated enclaves, and extracting for himself
such tolls as he could persuade them to pay. This
role involved no vision for the country, but simply
saw the leader acting as a broker among the conflicting demands of his countrymen, as long as all
remained willing to accept his control, or as a
tyrant holding power by force as people became
disillusioned with his rule.

For the 1960s and 1970s the accommodation
approach enjoyed mixed success, with those African
states which had begun with a relatively strong
hand, such as the Ivory Coast, Gabon, Cameroun and
Kenya, managing to satisfy their peoples' aspirations tolerably well, while those which offered
little to attract outside investors, such as Upper
Volta, Chad, or the Central African Republic, limped
along as the world's poorest states. As the 1980s
opened, however, the accommodation approach faced
its severest test since the African states' indepen-

dence. On top of two severe blows in the 1970s, the
drastic increase in world oil prices and the drought
which ravaged agriculture throughout the drier parts
of both West and East Africa, the industrial world's
most severe economic slump since the Great Depres-
sion of the 1930s hit African states in a number of
ways. Most seriously, it cut sharply their exports
of raw materials, particularly of minerals.
Secondly, it worsened their already deteriorating
terms of trade, since they were less well able to
control their selling prices than were the major
manufacturers of the West. Third, the Western
states' domestic economic problems led to a reduction of aid and an increase of commercial interest
rates to the Third World. All these factors came
together to produce a disastrous balance-of-payments
crisis, and the prospect that economic dislocations
would lead to the destablizing of even the most
firmly entrenched regimes.
    This economic crisis was particularly severe
for the accommodationist regimes since they tended
to depend upon material payoffs to maintain their
citizens' support, and were more closely integrated
into the Western industrialized states' economies.
Even states such as the Ivory Coast, which had managed to achieve a fair amount of diversification and
processing of their exports, faced problems as the
industrialized states strove to protect their own
economies. It remained in 1982 to be seen how
successful the accommodation strategy would be in a
world suddenly turned very hostile toward states
with limited economic power.

REQUISITES FOR A TRANSFORMATION STRATEGY

    The "transformation strategy" required major
commitments by the leader, by cadres of intermediaries, and by the mass of the people. It evolved out
of a perception that the colonial relationships of
the new African state had benefitted very few
Africans, and held little prospect of providing
wider benefits in the future. Specifically, the
economic exchange of raw materials for the manufactured consumer goods of the industrialized world
appeared to restrict severely the economic benefits
African states received, as well as limiting the
creation of technological skills and education, and
widening the gaps between a privileged few and the
bulk of the population. From a practical point of
view, the heavy reliance on imported consumer goods,
a long-term trend to worsening terms of trade

between these increasingly complex manufactures and the African states' raw material exports, and the consequent imbalance in foreign exchange, pointed to a politically excruciating belt-tightening some time in the future, particularly for those states whose products had no special leverage on world markets.

This view of the African economic situation suggested three possible routes to change. One route was to cut one's state off completely from the outside world, neither exporting nor importing goods, but relying entirely upon the energies and abilities of the country's own people. In that every African state had come to rely to some extent upon motorized transportation, and had a substantial population that liked manufactured cloth, metal goods, and construction materials such as cement, this course was just too politically painful for any government to pursue.[6] A second route would be to process one's major exports, and thus capture the considerable value added, as well as increasing the pool of domestic technological skills, and stimulating forward and backward linkages within the economy. However, the high cost of importing the technology and skilled persons to get processing started, coupled with the barriers to Third World manufacturers thrown up by most of the industrialized states, made this approach also a non-starter.

The third approach to transforming the economy was the more complex one of re-orienting agriculture to serve the domestic non-agricultural population, while developing manufacturing capacity to provide for the needs of the predominantly rural mass markets. Exports would provide foreign exchange to purchase complex manufactured goods such as trucks that were necessary for the economy as a whole, or better still, to purchase machinery that would allow the country to manufacture its own goods, but they were definitely subordinated to the need to develop the domestic economy. This down-playing of exports necessarily meant that imports would have to be reduced, and the main target was luxury consumer goods such as private automobiles.

The states which should most logically have been attracted to such a strategy were those which had little prospect of selling much in world markets in any case, whereas states which had one or more products which were firmly established in world markets seemingly had less incentive to undertake this kind of re-orientation of their economies. However, while some states with little to offer world markets, such as Somalia and Guiné-Bissau, did pursue a transformation strategy, others with equally poor prospects, such as Upper Volta and Chad, did not. Conversely, Guinea, Ghana, Mozambique and Tanzania could have carved themselves out tolerable niches in the world economy, yet chose to attempt the more difficult task of transforming their economies. This suggests that the pursuit of a transformation strategy was a decision consciously taken by a leader, rather than something made inevitable by circumstances. My contention is that it originated in each case with a leader's commitment to the goal of improving all his people's living standards, and that his success depended upon his skill in creating the means to carry his people with him, and in avoiding the various pitfalls that could lead his experiment astray.

To make a transformation strategy work, most of the population needed to be persuaded to change their ways of living. Farmers had to be persuaded to grow crops for domestic consumption rather than for export, and while these could provide them with as much income, there was no guarantee that they would provide more, or that incomes could still buy the range and quality of consumer goods to which they had become accustomed. Urban workers needed to move from those sectors which were essentially export- and import-oriented to jobs in the domestic sector, and to forego some of the imported luxuries they had enjoyed. The most substantial sacrifices, however, were asked of high-level civil servants and Africans in the private sector, who would have to forego their luxury imports and also the high level of salaries established under the influence of the colonial regime and the multinational corporations, yet would still have to provide their skills for building up domestic industry and for aiding the rural transformation.

If these changes were to effect an improvement in most peoples' standard of living, the leader had to persuade people to make them voluntarily. There was no way a government could force farmers to produce surplus food against their will, nor force unwilling executives to organize successful domestic industries. The leader had to persuade people to accept short-term material sacrifices for non-material satisfactions and the rather tentative hope of improved material well-being in the long run. For this, in turn, he needed not only clearly worked out goals of his own, but intermediaries who shared the same goals, and also had the ability to persuade and educate others. A strong commitment to shared goals, in short, was required by the leader, by party cadres, by people possessing the technical and administrative skills necessary to achieve these goals, and by the public at large.

If the leader and party could create this shared commitment, they might be able to build a state with a prospering internal economy, with a fairly egalitarian distribution of wealth, and with a sense of national identity. However, there were several obstacles to achieving these goals. The most immediate were that no matter how great their commitment, government and party officials might not have the skills to re-organize the economy to maintain a tolerable standard of living, and that in order to speed up changes, they might use force indiscriminately and alienate the people they needed to persuade. The disasters which befell Ghana's economy as a result of the attempts to use import controls in 1962-66, and the discontent engendered by Guinea's repeated use of coercion, served as warnings of these two dangers.

For the transformation approach to have a chance, then, the leader needed to know clearly where he was going and to be able to bring his people with him. Development needed to be carefully guided, and the leader needed to be prepared to act firmly to prevent plans being sabotaged by incompetence or corruption on the part of subordinates. Yet at the same time he could not fall into the trap of using coercion for its own sake against imagined "enemies of the revolution", or he would produce a regime which lived in fear of everyone. Such a leader had to be very much an activist, prepared to devote a great deal of effort to his goals; he needed also to be to some degree an ideologue, but not to the extent that he was blinded to the realities of his situation; and above all, he needed to have built a bond of trust with his people.

Since the transformation strategy requires a conscious and sustained effort by the leader, with the likelihood of short-term hardships for his people and risks for himself, and no guarantee of long-term success, it is not surprising that few leaders chose it. The three longest-running efforts at transformation are Sékou Touré's Guinea since 1958, Julius Nyerere's Tanzania since 1967, and Siad Barre's Somalia since 1969. The three ex-Portuguese colonies and Ethiopia under the military have been trying transformation strategies since 1975, but there is not yet sufficient data to evaluate the success of their experiments. Ghana under

66

Nkrumah from 1962 until 1966, and Mali under Modibo Keita from 1960 to 1968 tried the transformation approach, and Algeria, despite its continuing trade links with France and other industrialized states, has pursued elements of this strategy since 1962, but it is hard to see any other cases in Africa, unless one wants to include the drive for economic self-reliance (but within a capitalist framework) of the Rhodesian whites from 1965 to 1979.[7] '

Despite its hazards and difficulties, the transformation approach appeared to offer some potential advantages. It could to some extent insulate the state from the effect of world trade cycles, and thus reduce the danger posed to the leader by severe drops in his peoples' living standards. It could possibly also encourage people to develop their own productive methods for manufactured goods, methods adapted to local conditions, though how realistic this hope was remained to be seen. Finally, it could offer the psychological advantage of increasing self-confidence, although as a Ghanaian sadly remarked to me in 1978, "What is the effect of trying to do things for yourself when you fail?" The main question, however, is whether there is any transformation strategy that could succeed in realizing these potential advantages. Does it simply expect too much of a leader, of his cadres, and of the people of a country?

THE STRATEGIES COMPARED

How have the transformation states fared in comparison with the accommodation states? If we take Guinea, Tanzania and Somalia as our three main examples of the transformation strategy, and compare them with the over-all performance of African states by the criteria of wealth created, its distribution, the personal security of individuals, and the extent of national integration and commitment to the new state, the answer seems to be that there is no decisive difference. None of them has established a clear superiority according to these criteria, nor has any been markedly worse than their nontransformationist neighbours.

By the most easily measurable criterion, the rate of increase in the per capita Gross National Product, Tanzania's growth rate of 2.6% from 1960 to 1976 ranked 13th of 39 African states measured by the World Bank.[8] Guinea at 0.4% ranked 30th, and Somalia at -0.3% ranked 36th. It is also worth noting that for this period Tanzania's growth rate was identical to that of its capitalist neighbour, Kenya, often regarded as one of the "miracle" economies, and was considerably better than that of any of its other seven neighbours except Malawi. Guinea, by contrast, ranked below all its neighbours except Senegal, which achieved a negative growth rate of -0.7%, while the only states with worse over-all growth rates than Somalia were the other dry drought-stricken states, Senegal, Niger and Chad.

For the distribution of wealth, if we use the criterion proposed by Hicks and Streeten[9] of life expectancies, we find that the three transformation states increased the average life expectancy of their citizens by seven years from 1960 to 1975, against an average of 6.3 years for the accommodation states. In 1975 Tanzania, with an average 45-year life expectancy for its citizens, stood 11th of 39 states, while Guinea and Somalia, with 41 years, stood tied for 22nd.[10]

If we turn to the security of citizens against both spontaneous violence by other members of society and against severe oppression by their government, we find a rather mixed record. Tanzania seems to have been relatively free of violent crime, and has had little in the way of communal uprisings. The government for its part seems to have generally avoided the petty harassments and corruption that have been so marked a feature of neighbouring Zaire, as well as the political intimidation and atmosphere of fear that permeates Malawi. Its one major oppressive period came during villagization of some 11 million rural dwellers in the mid-1970s, when a number of cases of severe abuses arose. But even this seems to have been largely forgiven, and there is little to suggest seething discontent.

Guinea, by contrast, has been marked both by communal divisions in recent years, and by massive government repression. The fact that an estimated one-fifth of Guinea's population is in exile suggests the magnitude of this repression, as do the periodic purges and executions of Touré's critics. Yet neither the executions nor the numbers of exiles were on a scale comparable to those of the Macias Nguema regime in Equatorial Guinea, Micombero's government in Burundi, or Amin's regime in Uganda.

With respect to national integration and commitment to the state, again the record is mixed. Tanzania has had the advantage that it lacked any major ethnic group which could seek to dominate, and Nyerere has always managed to keep ethnic appeals from becoming a significant part of Tanzanian politics. The fact that most Tanzanian officials have accepted policies (such as the ban on private automobiles) that inflict a personal sacrifice on them, and have managed to remain surprisingly free from corrupt practices, suggests the strength of their commitment to the state and to the TANU ethos. Certainly in comparison to the ethnic conflicts in Kenya between Kikuyu and Luo, and the drive for personal enrichment among leading politicians and civil servants there, Tanzania seems a model polity, and the same could be said far more emphatically in comparing it with Zaire.

Guinea has been somewhat less successful in developing a commitment to the state, as Touré's attacks in 1976 on the Fulas as "disloyal" citizens suggested. While he has kept the political elite from the abuses of conspicuous consumption that undercut Nkrumah's regime, and maintained his personal reputation for honesty, Touré has had to cope with widespread problems of corruption among his officials.

Somalia is something of a special case, in that it is ethnically homogeneous, with the mission of liberating its brother Somalis from the control of Ethiopia and Kenya. Barre's regime, while puritanical and strict, has not had to be violently repressive against its own citizens, even though it did manage to embroil itself in an unsuccessful war with Ethiopia. Somalis started with a firm national identity, and this has been a mainstay of their state.

None of the criteria I have suggested for judging the contribution of a state to the well-being of its citizens sets the transformation states apart from the rest of Africa. As general strategies, neither transformation nor accommodation offers magic solutions to the multitude of problems facing each state at independence. However, if we look more closely at how specific states have coped with their problems, we may be able to discern some pattern, and within this pattern we may be able to see the effect of political leadership or its absence. It is to these specific cases that we will now turn.

NOTES

1. I have taken the terms "accommodation" and "transformation" strategy from Donald Rothchild and Robert Curry, Scarcity, Choice, and Public Policy

in Middle Africa (University of California Press, Berkeley, 1978). However, I have lumped their third type, the "reorganization" strategy, with the accommodation strategy because it seems to me that this strategy's attempt to give Africans more control of their economies through additional processing and manufacturing, and through participation in the management and ownership of companies, still leave these states firmly integrated into a capitalist world economy. What it represents essentially is a more successful bargaining position within the same general framework.

2. Sklar, Nigerian Political Parties, pp. 93, 101-2.

3. See Stephen Langdon, "Multinational Corporations, Taste Transfer and Underdevelopment: A Case Study from Kenya", Review of African Political Economy, 2 (1975), pp. 14-17, 22-23.

4. Peter Gutkind has been particularly emphatic on the growth of urban discontent. See especially his "From the Energy of Despair to the Anger of Despair", Canadian Journal of African Studies, 7, 2 (1973), pp. 179-98.

5. Even when they initiate changes, the officers may place more emphasis on protecting their own hold on power than on carrying through these changes. See, for example, the numerous radical critiques of the Ethiopian military regime, such as John Markakis and Nega Ayele, Class and Revolution in Ethiopia (Merlin, London, 1978), and Michael Chege, "The Revolution Betrayed: Ethiopia, 1974-9" Journal of Modern African Studies, 17, 3 (1979), pp. 359-80.

6. Almost the only example of this approach in recent years has been the Pol Pot regime in Cambodia, not one which would inspire imitators. The Burmese under General Ne Win also cut most of their ties with the outside world, but they did not attempt a massive restructuring of the domestic economy.

7. The Republic of the Congo under the late Marien Ngouabi, and the regime of Lt. Col. Kerekou in Benin, profess to be attempting total transformations of their societies, but the little information available suggests that these transformations are largely at the level of rhetoric.

8. World Development Indicators, Table 1.

9. Hicks and Streeten, World Development, 7, pp. 578-9.

10. World Development Indicators, Table 17.

Chapter Five

GHANA: A JOURNEY WITHOUT MAPS?

The man who shaped modern Ghana was independent Africa's first great tragic hero. Kwame Nkrumah deserves the title of "hero" because in pursuing his dream of making Ghana a modern industrialized state no longer dependent upon the West for either its material goods or its values, he made his countrymen aware of themselves as a nation and of their strength and dignity as Africans. But he was a tragic figure, and his country has suffered ever since, because he did not know how to achieve his dream. In his struggles to make Ghana economically prosperous and autonomous, he swung wildly from an unsuccessful search for private foreign investment to a disastrous attempt at a planned economy, while his major instrument for carrying the Ghanaian people with him, the Convention Peoples Party, degenerated into a corrupt patronage machine which turned people against Nkrumah and his government. By the end of his rule, the economic failure and the corruption that played a major part in it had so thoroughly disillusioned most of the people of Ghana that even the lead they enjoyed over almost every other African state in running all aspects of their country themselves seemed a dubious blessing, with many ordinary people wondering whether their affairs had been better managed under the British colonial masters.[1] A few years later, after a succession of further governments whose ineptitude and tawdriness matched that of Nkrumah's regime, a survey found that more than half the population not only saw their own lives as being worse than when they were children, but also saw their children's lives as being still worse than their own.[2]

Nkrumah's place in history is therefore an ambiguous one. By the cold measurement of economic growth statistics his regime was a miserable

failure, and the disillusionment just mentioned
suggested that at the human level also he signally
failed to achieve his goals. And yet he cannot be
dismissed as a failure quite so readily. Despite
the disillusionment, Ghanaians have shown a sense
of national identity stronger than most other
Africans, and they have been doing things, from
flying their own aeroplanes to developing their own
social insurance programmes, that few other African
states have as yet even contemplated. If Nkrumah
bears much of the responsibility for Ghana's economic and social problems today, he cannot be denied
some credit for the successes that Ghana has enjoyed.

The questions I wish to consider, then, are
how far and by what means did Kwame Nkrumah shape
present-day Ghana? To what extent could major
changes from the start of self-government in the
Gold Coast (as it then was) be attributed to actions
taken by Nkrumah rather than to events beyond his
control? If some of the major choices made by
Nkrumah were responsible for Ghana's economic hardships and for his own downfall, what kind of result
might alternative choices have produced? And to
what extent, in making these choices, did Nkrumah
succeed in persuading Ghanaians to support him,
rather than imposing his goals by force?

My argument is that much of Nkrumah's failure
was of his own making. He started, to be sure,
with the problem of not having all Ghanaians united
behind his nationalist movement, in that he came to
power by outbidding conservative upper-class
Ghanaians for mass support through his more vigorous attacks on colonial rule. However, he was so
obsessed with the goal of winning political independence that he did not develop an economic strategy
until well after independence. By then his failure
to mobilize and channel the popular anti-colonial
attitudes of earlier years into a comprehensive
transformation of key aspects of the economy and
the social structure had allowed the CPP to be
captured by opportunists who had no interest in mass
mobilization. Furthermore, he himself never seems
to have had such a clear grasp of what any developmental strategy might entail that he could settle
on specific goals, nor a sufficient commitment to a
strategy that he would risk his own political survival for its attainment.

THE NKRUMAH ERA: THE STAR OF AFRICA FADES

The story of post-war Ghana, and particularly
Nkrumah's rise and fall, has been told often enough
that I need give only a brief summary of the key
features relevant to my argument.[3] The Gold Coast,
comprising the Akan-speaking peoples of the south,
the linguistically related Ashanti Empire in the
centre, and the less numerous peoples of the northern savanna, enjoyed in the late 1940s the highest
per capita income of any tropical African territory,
as well as the largest proportion of educated persons and skilled workers. Its wealth derived largely from the initiative of the farmers of the south
and Ashanti, who in less than half a century had
built up cocoa growing to the point where the Gold
Coast supplied more than a third of total world
production, and cocoa provided about two-thirds of
the colony's export earnings. A capable and self-
confident elite of new professional groups with
links to the traditional rulers stood ready to take
up political power as the British handed it over,
and in 1947 formed the United Gold Coast Convention
to prod the British into hastening self-rule. Like
other British colonial people, and quite unlike the
francophone Africans, the Gold Coast elite saw their
country's future as an independent state expressing
its "African-ness", perhaps maintaining cordial ties
with Britain, but certainly not regarding it a
"mother country" or "homeland". They would show the
world just how well Africans could rule themselves,
enjoying prosperity and adopting institutions that
allowed political tolerance to flourish.
    To organize the UGCC into an effective polit-
ical movement, the lawyers and businessmen in 1947
brought home the 38-year-old Kwame Nkrumah, who
during his years in America and Britain had acquired
a reputation as a capable organizer. The Accra
riots in 1948 showed that there was a cauldron of
popular discontent over colonial rule just waiting
to be stirred, and after he and the UGCC leaders had
been imprisoned briefly for their alleged complicity
in the riots, Nkrumah built up a "Youth Wing" of
lower income, primary school leavers who became the
base of the Convention Peoples Party when he broke
with the "respectable" UGCC in 1949.
    The CPP's early success in Accra and other
towns owed a great deal to Nkrumah's personal dyna-
mism, and his ability to speak to ordinary peoples'
feelings in language they could readily understand.
His demands for "Free-dom!" and "Self-Government

NOW!", hard though they might be to achieve, offered a way of escape from the frustrations of colonial rule, and gave Nkrumah the image of the brave
warrior attacking the menacing British lion (even
though that poor beast would have liked nothing
better than to skulk quietly out of sight.) At
this time he could probably be called a charismatic
leader, a Messiah drawing people to break with the
past and accept the new values he personified.[4]
At the same time, his awareness of how much rested
on the personal basis of his appeal likely contributed to his personal insecurity, that was later to
drive him to make himself the centre of a cult of
personality, and to rely for counsel on soothsayers
and sycophants.

But for the first few years, there was little
reason to doubt the power of his appeal. Coupled
with his lieutenants' organizing skills and the
CPP's militant anti-colonial stance, his ability to
reach the common people carried the party to a
clear victory in the first national elections in
1951. In the next few years the militant radicalism subsided somewhat; Thomas Hodgkin noted as
early as 1954 that the CPP was growing "increasingly respectable" and "has undoubtedly lost some of
its old elan".[5] However, there was little doubt
through to 1957 that Nkrumah's slogan "Self-
government NOW" appealed to his countrymen powerful-
ly enough to sweep aside any opposition. Unfortunately this strategy of seeking first the political
kingdom, and adding other goals later, masked
Nkrumah's fatal weakness: that he did not know what
strategy to pursue once the political kingdom had
been gained.

Until independence, with the British insisting
on fair treatment for his opponents, Nkrumah had
little beyond his appeal to subdue successive
threats from local disintegrative forces. It was
enough; in 1954 the CPP triumphed over both a
northerners' party and a large number of CPP members standing as independents against its official
candidates, and in 1956 it overcame the more serious threat of a resurgent Ashanti nationalism allied to the more traditionalist chiefs and the dis-
gruntled upper class professionals who had been
shunted aside by the CPP. However, this election
showed the continuing challenge to the CPP from the
educated elite that felt it had been deprived of
the fruits of victory by a band of upstarts, as well
as the secessionist danger inherent in ethnic political movements.

Meanwhile, the prosperity that had bathed the country when cocoa prices moved up to a postwar peak of $1002 a ton in 1954 was eroded as the price slid gradually downward. By 1957 it was down to $692, and worse was to come. To be sure, the ordinary farmer had not been getting much of this wealth, since the Cocoa Market Board, which had been set up to cushion the farmers against severe price fluctuations, had put most of the receipts from the postwar commodities boom into its reserve funds. Thus, when the CMB was receiving $1002 for its cocoa in 1954 the farmer was getting only $375.[6] This disparity gave a very strong boost to the Ashanti-based National Liberation Movement in the 1956 election, although its ethnic base contributed to its inability to gain a foothold in the southern cocoa areas, where disaffection also ran high.

Once independence removed both British supervision and the rallying cry of "Freedom!" Nkrumah was able to deal more drastically with the growing challenges to CPP rule. Beginning with deportations and preventive detention, the government curtailed organized opposition to the point that in the 1960 elections, the opposition's share of the popular vote fell from the 40% of 1956 to just over 10%. Effectively Ghana had become a one-party state, though essentially by the opposition being coerced out of existence rather than by its being persuaded to join with Nkrumah.

Meanwhile, the economic situation continued to deteriorate. After a brief rally in 1958, the world price for cocoa again slid downward, to $633 a ton in 1960, and to $476 in 1962. This was disastrous for the very conventional economic development strategy that the government had followed since 1953, which had relied on foreign corporations to set up import substitution industries, while using cocoa revenues to build up infrastructure and cover imported consumer goods. Despite Ghana's scrupulously fair treatment of foreign investors, few came after independence; in fact, there was a net outflow of some $22 million of capital in the period 1957-1959.[7] Despite this danger signal, the government decided to use its own accumulated reserves to undertake in 1959 a Five-Year Plan doubling the previous seven years' annual investment rate to $84 million.[8] Since half these investments were for infrastructure and other services which provided no short term repayment, the major short-term effect was to send the import bill soaring, so that from slight surplusses in the 1950s, by 1961

Ghana had moved to a balance of payments deficit of
$146 million, an amount that if repeated would have
exhausted the foreign exchange reserves within two
years.

This looming disaster spurred the government to
more direct steps to promote economic growth, by
undertaking a massive programme of building state-
owned industries which would make the consumer goods
that had sent the import bill soaring, and by insti-
tuting a system of comprehensive planning for all
facets of the economy. Much of Ghana's investment
capital was thus committed to large-scale factories
and state farms, while strategic check points were
set up throughout the economy in the form of licences and exchange controls for all imports, including
vital parts for factories and other capital goods.

If Ghana had had the numbers of sophisticated
and skilled personnel available in industrialized
states, if these personnel had all been dedicated
to working for what they perceived to be the greatest good of the citizenry as a whole, and if the
government had had a clear sense of its over-all
priorities, then this type of " forced growth" might
have worked. However, while Ghana was better endowed with skilled persons than most other African
states, it fell woefully short of the numbers required for such a complicated exercise as planning
the entire economy, and a large number of those
available were interested mainly in benefitting
themselves or their immediate families. Equally
disruptive was Nkrumah's own lack of clear priorities, and his increasing tendency as problems worsened to over-rule his planners in erratic and non-
rational ways.

Nowhere was Nkrumah's lack of understanding of
the details which make the difference between economic success or failure more visible than in the
Volta River aluminum project. This project had
first been proposed by the British before Nkrumah
came to power, and by 1956 Nkrumah and his advisors
had worked out an integrated scheme using Ghana's
as yet untouched bauxite, smelting it with electricity from a power dam at Ajena, and providing spin-
offs of a fishery on the lake above, and irrigation
on the dry plains below. However, by this time
Britain had ample foreign exchange and aluminum supplies, and lost interest in the scheme. After independence Nkrumah sought American support for the
scheme, and eventually in 1961 secured an agreement
with the Kaiser Aluminum Corporation. The new plan,
however, had lost most of its linkages. All that

remained was a dam and power plant at Akosombo costing $196 million, half paid directly by Ghana and
half by loans from the West, and a smelter at the
new port of Tema, paid for and owned by Kaiser, and
using imported alumina rather than mining Ghana's
bauxite. Even more important was the fact that
Kaiser was to receive most of the project's electricity at scarcely over cost, meaning that the hydroelectric project would be hard put to pay for itself. Kaiser's smelter was expected to provide net
foreign exchange earnings of some $45-53 million a
year, but its contribution to employment was a modest 1,600 people at most.[9]
     Radical CPP members were appalled both by the
lack of structural change the final scheme would
make in Ghana's economy, and by the fact that the
key benefits were controlled by a foreign capitalist. More conservative observers also attacked the
scheme, mainly on the grounds that less grandiose
uses for this amount of capital which might have
brought a faster and a larger return were not considered. Nevertheless, Nkrumah pressed ahead. What
seemed most important in his mind was not a rational
calculation of costs and benefits, but that Ghana
should have the Volta Dam as a symbol of economic
progress.
     Although many of Nkrumah's subordinates talked
of building socialism, and the CPP's policy after
1961 was sometimes interpreted as the ascendancy of
left-wing ideologues over the more pragmatic older
cadres, the most significant feature of this
attempt at massive industrialization was the self-
seeking of the CPP elite. The personal corruption
which by now penetrated every level of public life
has been written about by so many observers[10] that I
need only note here how peculiarly dangerous it was
for a developmental approach which relied so heavily
upon key individuals being able to exercise control
over so many economic functions. If the factories,
machinery, and other imports being brought in were
to be measured by their social utility rather than
by potential profitability, the persons deciding on
this measure of utility needed to be strongly committed to seeking the good of the entire state. But
in fact most of the officials deciding what schemes
should go forward tended to judge by the criterion
of personal self-interest. Nkrumah had promised in
the famous "Dawn Broadcast" of April 1961 to clean
out the corrupt elements, but the clean-up never
materialized, and thus ordinary Ghanaians were left
feeling increasingly cynical about the "dedication"

of the CPP vanguard.[11]

Even if all the grandiose and ill-conceived schemes had been conceived soundly, and built and operated competently and honestly, their financing would have caused problems since most were financed through credit from foreign suppliers or contractors which came due before the projects could possibly pay for themselves.[12] But many projects were badly conceived, such as the Yugoslav-financed canning factories which simply assumed there would be suffi- cient crops of tomatoes, pineapples, and mangoes available to operate near capacity, and markets either within or outside Ghana for the output. Per- haps it was fortunate that the crops available were only a small portion of potential output, since the canned pineapple and mango would have had to be sold outside Ghana, and the former's quality was too low for world trade, while the latter would have tripled the total amount entering world markets.[13]

There were also a number of foreigners who deliberately defrauded Ghana, such as the French textile machine manufacturer who sold Ghana $9.8 million worth of looms whose production had been discontinued in France because of mechanical defects. And then, of course, there were the notor- ious contracts with the Drevici group, which left Ghana with such lasting monuments as four totally useless 50,000 ton cocoa-storage silos of solid con- crete.

The great spending spree from 1962-1965 not only left Ghana bankrupt, but created a great many hardships for ordinary people. For the three years, credit commitments totalled $423 million, enough to leave the country with debt-servicing commitments for the next five years of $92 million a year, equal to two-thirds of the cocoa crop at 1965 prices.[14] The spending spree produced rampant inflation, sharply cutting people's standard of living; the real value of the minimum wage, which by 1963 had declined to 82% of its 1960 value, fell to 57% of this value by 1965.[15] Clumsy and often corrupt han- dling of import controls aggravated this situation. Many widely used commodities were scarcely available, while in other cases poor quality substitutes from Eastern Europe replaced the goods to which Ghanaians had been accustomed. All of this hastened the disil- lusionment with the CPP and with Nkrumah himself.

The behaviour of CPP functionaries was even more important in destroying Nkrumah's support. The CPP had never been a party of dedicated revolution- aries; there was always a radical fringe, but particularly at the local level it had tended to be an aggregation of personally ambitious individuals who used it as a vehicle by which they might advance their own careers. The great increase in opportunities for exercising power and obtaining wealth through the proliferation of new state agencies, as well as through the control of imports and foreign exchange, produced many newly wealthy party functionaries, who were the subject of bitter comment by the ordinary workers who lacked such access to wealth. The long-time career civil servants did relatively well in resisting the temptation to concentrate on enriching themselves, and among the new managers of state enterprise there were also some dedicated individuals; but there were sufficiently large numbers of highly visible power-holders enjoying the sweets of office to make the regime appear the antithesis of socialism, which one Young Pioneer organizer succinctly defined as "No monkey dey wok baboon dey chop" ("Under socialism, clever opportunists are not allowed to steal all the wealth produced by working men").[16]

Under such circumstances, it is scarcely surprising that popular support for Nkrumah and the CPP had dwindled to scarcely perceptible levels by February 24, 1966. The rapid conversion of Young Pioneer leaders and even of his own entourage in Hanoi to an anti-Nkrumah stance after the military staged their coup while he was on a "peace-making" mission to Vietnam may have been a particularly opportunistic reaction,[17] but there seems little doubt that well before the coup most people had lost such enthusiasm as they had previously had for Nkrumah and were merely acquiescing in the rule of the CPP.

The party itself was becoming a tangle of factions intriguing against each other and sometimes against Nkrumah himself. The leading spokesmen of the left wing were implicated in 1962 when a grenade wounded Nkrumah in August at Kulungugu in the Northern Territories, and a month later a bomb exploded outside his residence. Tawia Adamafio, Nkrumah's chief propagandist and advisor, Coffie Crabbe, executive secretary of the CPP, and three other CPP men were arrested, tried, and eventually sentenced to death, although their sentences were then commuted. A different source of attacks was indicated when in January 1964 a policeman on duty at Nkrumah's residence tried to shoot him, but missed. Several senior police officials and leading members of the Opposition were detained as a result.

Clearly there were grounds for alarm here, although it can be debated whether the attempted assassinations provoked the government to tighten its grip or vice versa. Yet despite these direct threats on his life, Nkrumah did not turn to terror in the manner of, say, Sékou Touré. While increasing numbers of people were detained (and the "Grand Old Man" of Ghanaian politics, Dr. J. B. Danquah, died in prison), Nkrumah did not kill his enemies.[18]

However, while Nkrumah did not slaughter his enemies, he did complete the choking off of legal opportunities for a change of government. In January 1964, a referendum boasting a 92.8% turnout gave the proposal to turn Ghana into a one-party state 2,773,920 votes against 2,452 opposed[19] and the next year the election procedure was simplified still further, when following the approval of CPP candidates for the legislature by the Central Executive, Nkrumah declared the candidates elected without even the pretense of balloting.[20] The separation of the CPP from its popular base was completed. As Basil Davidson, the most sympathetic among the serious analysts of the regime, observed:

> "...he was terribly alone. He had to govern through a civil service or through party factions, playing off one against the other. Somewhere beyond this network of administrative intrigue stood the people of the country, watching with indifference a political game in which they had no part."[21]

In such a situation, with neither material payoffs nor spiritual hope to keep the populace faithful, his fall seemed almost inevitable. And yet, while he might be ousted from political control, Nkrumah could never be completely destroyed. As Trevor Jones, no admirer of Nkrumah, put it:

> "For all his faults, Nkrumah was the symbol of Ghana itself. It was he who gave his countrymen a genuine sense of pride in a common nationality. Such a memory is not easily excised. How can the birth of Ghana command respect, if the dead father is execrated? If he is discredited, what is left?"[22]

THE DESCENT AFTER NKRUMAH

Of those who have come after Nkrumah, far less
needs to be said. The National Liberation Council,
while unequivocal in its desire to undo as much as
it could of the Nkrumah regime, relied for direction
upon those senior civil servants who had remained
relatively untarred by the "misdeeds" of the Nkrumah
era.[23] The NLC's orientation was shown by its
favouring Dr. Busia and the old United Party opposition, and by its speedy honouring of Ghana's debts
to Western leaders, but apart from the initial jubil-
ation it aroused for having brought the CPP to an
end, it does not seem to have gained any deep support within Ghana.

Dr. Busia's ill-fated Progress Party government won a majority in the 1969 elections through
appearing to be most clearly the alternative to the
memory of the CPP; ethnic factors played a role as
well, although Komla Gbedemah's Ewe-based National
Alliance of Liberals also won a solid minority of
Akan votes.[24] There was no great surge of enthusiasm for Busia and the PP as there had been in the
previous free elections for Nkrumah; much of the
competition was built around local rivalries, with
the national parties and their policies very much a
secondary consideration for most voters.

The Busia regime was non-interventionist in
economic matters; it liberalized import controls,
but was reluctant to use state power to help lower-
income urban workers. It won some support by summarily expelling non-Ghanaians from many jobs, by
curbing higher civil servants' benefits, and by
channelling funds to rural development. However, a
flood of imports soon precipitated a foreign exchange crisis, and at the end of 1971 the government
devalued the currency by 44%. The effect on
people's consumption was drastic enough that when
the army used this as an excuse to oust Busia, none
of the groups who had originally supported him rallied to his regime's defence.[25]

Col. Acheampong's coup was seemingly inspired
more by personal and military considerations than
by any wider "good of the country". The soldiers
did restore many of the controls over the economy
abandoned by Busia, and also succeeded in getting
far better terms for repayment of Ghana's debts than
their predecessors by the simple expedient of announcing the terms on which they would repay.[26] Basically, they acted to benefit themselves first, and
the bourgeoisie second, drawing on lawyers,

businessmen and other relatively conservative groups to implement the "National Revolution", and refusing to lend money to small farmers when they began their major agricultural endeavour, Operation Feed Yourself.[27]

However, the soldiers managed to alienate these elite groups too, both by the regime's attempts to avoid restoring civilian rule and by the inflation which seriously hurt the elite's standards of living. When a <u>coup</u> from below ousted the senior officers in 1979 and eight officers were subsequently executed for corruption, few tears were shed over this departure from the usual gentle pattern of Ghanaian political change. Despite the record high prices for cocoa in the late 1970s the economy was a shambles, with ordinary people forced to pay a day and a half's wages for a single 10 lb. yam or other staples, while the upper class spent hours queueing for gasoline for their cars. The soldiers allowed elections for a civilian regime, but neither they nor the people had any great expectation of miracles. True to their expectations, the new government proved unable to deal with either the corruption and self-enrichment of its officials, or with the economic problems stemming from a declining agriculture and an over-valued currency. On New Year's Eve of 1981 Flight Lieutenant Jerry Rawlings, who had been the symbol of purifying force in the 1979 clean-out of the old officer corps, once again seized power, and this time threatened a more drastic purge to curb the corruption and the privileges of the elite. It remained to be seen, however, how long he and his military colleagues could remain above the morass.

NKRUMAH'S CHOICES: WAS THERE A BETTER PATH?

For better or worse, Kwame Nkrumah was the dominant figure in shaping present-day Ghana. Many of the subsequent economic and political problems facing the state could be traced back to his regime: heavy foreign debts, rampant corruption, severe inflation, and a grossly distorted economic base. But so could many of the advantages Ghanaians enjoyed over other African states: a solid educational system, widely distributed health services, African control over most domestic economic operations, and a strong sense of nationhood that overrode ethnic differences even in such stressful situations as elections. To be sure, neither the problems nor the benefits were totally attributable to Nkrumah's leadership; corruption and inflation, for example, became much more severe under Acheampong's regime, while the sense of nationhood could be attributed in part to the widely shared use of the Akan language, the fact that Ashanti had its own internal divisions, the political weakness of the north, and the fact that under colonial rule there had not been many occasions when different ethnic groups' interests conflicted. But even where we find other forces at work, we still find Nkrumah's actions contributing substantially to the subsequent course taken by Ghana.

However, this still leaves unanswered the question of how much influence the wishes of the leader had in shaping the new state. Would a leader with different goals and different effects have been possible in Ghana's circumstances? And did Nkrumah really have choices open to him at different stages, or was he forced along his path by the constraints within which his small, new and poor state operated?

My contentions are: first, that another type of leader with a much more "accommodationist" approach would have been quite likely in the late 1940s; second, that Nkrumah himself could have switched to an "accommodationist" strategy either before independence or at any time up to 1961; and third, that with some luck, he might have been able to move successfully to an all-out transformation strategy if he had taken the first critical move in 1954. As it was, he missed all these opportunities, and had the worst of two worlds; he was regarded as too "radical" to attract foreign private investment yet failed to maintain the base of popular support that was necessary if he was to make major structural changes.

In the Gold Coast after World War II, there was a great deal of discontent with the colonial system, but much of it was a generalized, unformulated resentment. The cocoa boycott of 1938, with its success in bringing together wealthy farmers and their labourers,[28] had already indicated the depth of feeling, but what was sought was not at all clear. There were few Marxists and little basis for a class-conscious movement either among urban wage labourers or among the cocoa workers. But there was a considerable base for any bourgeois movement demanding the right for Africans to get larger individual shares of the wealth that their colony was producing, among migrants to the towns, recent school leavers, traders small as well as large, and of course many of the farmers who had become heavily dependent upon cocoa as a cash crop. The UGCC had been formed in 1947 to appeal precisely to these groups and their aspirations, and in view of the way in which parties articulating essentially similar aspirations came to power in Nigeria and Sierra Leone as well as the Ivory Coast, it would not have been surprising to see the UGCC emerge as the spokesman for self-government in the Gold Coast.

That this did not happen is of course due to the fact that the party's General Secretary broke with it in 1949 and managed to outbid it with his militant demands for "Self-Government Now!" If Nkrumah had not been invited back by the UGCC in 1947 to take over the job of secretary, were the popular attitudes so far ahead of the UGCC's that some other leader would have emerged to build a dominant party through a similar insistence on speeding the process of change? Personally, I doubt it. If such a leader had tried to start outside the UGCC, he would have faced the problem that not only the educated elite, but also the chiefs, who were still influential opinion leaders in the rural areas, would have resisted him (as after 1949 they tried to resist the CPP). At the same time he would have lacked the patina of respectability that came from Nkrumah's earlier association with the UGCC, the "martyrdom" of detention in 1948, and the initial access to potential supporters that running the UGCC gave to Nkrumah. The UGCC, for its part, would likely have taken steps earlier to build its own organization. In other words, Nkrumah owed his initial success in creating the UGCC youth organization, which became the core of the CPP, partly to the umbrella that the UGCC provided him.

Similarly, if another individual had been organizing within the UGCC, he might have built up the same independent base of primary school leavers and might also have chafed at the UGCC leaders' caution in demanding changes. But it seems a rather long shot that any other such organizer would have had the combination of self-confidence in his own destiny, the magnetic attraction which could win mass support, and the ability to find skilled lieutenants that allowed Nkrumah to build the CPP in time for the 1951 elections.

Finally, we can note the obvious point that the issue on which the CPP outbid the UGCC in 1951 was the pace at which the Gold Coast should move toward independence. While their bases of activist supporters were different, and the CPP hinted at a more thorough reshaping of the social order than did the UGCC, most voters did not seem to be looking beyond the question of independence. The implication of this is that even if some other leader than Nkrumah had pushed aside the UGCC "Establishment" he would not necessarily have tried to reach socialism through massive industrialization. The case of Senegal, where Senghor in the 1940s became the champion of the "subjects" against the French citizen elite, but subsequently did nothing to free Senegal from its dependence on France, illustrates this point.[29]

In summary, then, if Nkrumah had not been the individual the UGCC leaders brought back to do their organizing in 1947, the odds were that the latter would have been the men to take the Gold Coast to independence. Most of the articulate and aspiring groups in the colony could have accepted their vision, although they would have had to make some concessions to the aspirations of lower-status groups such as the primary school leavers. Even if someone other than Nkrumah had succeeded in organizing a more militant movement for independence, there was no great likelihood that he would have pursued the same goal of industrialization.

Despite the achievements of his regime, it is the economic disaster of his last years in power for which Nkrumah is remembered. I have suggested this disaster had several roots: first, the drop in world cocoa prices from 1955 to 1964, which left Ghana chronically short of the foreign exchange needed to finance its ambitious plans for industrialization; second, the reluctance of foreign investors to support Ghana's import-substitution approach to industrialization; third, the wasteful and badly planned use of resources when the government tried to use its own reserves to finance industrialization; and fourth, the self-seeking and corruption at the top levels of the CPP, which vitiated any attempts to rally popular support for short-term sacrifices in order to achieve developmental goals.

Apart from the price of cocoa, all these factors were in part attributable to Nkrumah's leadership. I should like to consider here what he might have done to avoid these problems, and why he chose the course he did.

The "obvious" approach, in that it was the one followed by most leaders in both British and French Africa, was to work closely with the colonial power up to independence and with Western foreign investors generally afterwards. Such a strategy could involve inducing foreign firms to develop import-substituting industries, and even increasing Ghanaians' participation in the operation of these industries. In fact, this was the approach actually followed by Nkrumah's government up to 1961. But for such a strategy to work, it would be necessary for the Ghanaian government not only to provide quiet guarantees of protection for foreign investors, but to stop even rhetorical and symbolic assertions that it would like to curtail Western economic control. Given that Nkrumah himself in his "tactful" autobiography had written that Ghana needed economic independence from British control and "a socialistic society" backed by "emergency measures of a totalitarian kind"[30] and that his "tactical action" of stepping backward in order to reach compromises with the British overlords implied a (concealed) long-term strategy, it was not surprising that nervous foreign investors and critics remained unconvinced by Ghana's scrupulous treatment of private capital after independence, and that there was a net outflow of capital up to the end of 1960.[31] It would have taken an embarrassingly public about-face by Nkrumah on the role of Western capitalists to convince the latter that they really could expect their investments to be safe. Even then, the fact that Ghana was the first black African state to become independent was enough in itself to induce most investors to "wait and see"--and Nkrumah could not afford to wait for the material benefits of development to spread through the economy.

A further problem was that an "accommodationist" regime would have had a hard time justifying itself against the traditionalists and the old upper class of the UGCC, and if it failed to deliver material payoffs might well lose to them in a competitive election. On the other hand, as the first black African regime it was still very much on sufferance, and if it took the precaution of stifling its opponents to remain in power, the resulting criticism in the Western press would again likely hurt foreign investment.

Domestically, the costs of a switch to accommodation would have been high, but not fatally so. To CPP militants as well as to many ordinary Ghanaiams it would have appeared as a wholesale retreat from the CPP's original principles. Such a regime would have had a hard time instilling any sense of pride among Ghanaians; instead it likely would have produced the feeling that nothing really was changing.[32]

However, since the government controlled the access to wealth and power, it could be assured of support from key groups such as ambitious younger educated men who saw opportunities in business and government, and established traders and entrepreneurs who saw indigenization as opening opportunities for them. Radicals seeking a major restructuring of society would have been upset, but it would be hard for them to find another place to go. Over the long run, if development failed to materialize, they might have been able to challenge the CPP from a radical perspective, but this would take time.

What stopped the CPP from taking this route, particularly after it had secured its position in 1958? Certainly it was not the strength of the militants within the party, especially just after independence; by this time, not only had the CPP organization crumbled badly, but those controlling it tended to be largely opportunists with little commitment to a major restructuring of Ghanaian society.[33] I submit that the major barrier was Nkrumah himself. Although in practice he might solicit foreign investment, and even, as in the Volta River Project, abandon most of the real benefits to his country in order to obtain it, he could not bring himself to abandon the symbolic fight against "imperialism" and the capitalistic powers. This symbolic militance may have been simply a reflex from the years of anti-colonial struggle; more likely, however, it was the partially conscious strategy of an insecure man whose only way of justifying his holding power against the old, established elites was to show that he alone could be trusted to fight for Ghana's full independence.

Yet despite his avowed aim of fighting against imperialism, Nkrumah did not produce an economic strategy to promote Ghana's independence from foreign capitalist control until 1962, when the Programme for Work and Happiness and subsequently the Seven-Year Development Plan set out a strategy of heavy domestic investment in state-owned industry and state farms which would make the country largely self-sufficient in its basic needs. By this time he had largely forfeited the popular support that might have led people to accept the loss of imported consumer goods and the increasing taxes, as well as the need for working honestly and efficiently for the good of the state.

A major step in this collapse of his popular support had come in the aftermath of the Dawn Broadcast in 1961, when he had seemed on the point

of purging the most corrupt elements in the CPP.
But the purge never came. Within a month of the
broadcast, he had reassured the "Old Guard" that
they need not fear removal.[34] Even though the radicals such as Adamafio continued to ride high for
another year, there was no imposition of puritanical
values; corrupt party members continued to enjoy the
sweets of office while ordinary people suffered.

However, most of the loss of support had occurred long before this. Basil Davidson has suggested
that the turning point came in 1954, when the CPP
government decided not to raise the price paid to
the cocoa producers even though the world price was
more than double what the farmers were getting.
This action, Davidson claims, was

> "a major source of rural disillusionment
> with the CPP as a party of the masses.
> It ran directly counter to all that
> Nkrumah believed about social justice,
> as well as to what the CPP was supposed
> to stand for in that field; and from
> this standpoint it was undoubtedly a
> major blunder."[35]

The farmers' anger over the low cocoa prices
was a major source of support for the Ashanti-based
National Liberation Movement, which more than any
other opposition group frightened the CPP into using
authoritarian measures to protect its power, and led
Nkrumah and his Ministers to preoccupy themselves up
to 1958 with the political problem of holding the
new state together rather than building an economic
base. Furthermore, the farmers' readiness to turn
against the CPP over this "pocketbook" issue likely
reinforced Nkrumah's lack of sympathy for agricultural problems, an attitude which contributed to the
costly blunder of the state farming programme in the
1960s. More broadly, the failure to raise cocoa
prices helped show rural dwellers that the CPP was
no more "their" government and responsive to their
desires than the colonial government had been before
it, and thus helped ensure that few would participate in running the party out of idealistic motives.
The possibility of a check on the self-seekers and
opportunists whose control completed popular disillusionment with the CPP was thus destroyed, and the
CPP slid steadily away from its original role as a
party of the people.

What would have been the likely effects if the
government in 1954 had raised the producers' cocoa

prices? Suppose it had increased the payments by a third from 1953, and thereafter tied them to the "cost-of-living index"? Table 5.1 shows the effect up to 1958 upon the farmers' revenue and upon the government's revenue.

Table 5.1: Projected effect on farmers' incomes and on government revenues if government had tied cocoa price to cost-of-living index.

Year	Cocoa Output ('000 tons)	Cocoa prices ($ per ton)			Government Revenue ($ '000,000)		
		World	Ghana farmers'				
			Act-ual	Projec-ted	Act-ual	Projec-ted	Differ-ence
1954	214	$1002	$375	$498	$134	$108	$26
1955	206	988	375	529	126	95	31
1956	234	622	417	535	48	20	28
1957	260	529	417	540	29	- 3	32
1958	197	851	375	543	94	61	33

Source: data on actual cocoa prices taken from Killick, "Cocoa", in Walter Birmingham et al, A Study of Contemporary Ghana, Vol. I (Allen and Unwin, London, 1966), p. 369; projected prices calculated from Accra retail price index, ibid., p. 370.

      Since cocoa trees take seven years to come into production, output could not change quickly in response to higher producer prices; also, the Cocoa Marketing Board's costs would not be affected. The key point is that there would have been some $ 26-33 million a year less for government, and as much more for the cocoa farmers, if the government had raised the producer price.
      The potential political benefits of raising the price to producers were fairly obvious. Most important, it would greatly strengthen the CPP's rural base, and in doing so, would enhance Nkrumah's bargaining position with the British. Second, by improving the CPP's political hold, it would free Nkrumah and his Ministers to concentrate on the questions of economic development. Third, it might maintain popular enthusiasm for the CPP as a

populist party, and encourage ordinary people to
participate in it as a check on the self-seeking of
senior officials.

The need for strengthening the CPP's base was
not, to be sure, readily apparent in 1954. While
the Northern People's Party was strong in the
savanna belt, organized opposition had not yet erupted in the cocoa-growing areas. Nkrumah could be
forgiven for failing to foresee the protest that
would explode in the next two years.

In any case, there were also some highly visible costs to raising the producer prices. The
reason that Davidson advances for not acting, that
Nkrumah was concerned to appear prudent and cautious
in the eyes of the potential foreign investors whom
he and Komla Gbedemah, his Minister of Finance,
still saw as the key to industrialization, may have
been a factor.[36] But far more important, I suggest,
were Nkrumah's views on how the cocoa farmers would
have used their increased wealth. He shared the
general view that the cocoa farmers were relatively
well-to-do, and that such money as they did not
spend on increased imports would have been invested
in relatively unproductive uses as middle class urban
housing.[37] The imports themselves would not have
been a problem; Ghana's reserves were large enough
to allow them, and in any case the richer market
would have offered additional incentives to import-
substituting industries. However, what was dangerous in Nkrumah's eyes was the prospect of strengthening a class of "rural capitalists" as well as the
Ghanaian entrepreneurs who might develop through
providing consumer goods for them. Ghanaian capitalists could obstruct the development of a socialist
economy much more effectively than could foreign
ones, and even more serious, they could use their
wealth to threaten Nkrumah's personal hold on
power.[38] Any action that helped to build up this
potentially dangerous class, therefore, was to be
avoided.

In addition, Nkrumah had a strong bias against
rural-based economic development. As Killick has
noted, few nationalist leaders "have so deliberately
withdrawn assistance from the peasant farmers and
pinned their hopes so exclusively on state farms".[39]
Strengthening the cocoa farmers by giving them more
money would support a class which was not only capitalist in inclination, but also obscurantist and
anti-modernizing.

All these factors -- concern for his personal
position, a dislike of creating more Ghanaian

capitalists, and a bias against agriculture -- are enough to explain why in 1954 Nkrumah was unwilling to allow a significant shift of cocoa funds from the state to the producers. It could be argued, further-more, that strengthening the CPP's popular base in this manner would not necessarily help a later re-structuring of Ghanaian society; in fact, by diffus-ing wealth more broadly through the rural areas, it would have broadened the commitment to the status quo and made change harder to bring about.

Yet with all these qualifications, the fact remains that to bring about a successful transform-ation of Ghanaian society, Nkrumah needed two things: a clear idea in his own mind of the steps necessary to bring the transformation about, and the popular backing that would enable him to get people to take the successive steps, whether or not they were aware of the ultimate end. And in 1954 his government's failure to improve the position of the rural cocoa producers was the first major step in losing popular backing.

The record also suggests that he never really had a very clear idea of the steps necessary to bring about the transformation he desired, the suc-cessful industrialization of Ghana in order to enjoy the affluence and autonomy of the Western states. He seemed to think, and to have been reinforced in this view by the way it worked to bring political independence, that it was only necessary for him to exhort other Ghanaians to share his vision, and they would do what he wanted.

Until 1957 he was pre-occupied with winning the "political kingdom" and one gets the impression from his autobiography that once this was won, economic improvement would come almost automatically. His readiness to embrace first Sir Arthur Lewis' "con-ventional" development approach, then the radical (and Spartan) forced savings approach put forward by Nicholas Kaldor for the 1961 budget, then the plunge into supplier credits, not to mention the way in which he ignored the Seven-Year Plan's limits,[40] suggests that he had no commitment to any coher-ent economic strategy. Perhaps General Alexander best accounts for Nkrumah's vacillation in this area; he observes that in areas where Nkrumah knew little, he "was far too easily swayed by the last man he saw".[41]

There was perhaps another possible route to transforming Ghana, the route of terror and coer-cion to achieve a comprehensive goal. Whether this strategy can work in the small, weak state structures of Africa is doubtful, as we shall see from the Guinean example.[42] But it is to Nkrumah's credit that one of his best qualities stopped him from even trying it. After 1961, a leader of utter ruthlessness and duplicity might have been able to dispose of most of his rivals in order to achieve his goals of purging the CPP, installing a socialist regime, or simply maintaining himself in power. There were plenty of provocations which might have induced a leader to institute such tactics; the grenades at Kulungugu and at State House in 1962, and Amatwee's attempt at shooting Nkrumah in 1964, were certainly real enough and close enough that it would have been understandable if he had resorted to violence against both real and imagined enemies. Yet he did not: the only person executed for these attacks up to 1966 was Private Amatwee, and that was for killing another policeman, not for shooting at Nkrumah. Henry Bretton, who cannot be accused of being an apologist for Nkrumah, has noted that he was strongly committed to non-violence, and was "a forgiving person".[43]

The choices made by Kwame Nkrumah as leader of Ghana gave his country the worst of several possible worlds. The corruption and opportunism of most of his CPP associates gave political institutions a bad reputation, and disillusioned many Ghanaians with the possibilities of any kind of mass mobiliz- ation to transform society. The lesson learned by Ghanaians was that it paid to look out for yourself. However, this capitalist ethic was not given much chance to flower either, since Ghana's bankruptcy at the end of Nkrumah's regime meant that it could undertake very little development for itself, but would have to rely on foreign investors bringing their own investments on whatever terms they saw fit. Yet for this purpose, the pride and national- ism that had produced one of the highest rates of Africanization on the continent was a disadvantage, since most investors wanted their own nationals run- ning their business. All told, it was hard to see which way Ghana could go to extricate itself from the morass into which it had sunk by 1966.

It was thus a mixture of both his strengths and his weaknesses as a leader that allowed Nkrumah to lead Ghana into the morass of insolvency. His greatest strengths -- the ability to inspire Ghana- ians, and indeed all Africans, with a vision of the future greatness of the continent, and to fill them with pride in their Africanness -- left a legacy which still stirs the imagination. However, two of

92

his major weaknesses -- the lack of a clear goal
beyond political independence, and the lack of a
coherent economic strategy for attaining even his
apparent goals of industrialization and technological competence -- led him to flounder from one policy to another contradictory one. At the same time,
he believed so strongly in his own destiny, and in
the willingness of ordinary Ghanaians to follow him,
that he could shut his eyes and ears to the reality
of what was happening in his country. Even after
independence, he had been able to exercise genuine
leadership, but as he sought an ever greater transformation in Ghanaians' attitudes, he was losing
touch with what they felt and wanted. The result
was inevitable; as the people grew increasingly
disillusioned and cynical, Nkrumah grew more and
more frustrated and willing to use force. By the
time of the coup, his chances of ever again exercising political leadership had long since been
dissipated.

NOTES

        1. See Robert M. Price, Society and Bureaucra-
cy in Contemporary Ghana (University of California
Press, Berkeley and Los Angeles, 1975). p. 7, citing
the Ghana Government's 1967 Commission of Enquiry
on The Local Purchasing of Cocoa.
        2. Fred M. Hayward, "Perceptions of Well-being
in Ghana: 1970 and 1975", African Studies Review,
XXII, 1 (April 1979), p. 111.
        3. Studies focusing on Nkrumah's leadership
range from Basil Davidson's spirited defence, Black
Star (Allen Lane, London, 1973) through Dennis
Austin, Politics in Ghana, 1946-1960 (Oxford University Press, London, 1964) and Henry Bretton, The
Rise and Fall of Kwame Nkrumah (Praeger, New York,
1966), both of which see Nkrumah as having betrayed
originally good intentions, to T. Peter Omari,
Kwame Nkrumah: The Anatomy of an African Dictator-
ship (Hurst, London, 1970). A critical but under-
standing view is provided by Trevor Jones, Ghana's
First Republic, 1960-1966 (Methuen, London, 1976)
        4. Though in retrospect, it appears that this
charisma was already weakening by the time David
Apter argued that it would permit the transfer of
Ghanaians' loyalties to the new institutions of a
Parliamentary regime. See The Gold Coast in Trans-
ition (Princeton University Press, Princeton, 1955).
Some would argue that it never existed, that his

success was entirely due to his organizing skill. See Robert Dowse, "Professor Apter's Ghana", West African Journal of Sociology and Political Science, 1, 1 (October 1975) pp. 20-35.

5.   Thomas Hodgkin, "Ghana Votes", The Spectator, June 18, 1954, p. 731.
6.   Tony Killick, "Cocoa" in Walter Birmingham et al., A Study of Contemporary Ghana, Vol. I, (Allen and Unwin, London, 1966), p. 369.
7.   A. Krassowski, Development and the Debt Trap (Croom Helm, London, 1974), p. 54.
8.   Ibid., p. 37
9.   Tony Killick, "The Volta River Project" in Birmingham et al., pp. 391-410. See also David Hart, The Volta River Project (Edinburgh University Press, Edinburgh, 1980).
10.   A useful summary is Victor T. Levine, Political Corruption: The Ghana Case (Hoover Institute, Stanford, California, 1975). See also the brilliant novel by Ayi Kwei Armah, The Beautyful Ones Are Not Yet Born (Collier, New York, 1969).
11.   See especially Richard Jeffries, Class, Power and Ideology in Ghana: The Railwaymen of Sekondi (Cambridge University Press, Cambridge, 1978), passim.
12.   Krassowski, The Debt Trap, pp. 71-72
13.   Ibid., p. 88.
14.   Ibid., pp. 85, 105
15.   Jeffries, Class in Ghana, p. 104.
16.   Cited by Richard Sandbrook and Jack Arn, The Labouring Poor and Class Formation: The Case of Greater Accra (McGill University Centre for Developing Areas Studies, Montreal, 1977) p. 61.
17.   For an interesting account of on-the-street reactions to the coup, see Jack Goody, "Consensus and dissent in Ghana", Political Science Quarterly, 83, 3 (September 1968), pp. 337ff.
18.   Henry Bretton, "Non-Violent Leadership Response in a Violence-Inducing Setting: The Case of Kwame Nkrumah", in Robert S. Robins (ed.) Psychopathology and Political Leadership (Tulane University Press, New Orleans, 1977), pp. 113-150.
19.   Davidson, Black Star, p. 193.
20.   Jon Kraus, "Ghana's New Corporate Parliament", Africa Report, 10, 8 (August 1965), p. 6.
21.   Davidson, Black Star, p. 187.
22.   Jones, Ghana's First Republic, p. 292.
23.   For an account of the military's reliance on civil servants for policymaking during this period, see Robert Pinkney, Ghana Under Military Rule, 1966-1969 (Methuen, London, 1972).

24. See Dennis Austin, Ghana Observed: Essays on The Politics of a West African Republic (Manchester University Press, Manchester, 1976), p. 133.

25. For an overview of the economic policies pursued by the Busia regime, see Tony Killick, Development Economics in Action: A Study of Economic Policies in Ghana (St. Martins Press, New York, 1978), pp. 56-58.

26. Ibid., p. 112.

27. Sandbrook and Arn, The Labouring Poor, p. 39.

28. See Rhoda Howard, Colonialism and Underdevelopment in Ghana (Africana, New York, 1978), pp. 214-18.

29. See below, Chapter 7.

30. Ghana: The Autobiography of Kwame Nkrumah (Nelson, Edinburgh, 1957), p. x.

31. Krassowski, The Debt Trap, p. 54.

32. Such a feeling was to be found in other colonies, such as for example Sierra Leone. For that colony see Rt. Hon. Hilary Marquand "The ? Over Sierra Leone", New Commonwealth, 39 (April 1961), p. 216.

33. See, for example, Davidson, Black Star, pp. 24-25, 178, 185-87; Selwyn Ryan, "The Theory and Practice of African One-Partyism: The CPP Re-examined", Canadian Journal of African Studies, IV, 2 (Spring 1970), pp. 145-72.

34. See Ryan, "African One-Partyism", pp. 151-52.

35. Davidson, Black Star, p. 144.

36. Ibid., p. 146.

37. Killick, "Cocoa", p. 368.

38. Killick, Development Economics, pp. 37,40; also John D. Esseks, "Political Independence and Economic Decolonization: The Case of Ghana under Nkrumah", Western Political Quarterly, XXIV, 1 (March 1971), p. 61.

39. Killick, Development Economics, p. 41.

40. Ibid., esp. pp. 142-43; also the much harsher view of Douglas Rimmer, "The Abstraction from Politics", Journal of Development Studies, 5, 3 (April 1969), pp. 190-204.

41. Gen. H. T. Alexander, African Tightrope: My Two Years as Nkrumah's Chief of Staff (Pall Mall, London, 1965), p. 25.

42. See below, Chapter 9.

43. Bretton, "Non-Violent Leadership", pp. 140-41.

Chapter Six

THE IVORY COAST: IS ECONOMIC SUCCESS ENOUGH?

To the visitor, the Ivory Coast is plainly the
"miracle state" of Africa. From the glittering new
office towers of Abidjan to the neatly laid out
plantations and over-flowing markets of small up-
country towns, there is an air of prosperity pervad-
ing the country and forming a startling contrast
with the run-down appearance of, say, Senegal or
Ghana. The statistics bear out this impression of
wealth; the World Bank's figures for 1979 show the
Ivory Coast as having a per capita Gross National
Product of $1,040, higher than any other black
African state except Gabon.
     Yet the visitor soon notices other aspects of
the Ivory Coast. In many managerial and technical
posts, from government offices to banks, one finds
Frenchmen rather than Africans. Then too, one is
soon struck by the absence of any political comment,
whether in the form of publications criticising the
government, as in Senegal, or the heartfelt personal
comments of Ghanaians. There is no pervasive sense
of fear, as in Cameroun or Malawi, but rather a lack
of interest in the subject.
     The Ivory Coast's material prosperity derives
from its diversified agricultural exports, aided by
a growing manufacturing sector which includes a
number of goods for export as well as import substitutes. Even while it was overtaking Ghana as the
world's leading cocoa producer and expanding production of its other two major commodities, coffee and
timber, the Ivory Coast was developing new crops in
the 1960s and 1970s, such as pineapples, bananas,
rubber, sugar and cotton, and at the same time was
beginning to process these and other products.
While these crops were largely grown by a prosperous
African planter bourgeoisie, with the help of more
than a million migrant workers from other African

96

states (the country's total population is about eight million), most of the marketing and processing operations were controlled by the country's 45,000 Frenchmen, either working for French companies or for Ivorian state corporations. This heavy reliance upon expatriates as well as upon continuing foreign investment and access to world markets leaves the Ivory Coast somewhat vulnerable, although a good deal less so than most African states, thanks to its diversification.

The risks to the Ivory Coast of disastrously expensive mistakes have also been reduced by the fact that it has left most development projects to private entrepreneurs, so that there have been few massive single projects. At the same time, the economy has been carefully guided by state inducements, with the main goal being to maximize growth, but with some attention also to spreading development around the country.

This single-minded drive for economic growth through encouraging private investment has had some social costs. Despite its wealth, the Ivory Coast was rather laggard in improving its social capital, such as schools and health facilities, with the result that the life expectancy of its citizens and other indicators of general well-being are not significantly better than its less affluent neighbours. (See Table 6.1) Furthermore, there is a growing gap between the rich and the poor, with a political and business elite becoming very wealthy, a large middle class holding its own, and the purchasing power of a lower stratum steadily declining. The fact that much of this lower stratum consists of nationals of other African states eases the domestic political pressure, but leaves the Ivory Coast open to the charge that its prosperity is built on the backs of its poorer neighbours.

However, even Ivorian citizens have had their opportunities for political participation curtailed ever since 1951. The man who rode the post-war wave of nationalism to power, Felix Houphouet-Boigny, built a political system in which participation was confined to a small elite almost entirely under his control. There were occasional signs of restlessness during the period, and in late 1980 Houphouet took a small step toward easing the system, but for most of the period of the economic "miracle" few Ivorians even showed signs of wanting a more open system. As long as the economy prospered, and Houphouet continued to hold sway over the country's fortunes, this passive acceptance of elite control

was likely to continue. But if the economy falter-
ed, latent discontents and conflicts could easily
erupt, and once Houphouet, who was 75 and in frail
health by 1980, passed from the scene, it was difficult to imagine any successor who could so fully convince people they should accept his domination.

Table 6.1: Some indicators of wealth and well-being
for the Ivory Coast, Ghana, Senegal and Guinea

	Popu-lation ('000,000) 1978	GNP per capita 1978	Life expec-tancy 1960	1978	Safe water[a] 1975	Primary School[b] 1960	1977
Ivory Coast	7.8	$840	37	46	19%	46	92%
Ghana	11.0	390	40	48	35	38	74
Senegal	5.4	196	37	42	37	27	47
Guinea	5.1	210	35	43	10	30	[28[c]]

a: Pct. of population with access to safe drinking
   water
b: Pct. of children of primary school age actually
   enrolled

Sources: World Bank, World Development Report, 1980,
Tables 1, 21, 23, except (c) from World Bank, World
Development Indicators, 1978, Table 18 (1975 figure).

     How did this combination of economic prosperity
and political quiescence come about? To what extent
was President Houphouet-Boigny responsible? And
were there some points at which a leader with a different approach might have gained control in the
Ivory Coast, or could Houphouet-Boigny himself have
chosen a different path?
     This chapter argues that several of the most
critical features in the Ivory Coast's economic success are attributable to choices made by President
Houphouet-Boigny. His early fight against forced
labour and against racial repression established
his reputation as a militant champion of African
interests, even after he began conciliating the
French. In the period from 1951 to the present,
he was able to provide increasing material well-
being for a large number of Africans thanks to

three major policy decisions. First, he made the
Ivory Coast attractive to French investors by carefully protecting their interests against African
nationalism. Second, he concentrated on economic
development rather than on longer-term social
investments, although as the economy prospered the
government began to put more funds into schooling
and health. Third, he did not concentrate investment decisions in the hands of state officials.
Most productive investments were made by private
interests, while the state investments were guided
by French advisors, who in turn were checked by
Ivorians. The success of these policies in providing material payoffs allowed the President to
concentrate political participation in the hands
of a small elite, including a substantial number of
foreigners. Nationalist demands, which could
frighten away a large number of private investors,
were damped down by continuing prosperity.

THE UPRISING AGAINST FRENCH ABUSE

        The Ivory Coast, like Ghana, straddles the West
African forest belt and the drier northern tree
savanna. It can thus produce both forest crops like
cocoa, coffee and yams (by far the largest food
crop) and also savanna crops such as cotton, sugar
cane and millet. Unlike Ghana, it lacks major mineral deposits, although recently some oil has been
found off-shore.
        The French only began to develop the Ivory
Coast between the wars. By 1939 cocoa exports had
risen to 55,000 tons and coffee to 18,000 tons.[1]
A third of the cocoa and coffee trees, it was estimated, were in the hands of some 200 French planters,[2] whose main problem was obtaining African
labour against the greater economic attraction of
the Gold Coast. The administration was sympathetic
enough to their plight to impose forced labour
obligations on Africans. The large number of
African planters were denied access to this pool of
cheap semi-slave labour, and also suffered discrimination in their access to loans, and to technical
assistance. The wartime Vichy regime was particularly open in its racialism, and found a sympathetic
response among the French colons.
        The comparatively well-to-do African planters
were pushed into an alignment with their less prosperous brothers against the French planters. When
a Free French governor took over in 1944, he

encouraged the formation of a Syndicat Agricole African to offset the pro-Vichy French planters' association.[3] From eight founder-members, the SAA quickly grew to 8,000 by the end of 1944, with half of these from Baoulé districts. Since Felix Houphouet-Boigny was the only Baoulé among the founding members, it was not surprising that at the first SAA congress in September 1944, he was elected President.

The SAA was essentially an organization of wealthy African planters. Still it provided one of the few vehicles for African political expression. Urbanization was slower in the Ivory Coast than in the Gold Coast, with Abidjan having perhaps half the population of Accra at the end of World War II.[4] Formal education, the greatest stimulus to organized political action, lagged far behind the Gold Coast; by 1945 there were only 4 university graduates and about 200 to 300 diploma-holders from Ecole William Ponty in Dakar, while in 1948 it was estimated that only one of 20 schoolage children attended primary school.[5] There was neither the large body of professional men who organized the United Gold Coast Convention, nor the mass of primary school leavers who furnished the cadres for the Convention Peoples Party. The pool of potential political activists who could articulate and organize movements around grievances was much smaller in the Ivory Coast than in the Gold Coast or in Senegal.

But the burning question of forced labour, as well as the lack of educational facilities, the numerous forms of discrimination against African planters, and the stranglehold over trade held by the French firms and the Lebanese, made most Africans receptive to any political organization which promised to fight these problems. Houphouet-Boigny quickly sensed this political potential, and by militantly championing these causes on which most Africans could unite, managed to expand his original SAA base into an effective political coalition. In the 1945 Abidjan municipal elections, he rejected the practice of other African parties of forming slates including both Europeans and Africans, and instead built a Bloc Africain excluding the European minority altogether, but carefully balancing the different African groups in the city. Most of the other African slates then withdrew, and the Europeans boycotted the election in protest, with the result that Houphouet's slate won all but 28 of the 1,523 votes cast.[6]

Shortly thereafter, he won a tightly contested

election against an Administration-sponsored candidate for the Ivory Coast seat in the first French Constituent Assembly. In the Assembly, he concentrated on African issues, and early in 1946 he managed to put through a bill abolishing forced labour in the overseas territories. Such a bill was of no great concern to metropolitan France, but in the Ivory Coast it gave him a heroic stature which enabled him to win an easy re-election to the Second Constituent Assembly, and subsequently to the French National Assembly, where he held a seat continuously until 1960.

His prestige as the man who ended forced labour and his membership in the National Assembly soon became vitally important, because from 1947 to 1951 the Ivory Coast was the scene of the most intense struggle in West Africa between French administrators and African nationalists for supremacy. Houphouet had worked to form the inter-territorial Rassemblement Democratique Africaine (RDA) in 1946, and the Ivorian branch, the Parti Democratique de la Cote d'Ivoire (PDCI) shortly afterwards, becoming President of both.

The RDA received considerable help from the French Communist Party both in organizing and in fighting African issues in the Assembly, and formally allied itself with the Communists. However, after the Communists were driven out of the French government coalition in 1947, successive French administrators tried to destroy the Communists' African nationalist allies. In the Ivory Coast, the settlers' bloc egged on a new hard-line governor to try first to establish a new anti-PDCI party, and when that failed, to harass, intimidate and eventually arrest most of the top PDCI leadership. By 1950 most PDCI leaders were in jail; Houphouet and his close associate Ouezzin Coulibaly were free only because as Deputies they enjoyed Parliamentary immunity. It was becoming "increasingly clear that [the PDCI] could not hold out much longer",[7] while on the French side more liberal members of the government such as François Mitterand were aware of the dangers of repressing a movement which had clearly demonstrated its broad support among the populace.[8] In 1951 a deal was struck; Houphouet agreed to end the RDA's alliance with the Communists, while the French agreed to end their persecution. The way was now clear for the PDCI to consolidate its hegemony over the Ivory Coast.

The French repression further enhanced Houphouet-Boigny's heroic stature. Not only had he

fought for and won African rights, but in doing so
he had not been arrested, and thus had showed himself to be as powerful as the Frenchmen. With these
credentials, he could afford to compromise with the
French and yet remain secure from most attacks.

In retrospect, it seems something of an aberra-
tion that this small, quiet son of a chief, "African
doctor"[9] and wealthy planter should have emerged as
a militant fighter against French colonial rule.
Yet Houphouet had never accepted that Africans
should be subordinate to Europeans on account of
their race. His readiness to fight for equal treatment was shown in his first posting as a medical
auxiliary in the 1930s when he was denied a government house by the French administrator because it
was "too good for a native". Rather than argue, he
simply moved into the house, then informed the administrator. The latter backed down.[10] In the
French Assembly in 1946 he warned that the position
was simply a means by which Africans could "contribute effectively to the evolution of the territories
that we represent"[11] and despite regarding France as
a "second homeland" he kept his rural Ivorian roots,
and later styled himself "President-paysan".[12] It
would be wrong, in other words, to regard Houphouet-
Boigny as a French stooge, even if his actions after
1951 so often seemed to support continuing French
control in Africa. He had his own vision of what
the Ivory Coast should become, and if his vision of
an inegalitarian, capitalist society closely associated with the former colonial power was not a
fashionable one, still it was his own and it seemed
to produce results.

It was not, in any case, his vision of what the
Ivory Coast should become that won Houphouet-Boigny
his massive support, it was what he actually produced. He was not a charismatic, prophetic figure
in the manner of Nkrumah, although his quiet self-
assurance helped to bring people around to his view.
But it was the fact that he could point to what he
had accomplished, the abolition of forced labour,
the bringing about of reconciliation with the French
administration, and then the long string of successful economic projects, that steadily built up his
reputation as the almost supernaturally "wise old
man" of the country. Even the lack of flamboyant
gestures, the care he took not to push any further
than was necessary to accomplish his ends, worked to
enhance this appearance.

There are two crucial turning-points in this
period where events might have gone very differently.

First, in the immediate post-war period, a much more radical leader than Houphouet-Boigny might well have emerged, and second, in 1951 Houphouet-Boigny or any other nationalist leader might well have been driven to a much more militant approach.

It was largely the fact that the wealthier African planters were denied the forced labour of their countrymen that encouraged them to align themselves with ordinary Africans against the French. Had the French administration not discriminated on a racial basis, the conflict of interest between African planters and labourers would have been politically far more salient, with a consequent political alignment more like that of the Gold Coast. Furthermore, the abolition of forced labour was a demand which could be achieved only in the metropolitan forum; had Houphouet had to fight within a French West African political structure giving French administrators and <u>colons</u> substantial control, success would have been far less likely, and consequently there would have been a much more profound struggle to uproot French institutions. Finally, the alliance with the Communists and the French repression helped give the RDA an aura of militancy which protected it from being outflanked by a more radical movement. In the absence of these factors, it seems improbable that Houphouet could have put together a party reaching much beyond the circle of wealthy African planters.

Yet equally important for the subsequent history of the Ivory Coast was the fact that Houphouet-Boigny was not "radicalized" beyond compromise by the French repression from 1947 to 1951. The behaviour of French administrators toward the PDCI was certainly provocative enough that even a leader well-disposed toward France must have had a hard time maintaining his belief in that country's good intentions. It is not hard to imagine the PDCI being driven toward an armed guerrilla uprising along the lines followed by the Union des Populations du Cameroun under similar provocation a few years later.[13] From the French point of view there were two factors working for compromise in the Ivory Coast: first, the fact that the PDCI's support was so widespread that they could not play off different groups in order to undermine it, as they did in Cameroun; and second, the fact that the PDCI, unlike the UPC, did not seek complete independence, but only a more equal relationship for Africans within a French hegemony. Nevertheless, the PDCI too needed to compromise, and here I think Houphouet-Boigny's own views were decisive. He was no Marxist, and his personal experience with the French government encouraged him to maintain a good relationship. At the same time, he could see the cost of a prolonged struggle, both in African lives and in the likely loss of any chance at increased material prosperity. His pragmatic evaluation thus tipped the balance toward compromise.

His accommodation with the French administration cleared the way for Houphouet-Boigny to concentrate on his primary goal of increasing the Ivory Coast's wealth. Beyond this economic goal, he seemed to envision the Ivory Coast developing as an industrial society with its own political identity, but still closely linked to France; but no other goals come out as clearly as the economic one. In the next decade and beyond, he succeeded admirably in achieving his economic goal, even though political events outside the Ivory Coast created a new situation he had scarcely anticipated.

From 1950 to 1960, the Ivory Coast enjoyed an impressive growth rate of 7-8% per year,[14] with coffee, cocoa and timber exports leading the way (see Table 6.2). At the same time, structural changes began to occur, with the share of industry and construction in the gross domestic product rising from 8.7% in 1950 to 11.4% in 1960, while agriculture, forestry and fishing fell from 52% to 41.2%.[15] Much of this increase in the manufacturing sector was concentrated in large businesses, predominantly French-owned.[16] The number of wage-earners rose from 78,000 in 1947 to an estimated 171,000 in 1957; of these, 90,000 were working in agriculture, mostly for African employers.[17]

The investments which powered this growth came from a variety of sources. The Ivory Coast public sector itself provided a substantial portion, rising from $7.2 million in 1950 to $26 million in 1960, while the French government contributed for the same period more than $14 million per year.[18] The private sector increased even more substantially, passing the public sector's investment in 1955.[19] Ivorians naturally predominated in agriculture and housing, but in industry, forestry and heavy construction, where large sums of capital were needed, French firms made most of the investments, including substantial amounts ploughed back.[20] The total foreign private investments in this period amounted to some $400-480 million, an impressive sum when one recalls that this is more than twice the amount that Ghana invested in the huge Volta Dam project,

or that it means average annual investments were
about a quarter of the total value of the Ivory
Coast's exports for 1960.

Table 6.2:   Changes in exports of coffee, cocoa and
timber from Ivory Coast, selected years, 1947-1960.

Year	Coffee (tons)	Cocoa (tons)	Timber (tons)	Value of all exports ($'000,000)	Top three as percentage of total
1947	42,677	28,048	48,724	$ 11.0	79.7%
1950	54,189	61,686	108,709		
1956	118,794	75,745	212,000	150.2	94.3%
1960	147,500	62,900	654,900	222.8	86 %

Sources: Quantities, Morgenthau, Political Parties,
p. 168; value, Zolberg, One-Party Government, p. 163,
Jean M. Due, "Agricultural Development in The Ivory
Coast and Ghana", Journal of Modern African Studies,
7, 4 (1969), p. 640.

Economically, the Ivory Coast by 1960 had pulled well ahead of all other French West African
states, and was beginning to close in on Ghana,
still the richest and most developed state in West
Africa. It was already planning to diversify its
primary product exports, thus giving itself more
protection against the possible collapse of any one
commodity's markets, and it had already begun to
strengthen its manufacturing sector. Its main weakness appeared to be its reliance on a continuing
stream of foreign investment, which could suddenly
reverse itself and disappear. Repatriated profits
of foreign firms and the costs of providing expatriates with imported goods and services kept a steady
pressure on the balance of payments, and would not
cease even if exports and new capital inflows slowed
down. The main political challenge for Houphouet-
Boigny and the PDCI thus appeared to be how to maintain the confidence of foreign investors, so that
the boom could continue.
While the Ivory Coast's wealth of natural assets
was a necessary condition for attracting foreign investors, sufficient conditions had to include a
political climate that they would regard as "safe".
Houphouet-Boigny worked quickly after 1951 to

establish such a climate, emphasizing repeatedly that the economy was an open one, that investors could withdraw their earning as well as enter freely. To conciliate the French settlers and businessmen in the Ivory Coast, he brought some of their number onto the government's electoral slate, dropping PDCI militants in order to make room for these former opponents.[21] The value of the Ivory Coast to France, coupled with his own supremacy there, led to his becoming a Minister in the French government in 1956, a position he retained through successive governments even after the collapse of the Fourth Republic. His Ministerial office also benefitted the Ivory Coast, by providing it with a lobbyist ensconced within the French government's innermost councils.

Despite the time he had to spend in Paris, Houphouet-Boigny was able to use the French custom of multiple office-holding to maintain his grip on the government of the Ivory Coast, as well as a powerful voice in French West Africa. By 1957 he held offices at four levels; mayor of Abidjan, member and President of the Ivory Coast Territorial Assembly, member and President of the Grand Council of French West Africa, and Deputy in the French National Assembly and Minister in the French government.[22] Within the Ivory Coast he allowed the PDCI to develop more and more into a machine for the distribution of patronage rather than an organization concerned with policies. The district secretaries, who handled patronage, tended to be "strangers" in their districts, whereas the Assembly representatives, who usually had some personal local base, had to work through the party organization to obtain benefits for their constituents. The frequent disputes between party secretaries and Assemblymen could, of course, only be resolved by top-level members of the party, and thus central control was strengthened behind a facade of participation. At the same time, Houphouet-Boigny gradually eliminated leading opponents, though generally by bringing them into the party rather than by coercing them.

While events within the Ivory Coast remained under firm control, elsewhere in Africa and in France changes were occurring that would force Houphouet to shift his comfortable position. The first of these changes occurring in 1956, when the French government, responding to increasing demands among Africans for self-determination, introduced the Loi-Cadre which decentralized power to the territorial units of West and Equatorial Africa while gutting the federation governments. The territories each received a fully elective assembly with control over government expenditures, and an executive elected by the Assembly. The federation governments, by contrast, were given no executive, and were left dependent on the territorial assemblies to vote them funds.[23] Most African leaders rightly saw this as an attempt to "Balkanize" their area, but for the Ivory Coast, "Balkanization" was an eminently desirable policy. As the richest territory in French West Africa the Ivory Coast was already putting far more into the federation than it was extracting in material benefits,[24] and if a true federation had been created, its role as milch cow for the poorer territories would have been expanded. Houphouet's terms for continuing French West African Federation were simple: largely autonomous territories, capitalist economies, and close relations with France. Otherwise, the Ivory Coast would happily go its own way.[25] Eventually, when the rest of the RDA insisted on pressing for a federation in West Africa and on demanding that France negotiate with the Algerian FLN, Houphouet withdrew from the Presidency of the RDA and took the PDCI out of the organization.[26]

Meanwhile, the Algerian problem suddenly forced a drastic change in the Franco-African political system. In May 1958 the French generals in Algeria attempted their coup, the Fourth Republic collapsed, and General de Gaulle at last received his long-awaited call to save France from the politicians. In dealing with France's West and Equatorial African territories, the Fifth Republic constitution proposed a Community which would look after foreign affairs, defence, common financial and economic policies, justice, and higher education.[27] The Community's organs were not clearly defined; representatives from the overseas territories were to be included in the French upper house, but neither the form of the executive nor the court arbitration which would settle disputes between members were settled. The alternative to accepting this arrangement, as de Gaulle made clear in Guinea, was to have all links with France completely severed.

Most African leaders were unhappy about this choice, particularly about the lack of any possibility of an amicable independence. But for Houphouet, there was no problem. He did not want independence for the Ivory Coast in 1958, despite the pressure from students and other younger Ivorians. He had a great admiration for de Gaulle, an admiration which

the latter reciprocated.[28] Despite his association
with the Fourth Republic, he had been taken into
de Gaulle's cabinet, and was the sole African member of the advisory commission which produced the
first constitutional draft, embodying proposals essentially along the lines he had long advocated.[29]

INDEPENDENCE: THE NON-CELEBRATION OF A NON-EVENT

    Houphouet-Boigny was soon to be disillusioned
with the new Community. The examples of Ghana and
Guinea proved too strong for other French African
leaders to withstand, and in May 1960 Madagascar and
the Mali Federation (Senegal and the Soudan) secured
the right to enjoy sovereignty while remaining members of the Community. For Houphouet, who had
claimed members of the Community did not need independence, this was a blow to his prestige. His response was to outbid the nationalists by announcing
that the Ivory Coast would leave the Community completely, which it formally did on August 7, 1960.
Unlike Guinea, however, the Ivory Coast retained
relations with France; the latter sponsored the
Ivory Coast's membership in the United Nations, and
agreements for aid and co-operation were quickly
negotiated over the next few months.
    While he had no particular desire for political
independence, and indeed in his wager with Kwame
Nkrumah in 1957 had seemed to imply that the Ivory
Coast would surpass Ghana by remaining a member of
the French Community[30] Houphouet was able to handle
the new situation. Turning the Ivory Coast into an
independent state did have the advantage of under-
cutting the radical critics in the student movement
and the trade unions who had criticized the government for being far too subservient to the French,
and who regarded Kwame Nkrumah and Sékou Touré as
their heroes.[31] Even here, however, he subordinated
political symbols to economics. For example, the
government postponed choosing a national flag for a
year, at least partly on the grounds that the
Tricolour was more attractive to investors.[32]
    While there was no organized political chal-
lenge to the PDCI, there was some uncertainty about
the strength of its hold on the country. Riots
against non-Ivorian Africans in Abidjan in 1959 following a slow-down in economic growth had suggested
that considerable tensions lay dormant. Equally
worrying was the claim by critics that the low turn-
outs at elections (in which only a single slate of

PDCI candidates was presented) indicated a "silent opposition", which by hinting at future difficulties could also alarm foreign investors.[33] The PDCI's practice of organizing through ethnic groups had done little to build a sense of nationhood; and there were occasional protests in peripheral areas over the distribution of wealth. Most important of all was the fact that Houphouet's own stress on material well-being had led to Ivorians judging him and his regime on their ability to continue to produce material payoffs, without any of the symbolic attachments that could help sustain Kwame Nkrumah or Sékou Touré over some hard times.

Houphouet-Boigny by 1960 had thoroughly committed himself to a policy of economic growth without end, based upon continuing foreign investment. A radical attack on foreign investors, such as Guinea's 1960 nationalization of the banks and freezing of its currency, would certainly bring a complete halt to such investment, and even too much pressure for "Ivorianization" of higher-level jobs in the government as well as in private businesses, would have frightened investors with the spectres of inefficiency and corruption. Similarly, too much pressure for processing of Ivorian exports, or any hint of exchange controls, would likely have meant a fairly dramatic slow-down in foreign investment, and even of foreign firms' ploughing back of their profits. In short, to keep its prosperity the Ivory Coast had to maintain its "open" economy and leeway for expatriates to run businesses much as they pleased.

In the two decades following independence a combination of some luck and considerable skill in taking advantage of opportunities allowed the Ivory Coast to enjoy one of the most remarkable runs of economic growth in Africa. Without the oil that so enriched Nigeria, Gabon, Libya and Algeria, and concentrating its exports in the despised agricultural sector, it enjoyed a rate of growth estimated at 10-12% in the 1960s, and even in the world economic slow-down of the late 1970s was still enjoying a growth rate of some 6-8% per annum.[34] Some danger signs were appearing by 1980. Foreign private capital investment had almost stopped, while the state in 1979 financed 34% of total investment by borrowing abroad, contributing to a growing weight of debt which had to be financed out of export earnings.[35] However, the diversification of exports seemed likely to ensure that this situation did not deteriorate into a disaster, even though it might involve a fairly painful slow-down in economic activity. By the mid-1970s the state was taking an increasing role in financing development projects, such as the Koussou Dam, an Ivorian shipping firm, and the huge cane sugar project intended to bring development to the backward North. However, it was taking the same approach as a private entrepreneur, investing in projects which would provide a quick and high economic return, rather than the less tangible and longer-term social benefits.[36]

In most of these projects, the Ivory Coast was lucky. Shortly after independence, when EEC regulations stopped it receiving higher than world market prices from France for its coffee, poor Brazilian crops of <u>robusta</u> at a time when United States demand for instant coffee was growing allowed the Ivory Coast to keep expanding its output until 1965.[37] A decade later, massive government investments in palm oil plantations came on stream just when world vegetable oil prices were beginning a long upward movement, while the Koussou hydroelectric project, which Berg had suggested in 1971 was a dubious investment,[38] began to operate just before world oil prices tripled. On the other hand, the sugar-producing scheme, whose original goal was 600,000 tons a year, was cut back by slumping world prices to 100,000 tons a year by 1980. Even at this rate it was costing the state corporation running the scheme a subsidy of $73 million a year.[39] However, unlike Ghana, the Ivory Coast was prepared to cut back this uneconomic project.

The development strategy of building on agriculture and relying largely on private enterprise offered several advantages. I think Elliott Berg is right to argue that leaving productive projects to private entrepreneurs and investing in export-oriented industries that have to compete in world markets to survive provides "built-in safeguards against massive resources misallocation",[40] at least if this allocation is to be determined by economic criteria. Furthermore, emphasizing coffee and cocoa as leading crops meant that economic well-being was diffused among a numerous class of modest farmers who provided the core of support for the regime. Finally, the large number of private enterprises, and the lack of government restriction in such areas as importing materials and exporting earnings, reduced the opportunities for personal corruption among officials.

This is not to say that the Ivory Coast was free of such problems. Some officials took cuts on contracts, many more benefitted from leasing government houses, or providing private services such as trucking to the government, while PDCI secretaries and other power-holders were sometimes charged with extorting funds. But compared to Ghana, or indeed most African states where bureaucrats could use their gate-keeping powers for self-enrichment, the Ivory Coast had relatively few problems.[41]

One expensive problem was the tendency of leading politicians to glorify themselves by having grandiose projects built in their home areas. By far the grandest of all was the transformation of the President's home village of Yamoussoukro into a "Versailles in the bush" (as a French economist put it to me), complete with a Presidential palace and immense "guest residence" finished in marble, as well as a party headquarters for the PDCI, and miles of sub-division streets laid out with curbs and street lamps.

The most visible problem facing the Ivory Coast was the extent to which foreigners, mostly Frenchmen, dominated the economy, and even the government. Even at the end of the 1970s there were still some 12,000 Frenchmen in high-and middle-level positions in both government and private sectors.[42] One foreign official told me that every time he talked business to an Ivorian official, there was a French "advisor" lurking in the background, a situation unimaginable in most African states. The costs of this domination were several. The French staffs in ministries concerned with development made it difficult for non-French investors to get their plans approved, even though the Ivorians were keen to diversify their sources of capital. Further, the provision of imported goods and services for these high-priced workers imposed a substantial drain on the Ivory Coast's balance of payments, as did their repatriation of part of their salaries.[43] One could also argue that as long as foreigners made key decisions, Ivorians would lack the opportunity to learn by their own mistakes and to gain confidence in their own abilities.

A key aspect of foreign domination was the fuel it gave to discontented Ivorians demanding more rapid access to jobs. This problem was becoming increasingly severe during the 1970s. Den Tuinder estimated in 1978 that even at existing growth rates, there would be some 1,900 Ivorians a year with post-secondary education seeking less than 700 jobs at this level, and 18,000 with secondary education seeking some 4,600 jobs.[44] Already there had been agitation in 1969 over this issue, and in 1973 the government had initiated a voluntary scheme with little effect. In 1978 it introduced a "charter of Ivorianisation" requiring firms to submit long-term plans for placing Ivorians in their top posts.[45] But the President still resisted "cut-rate Africanization" on the grounds that this would jeopardize the economy and that he wanted Ivorians to take over only when they were capable of doing the jobs.[46]

Another foreign influx created problems of a different type. During the entire period of prosperity, foreign migrant workers had played a key role, especially in agriculture, where in 1970 "more than half the agricultural wage-workers were non-Ivorians".[47] The direct effect of these workers was to help the competitiveness of Ivorian agricultural exports by keeping wages low. But by keeping rural wages low, they encouraged young Ivorians to migrate to the cities, where many joined the ranks of the unemployed, and contributed both to crime and to antagonisms directed against foreign Africans, antagonisms manifested in riots in 1959 and 1969. However, Ivorians were perceptively selective in their antagonisms, according to a 1969 survey. Voltaics (who comprised by far the largest group), Ghanaians, Senegalese and Biafrans were generally well regarded, while the Togolese, Guineans and Dahomeans, who tended to be most visibly involved in petty trade, drew more negative than positive comments. The dominant group in petty trade, however, were the Lebanese, whom Cohen described as "the most hated non-Africans in the country."[48]

We have already noted that the Ivorian boom was built largely on a steady increase in the output of agricultural exports. By 1978 it had surpassed Ghana as the world's leading cocoa producer with a crop of 297,000 tons, and had reached the coffee production limit allowed under the international coffee agreement at 197,000 tons.[49] Production of palm oil, pineapples, rubber, cotton, and sugar had also greatly increased. These increases, however, did not come about through improved farming methods; rather, they were due to the fact that more and more of the southern forest region was being brought under cultivation.[50] While this region had some 14,000 large farms of more than 20 hectares, some three-fifths of the total farming area was in some 353,000 medium or "family"-sized farms of 2 to 10 hectares[51] which normally did not have paid labourers outside the family working for them.[52] These farms, which comprised nearly two-thirds of the total farms in the southern region, typically grew coffee, cocoa or both, and sold more produce as either exports or food crops than they consumed themselves, enjoying in the process an average cash income per farm of $1,083 in 1978.[53] While this was a good deal less than the $7,521 enjoyed by the large farms of 20-100 hectares, and even on a per capita basis represented only about a third of the income of the larger farms (the latter had more family members living on them), still it represented a reasonably comfortable income.

It was also of importance to this group that the producer prices paid for coffee and cocoa tracked the world prices fairly well, with producers receiving on average a little more than half the world price for each of these commodities.[54] Overall, it appears that small farmers' incomes probably held up or even improved slightly in real terms during the 1960s and 1970s.

Landless labourers fared less well. Their incomes appear to have declined in real terms fairly steadily from 1960 to 1976 until by 1976 their wages had only two-thirds the purchasing power they had had in 1960.[55] However, since half of these labourers were from other African states, and they were in any case outnumbered by the farmers working small to medium sized holdings, their political influence was small.

Production of domestic food crops was less impressive than that of export crops. The total output of the main food crops, yam and cassava, increased from 1960 to 1976 at a rate well below the rate of population increase, 0.8% per annum and 1.4% per annum respectively.[56] Rice and maize outputs grew more rapidly, but not enough to meet the increased demand. Rice and wheat became two of the Ivory Coast's main imports, rising from 27,000 tons in 1950 to 107,000 tons in 1965[56] and 270,000 tons in 1977, at a cost in that year of $57.6 million.[57] It could be taken as a sign of affluence, irrationality or both that ordinary labourers in towns breakfasted on French bread made from imported wheat and cafe au lait using imported tinned milk. Certainly this shift in taste helped tie the Ivory Coast even more firmly into a trading economy with Europe and North America.

Perhaps the most important long-term problem of Houphouet-Boigny's regime is the way in which channels for the articulation of political views have been blocked by the concentration of power in

the hands of a very small "old guard".[58] Within the
party, power was concentrated by 1951 in Houphouet's
own hands, and it has remained there ever since,
with a small inner circle of faithful militants
seemingly the only persons who share any degree of
decision-making with him. Even they can be dropped
if they seem too independent, as was shown by the
trial of Interior Minister Jean-Baptiste Mockey in
1963 for allegedly plotting against Houphouet, a
plot which the President later acknowledged was a
frame-up.[59] Auxiliary organizations such as youth
movements and the labour unions were also brought
under tight control.[60] By 1959, popular participation in elections had become a farce; Houphouet and
his associates determined the PDCI slate of candidates, and the electoral rules effectively kept any
other slate from running.[61] This system persisted,
with the determined support of the "old guard", until 1980, when a cautiously controlled experiment
allowed candidates to compete for Assembly seats,
although all had to run under the PDCI banner.[62]
While less than 40% of the electorate turned out,
those who voted did reject 54 of the former deputies, while re-electing only 21.[63] The results
suggested a marked lack of enthusiasm for the political elite, though whether the experiment would be
repeated remained to be seen.

Information about domestic events was tightly
controlled, although foreign newspapers and jour-
nals circulated freely. The only domestic news-
paper after 1964 was the government-owned
Fraternité-Matin, which provided a bland and inoffensive commentary on local events. Radio and tele-
vision were even more inoffensive, with scarcely any
commentary on government plans.[64] In its press, as
in so many other things, the Ivory Coast pursued a
middle path, with neither the sycophantic excess of
praise for the leader characteristic of Malawian
newspapers, nor the frequent references to government short-comings to be found in the press of
Senegal, Ghana, or Zambia. The possibilities for
informed public discussion of problems, however,
were slight.

Developmental activities in small communities
was invariably "top-down" with prominent politicians
bringing benefits to favoured towns and villages.
The President's home town of Yamoussoukro was only
the most spectacular example of this tendency by
notables to create monuments to their own political
power. At the same time, the government consistently refused to support projects involving local

114

self-help.[65]
     Still, despite Yamoussoukro, it would be hard
to say that Houphouet-Boigny had succumbed to the
megalomania of a Dr. Banda or an "Emperor" Bokassa.
He did remain ready to listen to serious grievances,
and even on rare occasions to modify policies. Thus
in 1966, when he tried to introduce dual citizenship
with neighbouring francophone states, which would
have allowed migrants to settle securely in the
Ivory Coast, he was taken aback by the angry reaction from most levels of Ivorian society, and consequently dropped the scheme.[66] Then in 1969 unemployed youths in Abidjan went on a rampage to publi-
cize their long-standing grievance against foreigners taking jobs from Ivorians. The initial government response was to surround the demonstrators
with troops and incarcerate 1,600 of them for up to
three months. But then Houphouet announced a major
"Dialogue", a series of 33 mass meetings with different sections of Ivorian society, at which he
listened to complaints and grievances, outlined his
government's position, and in some cases took steps
to remedy the grievances. As a means of assuaging
discontent, these "Dialogues" seem to have succeeded, and were used again on later occasions. Even
the students, who emphasized their concern over the
slow rate of Ivorianization, seem to have been
brought round to see Houphouet's viewpoint.[67] For
his part, the President seems to have been surprised at the depth and variety of criticisms unleashed[68] and while his response to these criticisms was
limited and cautious, he did not take any retribu-
tion against those who spoke out frankly.
     While it is hard to see such "Dialogues" as an
effective continuing channel for contact between a
leader and the public, still they offered far more
opportunity for such contact than most other African
heads of government made available. One has only
to think of the executions and purges of anyone
criticizing Sékou Touré's or Kamazu Banda's regimes
to realize that Ivorians' opportunities for political expression could have been much more circumscribed.
     Still, the tight control on behalf of a privi-
leged elite did sharply skew the distribution of
goods and services, and contributed to widespread
disaffection toward high officials. During the
boom period of the 1960s the gap between the richest and poorest widened considerably, with the top
5% of Ivorians increasing their share of national
income from 29% to 30% from 1960 to 1970, while the

bottom 20% saw their share fall from 7% to 4%.[69]
There were many specific illustrations of the government's tendency to aid the most affluent. For
example, rather than build twelve regional hospitals around the countryside, the government concentrated health resources in a single modern hospital in the luxurious Abidjan suburb of Cocody.[70]
When pressure grew in the 1960s for government to
build housing in Abidjan, the housing corporation's
response was to build units in Cocody at rents of
$50 to $75 a month, at a time when the average income in Abidjan was less than $100 a month.[71] At
the same time, it restricted private building by
insisting on standards that placed the cost beyond
the reach of anyone not holding a middle-level
job.[72] The result was that many Abidjanais were
pushed through the absence of intermediate levels
of housing into the muddy slums of Adjamé and
Marcory.

Much of this growth in social inequalities was
an inadvertent but inevitable by-product of the government's desire to maximize economic growth, an
approach which necessarily entailed choosing projects on the criteria of economic "efficiency" and
"rationality". For example, in order to increase
agricultural output, the government concentrated
its attention on large-scale plantations and farmers who had already built up farms big enough to
move toward mechanization. Smaller farmers whose
scale of production was not large enough to justify
either mechanical aids or the time of extension officers tended to be overlooked.[73]

It is not surprising in such a situation that
even a government study found that Ministers and
PDCI officials were considered to be interested
mostly in their own good, and that buying a party
card was a form of tax. Even the local PDCI secretary was generally regarded as having "friends in
politics" to help him get rich, while the only protection for the ordinary man was the village chief,
who could to some extent act as a buffer against
the PDCI and the government's spies.[74]

Still despite all this evidence of elite privilege, one does have to note that material well-
being also trickled down to the lower levels of the
society. To be sure, the sight of some of their
countrymen enjoying luxuries that they can scarcely
imagine may stimulate envy among ordinary Ivorians,
but it can also act as an incentive for them to
work for their children's sakes, even if such affluence is beyond their own reach. The most convincing

evidence that for all its problems the Ivory Coast
"miracle" does offer a better life than other parts
of Africa is the presence of two million non-
Ivorian Africans, who though they may grumble about
the high cost of living in Abidjan, show no sign of
rushing back to their homelands.[75] Whatever their
motives, they clearly like something the Ivory
Coast offers better than they like life in their
own villages. Conversely, one finds very few
Ivorians seeking a better life in other African
states.

Nor has the Ivory Coast suffered the disruption of constant intrigues within the civilian and
military elites. The only two plots against
Houphouet-Boigny which were taken seriously were
the one in 1963 involving the Minister of the Interior and a few other high officials, and one in 1973
when some junior army officers were condemned to
death for plotting to overthrow the regime. The
1963 plot, we may recall, was later described by
Houphouet himself as a frame-up and its "participants" restored to favour.[76] There was also a
small-scale uprising in the west-central region in
1970, with a self-proclaimed prophet announcing an
independent "Bété Republic" in Gagnoa, but this
only lasted a few hours.[77] Otherwise, there has
been little to disturb the calm pursuit of national
wealth.

THE "MIRACLE": LUCK OR LEADERSHIP?

It is time to consider the extent to which
political leadership contributed to the path pursued by the Ivory Coast, and to the success enjoyed
in pursuing that path. Could a leader have pursued
different goals in the Ivory Coast, or would any
leaders have been constrained by social and economic
forces to follow the path pursued by Houphouet?
And was the degree of success achieved along this
path produced by forces which would have worked regardless of any political leader's actions, or did
Houphouet's behaviour make a significant contribution?

I would suggest that there were two points at
which a leader pursuing quite different goals could
have emerged, and that the subsequent history of
the Ivory Coast would have been very different had
such leaders appeared. These two points were,
first, the period in 1946 when Houphouet-Boigny took
the PDCI into a position of militantly pro-African

opposition to the French administration, and second, his move back to close collaboration with the French in 1951.

The phase of militant opposition to widely disliked aspects of French colonialism was signalled by the all-African slate in the 1945 Abidjan municipal elections, by the formation of the RDA and the link with the French Communist Party, and above all, by Houphouet's success in securing the prohibition of forced labour in the African territories. All these actions gave the PDCI and Houphouet-Boigny wide popular support far beyond the well-to-do African planters who gave him his start, and focussed Africans' interests on their shared concerns as colonial subjects rather than on more specific class or ethnic interests. Had Houphouet not succeeded in creating this mass base, his PDCI would likely have become an "administration" party, either coming to power with French backing like Grunitzsky's Parti Togolais du Progrès or swept aside by a more radical "Nkrumahist" movement as African nationalism gained force in the 1950s.

With the backing of this mass popular base, and with the PDCI organization largely destroyed as a potential restraining force during the French repression from 1947 to 1951, Houphouet-Boigny had a wide range of choices after he broke with the Communists. Certainly the most articulate and organized sections of Ivorian society, notably the wealthier farmers, acted as a conservative force, but Houphouet's personal stature in 1951 was such that he could easily have "betrayed" his class and sought more egalitarian or more communal goals, or greater autonomy from France, especially if he had pursued these goals by "Tactical Action" or discreet piecemeal steps. There is certainly some truth in the claim that the desire for personal acquisitions and "the capitalist mentality" had taken firm root among Ivorians, and that Houphouet felt he had to work with this mentality rather than oppose it,[78] but he also did a good deal to promote this value system against older, more communal beliefs. For example, a few years later the 1964 Civil Code dismissed traditional collective family claims by such means as a declaration that marriage was "a law that applied to two individuals" and that inheritance ran from father to son rather than from uncle to nephew.[79] Over-all he took the most individualist, pro-capitalist position from the range open to him.

That this choice paid off by providing a wave of prosperity that maintained Houphouet's support is beyond dispute. Further, the potential riches of the Ivory Coast would not have been realized without a climate that encouraged both private investors and the French government to be lavish in their infusion of money and personnel. In turn, Houphouet would have had difficulty allowing such concessions had he not been able to maintain a strong basis of respect among Ivorians. Economic prosperity, of course, helped maintain this respect; but more important was the combination of his reputation for power in defying the French during the repression, his age, and the deliberateness which enhanced his aura of wisdom.[80] He also took care to emphasize his concern with farmers' well-being, and to maintain contact with the countryside.[81] Finally, the very fact of his peasant caution supported his ideological belief that state intervention was a last rather than a first resort for achieving goals, and this self-restraint helped save the Ivory Coast from the kind of well-intentioned but disastrous interventions that marked most African states' development efforts.

I do not wish to suggest that the range of choices open to Houphouet-Boigny in 1951 was unlimited. To take the most obvious illustration, he would have had a very difficult time pursuing a course similar to that of Nkrumah and the CPP in Ghana, simply because such a course implied substantial independence from the metropolitan power. Whereas for Nkrumah to demand "Self-Government Now" was merely to speed up the British timetable for their African colonies' independence, for Houphouet-Boigny to have stated such a goal would have been to challenge directly the French assumption that their colonies were inseparably a part of a Greater France. It seems hard to believe that three years before Dien Bien Phu the French would have ceased their attacks on the PDCI if Houphouet-Boigny had espoused Ivorian independence from France. Similarly, the radical break with France that Guinea made in 1958 was facilitated by Guinea's lack of a planter class dependent on French markets; strong as Houphouet's position was, he probably could not have championed such a course in the Ivory Coast in 1958 or at any earlier time.

Yet short of these extremes, Houphouet could have taken many positions that would have been quite acceptable. A stepped-up Ivorianization programme for high-level jobs, even though it would have impaired efficiency and reduced foreign investment, would have probably increased the regime's

popularity. More emphasis on import substituting
industries, even financed from farmers' crop production, would have been widely accepted, especially in
urban areas. Politically, more nationalist rhetoric
and more support for Pan-African causes would have
been well received. Domestically, attempts to build
cross ethnic links, and to encourage a greater sense
of Ivorian nationhood, would have reduced the sense
of alienation noted earlier, as would the encouragement of self-help schemes for economic development,
even though this last might have made the task of
central political management more difficult.

When we look at the problems facing the Ivory
Coast -- inequalities, foreign control of much of
the economy, lack of political participation -- and
set them against the problems of other African
states, it is hard to fault Houphouet's choices.
When one looks at states which pursued indigenization more rapidly, such as Zambia or Zaire, it is
very hard to argue that they have in any way improved the opportunities for ordinary Africans to
have a say in how their countries' economies are run,
and certainly they have not improved ordinary
Africans' standard of living. Similarly, the record
of states trying to develop through state enterprises has not been encouraging. And while a number
of states -- Tanzania, Botswana, or Sierra Leone,
for example, -- have provided more opportunities for
people to participate politically at either the local or national level, participation has not necessarily contributed to development, nor has it acted
as an effective check on rulers' behaviour.

Perhaps the most important question concerning
the path chosen by the Ivory Coast is whether its
commitment to a "bourgeois" regime tied firmly into
the world capitalist system will prevent it developing the capability for making its own choices of
economic, social and political policies. Do the
"dependency" theorists have a case when they contend
that the result of development like that in the
Ivory Coast is the creation of a ruling group so
desirous of preserving its own life-style and the
links to the capitalist states that support it, that
it deliberately keeps its economy from satisfying
and shaping its own consumer demands and leaves the
major choices regarding the nature and extent of
economic activity in foreign hands?

Certainly the Ivorian bourgeoisie has developed
a great appetite for European consumer goods, and
regards European capitalist society as its model for
emulation. And yet, the government has also taken

120

steps which give the Ivory Coast the ability to create more prosperity for itself. The attempt to meet its own refined sugar needs, the establishment of textile mills, and the setting up of its own merchant marine, all point toward creating within the country more skills which will put it on a footing of equality with the industrialized states. It appears that the Ivory Coast has been doing a good deal to use the prosperity generated by its primary product exports to widen its economic choices, and that it has done nothing yet to foreclose the possibility of attaining the level of industrial skills enjoyed by, say, Costa Rica, or looking much further into the future, Finland or Norway. Obviously there are many hazards still ahead, the most immediate of which is how to keep a tightly controlled system going under successors who cannot hope to achieve the moral authority that Houphouet's successes have built up over the years. Without such a strongly entrenched leader, there is a great risk that the government will succumb to pressure to take more popular but risky steps such as grandiose megaprojects or premature Africanization, or that to contain popular pressure it will resort to much more overt coercion than Houphouet has ever had to practise. Whatever his faults, Felix Houphouet-Boigny's cautious approach has managed to avoid the disasters that have disrupted the economies or the social fabric of other African states, and his legacy is a state with at least the possibility of enjoying a living standard comparable to that of the industrialized states.

NOTES

1. Ruth Schacter Morgenthau, Political Parties in French-Speaking West Africa (Clarendon Press, Oxford, 1964), p. 168.
2. Hubert Frechou, "Les plantations européenes en Côte d'Ivoire", cited in Aristide Zolberg, One-Party Government in the Ivory Coast (Princeton University Press, Princeton, 1964), p. 58.
3. Zolberg, One-Party Government, p. 66.
4. Immanuel Wallerstein, The Road to Independence: Ghana and the Ivory Coast (Mouton, London, 1964), p. 8.
5. Zolberg, One-Party Government, pp. 29, 30.
6. Ibid., p. 69; also Jon Woronoff, West African Wager (Scarecrow Press, Metuchen, N. J.,

1972), p. 35.
    7. Woronoff, African Wager, p. 42.
    8. For a detailed participant's account of the attitudes on both sides and the negotiations, see Paul-Henri Siriex, Felix Houphouet-Boigny (Seghers, Paris, 1975), pp. 126-39.
    9. He took three years' training in medicine beyond secondary school.
    10. See Siriex, Houphouet-Boigny, p. 29.
    11. Ibid., p. 77.
    12. Ibid., p. 294; also Woronoff, African Wager, p. 294.
    13. For the UPC, see Richard Joseph, Radical Nationalism in Cameroun (Clarendon, Oxford, 1977), esp. pp. 243-92.
    14. See Samir Amin, Le Développement du Capitalisme en Côte d'Ivoire (Editions de Minuit, Paris, 1967), p. 8.
    15. Ibid., p. 297.
    16. Calculated from ibid., p. 294.
    17. Morgenthau, Political Parties, p. 414.
    18. Amin, Capitalisme, pp. 200, 300; he notes on p. 200 that France gave a total of Fr. CFA 40,600 million (about $U.S. 232 million) for the entire period. (I am taking CFA francs at their official exchange rate of 175=$U.S. 1.00; however, the CFA franc was over-valued during this period, and thus the value of French investment could be reduced by about a quarter.)
    19. Ibid., p. 226.
    20. Ibid., p. 225.
    21. See Zolberg, One-Party Government, pp. 152-55, 188-92.
    22. Ibid., p. 197.
    23. For the workings of the Loi-Cadre, see Kenneth Robinson, "Constitutional Reform in French Tropical Africa", Political Studies, VI, 1 (1958), pp. 45-69.
    24. See Elliot Berg, "The Economic Basis of Political Choice in French West Africa", American Political Science Review, LIV, 2 (June 1960), pp. 391-405.
    25. Cf. Bonnie Campbell, "L'idéologie de la croissance", Canadian Journal of African Studies, X, 2 (1976), p. 225, for the government's continuing opposition to regionalism in the 1970s.
    26. See Zolberg, One-Party Government, pp. 222-24.
    27. Ibid., p. 227.
    28. General de Gaulle in his Memoirs described Houphouet as having a "first-class political mind,

122

up to all the questions which concerned not only his own country but also Africa and the entire world, and possessing an exceptional authority and above all, an unquestionable influence, and using them to serve the cause of reason." Quoted in Siriex, Houphouet-Boigny, p. 171.

29. See Zolberg, One-Party Government, p. 226.

30. For the wager, see Woronoff, African Wager, p. 13; for Houphouet's views, Zolberg, One-Party Government, pp. 233-36, and Siriex, Houphouet-Boigny, p. 163.

31. See Woronoff, African Wager, pp. 88-91.

32. Zolberg, One-Party Government, p. 244.

33. Ibid., pp. 212-15.

34. For 1960-1965, Amin notes a growth rate of some 11-12% (Developpement du Capitalisme, p. 7); for the later period, see Jean-Claude Pomonti, "Black African Showcase", Guardian Weekly, February 24, 1980.

35. Pomonti, "The Ivory Coast: Clouds over a Model State", Guardian Weekley, March 2, 1980.

36. See Woronoff, African Wager, p. 209.

37. See V. L. Galbraith, "When Trade Does Act as an Engine of Growth: The Case of the Ivory Coast", in Sayre Schatz (ed.), South of the Sahara: Development in African Economics (Temple University Press, Philadelphia, 1972), p. 304.

38. Elliot Berg, "Structural Transformation versus Gradualism", in Aristide Zolberg and Philip Foster (eds.), Ghana and the Ivory Coast (University of Chicago Press, Chicago, 1971), p. 220.

39. Pomonti, "Clouds over a Model State"; see also Vincent Tickner, "International-Local Capital: The Ivory Coast Sugar Industry", Review of African Political Economy, 8, pp. 119-21.

40. "Structural Transformation versus Gradualism", pp. 219-20.

41. See Woronoff, African Wager, p. 282: also Tamar Golan, "The Iceberg that is Ivory Coast," West Africa, September 6 and September 13, 1975, pp. 1288-89 and 1321-23.

42. See Bastien den Tuinder, Ivory Coast: The Challenge of Success (John Hopkins University Press for the World Bank, Baltimore, 1978), p. 294.

43. See ibid., p. 113. He estimated that an amount equal to 8% of foreign exchange earnings was remitted as personal transfers by non-Africans.

44. Ibid., pp. 293-94.

45. Africa Confidential, August 1, 1979.

46. See Woronoff, African Wager, p. 275; Siriex, Houphouet-Boigny, p. 210.

47. Bonnie Campbell, "Idéologie de la Croissance", p. 223.

48. Michael Cohen, Urban Policy and Political Conflict in Africa: A Study of the Ivory Coast (University of Chicago Press, Chicago, 1974), p. 128. We should note, however, that there were few other non-Africans besides the French.

49. Africa Confidential, October 17, 1979.

50. See the excellent analysis of the Ivory Coast's agricultural sector by Eddie Lee, "Export-led Rural Development: The Ivory Coast", Development and Change, 11, 4 (1980), pp. 611-12.

51. Ibid., p. 629.

52. Ibid., p. 633, cites data from the 1974-75 Census of Agriculture showing that farms up to 5 hectares had an average of 0.1 permanent (non-family) labourers, while those of 5 to 10 hectares had 0.4 labourers. In other words, about one in five of these farms might have had one labourer working on it.

53. Calculated from Lee's Table 7, p. 629.

54. Ibid., p. 636.

55. Ibid., p. 626.

56. Amin, Capitalisme, p. 287, Table 2.

57. United Nations 1978 Yearbook, International Trade Statistics, Vol. I, p. 636.

58. See Dennis Austin, Politics in Africa, (University Press of New England, Hanover, N. H., 1978), P. 43.

59. Golan, West Africa, September 6, 1976, p. 1287.

60. For the youth movements, see Naomi Chazan, "The Manipulation of Youth Politics in Ghana and the Ivory Coast," Génève-Afrique, 9, 2 (1976) pp. 38-63.

61. See Zolberg, One-Party Government, pp. 264-65.

62. Le Devoir (Montreal), November 8, 1980.

63. West Africa, December 1, 1980, p. 2459.

64. See W. A. Hatchen, "The Press in a One-Party State" Journalism Quarterly, 44 (Spring 1967), pp. 11-12.

65. See Cohen, Urban Policy, p. 212.

66. See ibid., p. 75, citing Afrique Nouvelle, 6-12 January 1966 and 27 January-3 February 1966.

67. See ibid., Ch. 6, for the fullest description of the "Dialogues"; also Siriex, Houphouet-Boigny, p. 210 and Woronoff, African Wager, pp. 284-85.

68. Cohen, Urban Policy, p. 121

69. See World Bank, World Tables 1976 (published for the World Bank by John Hopkins Press,

Baltimore, 1976), p. 515.

70. Cohen, Urban Policy, p. 57.

71. Ibid., p. 38.

72. Ibid., p. 35.

73. For an illustration of this tendency, see J. Hinderink and G. J. Tempelman, "Rural inequality and government policy: the Bou River basin, Ivory Coast", Tijdschrift Economische en Sociale Geographie, 69, 1/2 (1978), pp. 58-67.

74. Côte d'Ivoire Ministère de Plan, Rapport de Synthèse, pp. 13-14, 18.

75. This figure of two million includes both those Africans who themselves were born outside the Ivory Coast, and the children of these foreign-born Africans. See den Tuinder, Ivory Coast, p. 124.

76. Tamar Golan, West Africa, September 6, 1976.

77. See West Africa, December 5, 1970, p. 1417.

78. Woronoff, African Wager, p. 201: also Ministere de Plan, pp. 18, 21, 27.

79. Mireille Laporte, "La Pensée sociale du President Felix Houphouet-Boigny", (Centre d'Etude d'Afrique noire, Bordeaux, 1970), p. 17.

80. Tamar Golan, West Africa, September 13, 1976, pp. 1321-23 has a good description of his style.

81. Woronoff, African Wager, p. 294.

Chapter Seven

SENEGAL: THE PHILOSOPHY OF ACQUIESCENCE?

At the end of 1980, Léopold Sédar Senghor retired after twenty years as President of Senegal.
When he first entered the Senegalese political arena
in 1946, it would have been hard to imagine anyone
less likely to survive the rough-and-tumble that
African politics was to become in the succeeding
three decades. A forty-year-old university teacher
who had lived in France for nearly twenty years, who
had acquired a French wife and citizenship, and
whose claim to prominence was his reputation as one
of France's leading young poets, hardly seemed the
man who would come to master brokerage politics with
a subtlety and skill matched by few other African
leaders. Yet Senghor managed to build his political
base on the rural masses rather than the sophisticated elites of Dakar, and even after independence
maintained Senegal as one of the more tranquil and
conflict-free states in Africa. Partly in consequence of this, it enjoyed one of Africa's more open
and tolerant political systems. However, it also
had one of the poorest records in Africa in economic
development, both in aggregate terms and in terms of
the standard of living of ordinary citizens.
Senegal had had little success in diversifying its
heavy dependence upon peanuts for its export earnings, nor had it managed to improve greatly its own
capacities for providing a better life for its citizens, in large measure because it had never succeeded in breaking down the authoritarian social structures which dominated the rural areas. It furnished, in short, almost a classic illustration of the
neo-colonial state.

Yet Léopold Senghor was no mere neo-colonial
puppet. The most intellectual of African political
leaders, he had a vision of a new society based on a
synthesis of European technology and African communal

126

values, a synthesis which he claimed would produce a humane socialism. What he achieved, however, was almost the antithesis of this: a society lacking any significant control over its technological development, but permeated by a spirit of individualism and acquisitiveness well captured by the novels and films of one of its leading artists, Ousmane Sembene.[1] Senghor's tragedy was that in focussing on cultural values, he lost touch with the mundane realities of economic and social power, and as a result the latter were used for ends quite different than those which he professed to believe were desirable.[2]

Yet somehow Senghor survived these failures, and even retained a substantial degree of respect and admiration within his own country. After independence he never did try to lead his country in new directions, nor even to inspire his people with his vision; but he did manage to keep conflicts under control and to maintain a reasonably peaceful society. His role was certainly not a heroic one; one of the many ironies for a man who took his intellectualism so seriously was that his political model could have been the good soldier Schweik. But was he really a failure? The ambiguous legacy he left to his successor can be interpreted in many ways.

No matter what his goals, any would-be Senegalese leader faced severe constraints. Nature and the colonial heritage left Senegal with five major problems at independence: a dry land vulnerable to droughts, a great gap between urban and rural ways of life, reliance on a single major export crop, a dominant role for wealthy Muslim religious leaders in the countryside, and a pervasive French influence over government and society. None of these problems was insurmountable, but together they looked daunting to any leader cautious about taking political risks.

Senegal's location at the western end of the Sahel meant that its rainfall was never high and was subject to considerable fluctuation; the drought from 1968 to 1973, while not as severe as in inland states, underlined this vulnerability. Its two major rivers, the Senegal and the Gambia, were shared with other states, which meant that utilizing their waters for agriculture involved rather complicated international arrangements, as well as imposing an additional limit on the amount of water they could provide.

The territory's location also gave it an earlier and more thorough contact than most of Africa to

European expansion. French settlements were established in the 18th century, and during the French
Revolution the inhabitants of the French settlements, including Africans, were given French citizenship.[3] The distinction thus established between
the small group of African "citizens" and the great
bulk of hinterland "subjects" retained its significance for Senegalese politics until well into the
1950s. The citizens set the cultural tone for the
territory, and not surprisingly, they favoured assimilation into France.[4]
    In 1902, after France had extended its control
over all French West Africa, Dakar was designated
the capital of the region. This role as the political and administrative centre of an area possessing
eight times the population of Senegal alone encouraged an extensive development of the services auxiliary to running an empire, such as the Ecole William
Ponty, which educated most of French West Africa's
first generation of African administrators and teachers. Dakar also became the major port and commercial centre not only for Senegal, but also for the
Soudan, to which it was linked in 1923 by the 720-
mile Dakar-Bamako railway. Its central area was
built in a French monumental style, with broad tree-
lined boulevards, imposing public buildings, and
large numbers of sidewalk cafes to solace expatriate
Frenchmen. Its opportunities for jobs in trade and
administration made Dakar a magnet for rural
Senegalese, until by 1978 it contained one-fifth of
Senegal's inhabitants, although many of these remained jobless and in dusty slums. Like many other
capitals, it enjoyed a disproportionate share of
social services; for example, it had three quarters
of all Senegal's doctors in 1978.[5]
    In contrast to the affluence on display in
Dakar, the Senegalese countryside is poor and dry.
However, ever since the French discovered in the
mid-19th century that Senegal's soil could grow
peanuts, it has been the countryside that has provided the basis for much of the city's prosperity.
As an export crop whose revenues could be tapped at
several points in its journey from "the bush" to
France, the peanut financed among other things the
remarkable growth of the Senegalese bureaucracy from
some 10,000 civil servants at independence in 1960
to some 61,000 in 1973.[6] This concentration on peanut monoculture had its costs. So much land was devoted to peanut cultivation that in the mid-1970s
Senegal was importing between $53 and $95 million
worth of cereals a year.[7] Furthermore, drought

could be disastrous; after running around 800,000
tons per year from 1960 to 1968, the crop slid down
to a post-war record low of 428,000 tons in 1973,
then rebounded to an all-time record of 1,180,000
tons in 1977, only to crash again to 480,000 tons in
1978.[8] During most of this time the farmers received only a modest portion of the revenues. For most
of the 1960s they were paid about $89 a ton, with
the price dropping to $61 a ton in 1970 and creep-
ing back to $83 in 1973. Then, faced with the
threat of massive withdrawals from peanut cultivation, the government nearly doubled the producer
price in 1974, to $155 per ton.[9] Meanwhile, the
price that Senegal was receiving on world markets
for raw peanuts was about $175 a ton during the
1960s, rising to $189 in 1970, $275 in 1972, and
$502 in 1974.[10]

Much of the explanation for the willingness of
peasant producers to accept such a distribution of
wealth for so long lies in the social structure of
Senegal. The major social organizations in rural
Senegal are the patronage networks called "clans",
and the Muslim brotherhoods. Both of these organizations limit ethnic divisions, and even more important, class conflict.

Ethnicity in Senegal has never been the basis
of major conflicts. The "core" group, the Wolof,
comprises about a third of the population, concentrated in Dakar and the richest peanut-growing
areas, but it has remained open and able to assimi-
late individuals from other groups, so that about
60% of Senegalese speak Wolof. Like other ethnic
groups the Wolof are internally divided by the
"clans", which provide competing alliances within
each ethnic group and thus prevent the latter from
forming united blocs.[11] These clans unite the ordinary peasants with rich patrons by allowing some
wealth to trickle down, and thus also limit class
conflict.

The Muslim brotherhoods also cut across class
lines, but they also cut across both ethnic groups
and clans, and for most rural dwellers, override
both in importance.[12] Most of the 80% of Senegalese
who are Muslims consider themselves as members of
one or other brotherhoods, giving these organizations the potential to be the most powerful force in
Senegalese politics. The brotherhoods, or tariqas,
were based on the mystical Sufi strain of Islam,
which maintained that if followers were to give
total obedience to their religious leader, he could
bring them into Paradise through prayer. Tariqas

are hierarchical in structure, with <u>marabouts</u> as the major leaders of specific regions, and a Grand Marabout or <u>Khalif</u> as leader of a <u>tariqa</u> in a territory such as Senegal. The marabouts of the most powerful brotherhood, the Murids, managed to enhance their spiritual role by having their followers work in their peanut fields as a religious obligation, so that the Grand Marabout, Falilou M'Backé, enjoyed an income of well over $100,000 a year. Leading marabouts had large enough holdings that they could experiment with new varieties of seed, fertilizer and other innovations, and could then use their influence to have their followers to do the same.

While the Murids' interest in economic improvements endeared them to the French, they were far less interested in any social changes. Schooling, which many marabouts perceived as a secular and rationalist threat to the obedience they received from their followers, was least advanced in those areas in which the marabouts were strongest.[14] Government administrators generally had to be acceptable to the marabouts in their region, and often the administrators would call on the marabouts to help them carry out governmental duties.[15] Marabouts operated almost above the law in some cases. For example, in 1965 the United States gave Senegal surplus grain for free distribution. Some marabouts sold the grain, greatly embarrassing the government in its dealings with the United States, but none was ever punished. All the government could do was to ensure that in future only trustworthy marabouts received the grain for distribution.[16]

Fortunately for President Senghor, the marabouts were usually divided among themselves by personal rivalries, and they could also be persuaded to abandon their followers to further their personal interests. Thus in 1965 Falilou M'Backé called on his followers to withhold their peanuts from the government in response to a government decision to hold back 10% of the price it had earlier promised to pay. The government eventually exempted M'Backé, though not his followers, from the 10% withholding. M'Backé then ordered his followers to sell their peanuts.[17]

The marabouts, then, while powerful, are not omnipotent. The government can generally play them off against each other, and can balance their claims to some extent against the demands of the growing body of educated youth and urban dwellers who lack the strong devotion which underpins the marabouts' strength. Still, the urban and educated persons

form small minorities in present-day Senegal, and in
the countryside the marabouts' hold shows little
sign of weakening.

A further enduring feature of Senegal is the
pervasiveness of the French. Dakar, as the capital
of the AOF and until the 1950s its largest commercial centre, had always attracted a disproportionate
number of expatriates, in business as well as government service. Even today one sees large numbers
of "petits blancs", the French shopgirls and others
in relatively menial employment, in the central business district. In 1956 one observer noted that the
number of French people in Senegal was as great as
those in all the rest of French West Africa combined,
and approached the white settler population of
Kenya.[18] However, he went on to note that none of
the French considered themselves as settlers; all
assumed that some day they would retire to France.
They would not, in other words, be expected to cling
as intransigeantly to their position as East African
settlers, and thus act as such a barrier to African
advancement.

Nevertheless, the French presence was formid-
able. Although Senghor was able to boast in 1961
that thanks to Senegal's long association with
France and consequent opportunities for Senegalese
to acquire technical and military skills, there
were "only 1,500 foreign technicians"[19] this still
meant that even in the public sector 120 out of 273
high level civil servants were Frenchmen. In the
private sector "Senegalization" had made far less
impact: in the industrial sector in 1964, all but 60
of the 889 managerial posts were held by expatriates,[21] while in the commercial sector, despite a
growing body of young Senegalese entrepreneurs,
French firms still predominated, with the Lebanese
also holding a substantial share of business.

Most critical of all in providing Senghor with
security was the presence of a French garrison just
outside Dakar. Though the numbers of this garrison
diminished over the years, from 27,000 in 1960 to
6,600 in 1965 and (officially) only 900 in 1976[22]
their presence provided important insurance for
Senghor against a <u>coup</u> by more nationalist opponents.
While the French troops have never actually fought
against the Senegalese army (as they did in Gabon in
1964 to restore President M'Ba after his army had
apparently staged a successful <u>coup</u>) their very presence at the nerve centre of the country has served
to dampen any political ambition that may lurk among
Senegalese officers, as well as to provide a

praetorian guard against such civil threats to
Senghor as Prime Minister Mamadou Dia's challenge in
1962 or the general strike of 1968.[24]

These constant elements in the Senegalese polity all set limits to the freedom of manoeuvre open
to any Senegalese leader, yet they were not unalter-
able constraints; a leader could still make some
choices, provided he was prepared to make an effort
and take some risks in order to bring changes. Let
us examine, then, some key events in Senegal's political evolution since 1945, particularly those at
which a leader might have followed a course other
than that chosen by Senghor.

SENGHOR: FRENCH POET OR SENEGALESE MAN OF THE BUSH?

We have already noted that since 1792 a small
number of Senegalese had enjoyed the privileges of
French citizens, although it was not until 1914 that
the first African, Blaise Diagne, won a seat in the
French National Assembly. Inter-war politics was
essentially a competition among patron-client networks within this citizen elite, with little trickling down to the 96% of the Senegalese who were mere
subjects.

However, in the liberal flush of the post-1945
Constituent Assembly the leader of the Senegalese
branch of the French Socialist Party (SFIO) succeeded in gaining the vote and other privileges of citizenship for the erstwhile subjects. This achievement reinforced the reputation Lamine Gueye, himself
a citizen, had already gained among subjects for his
legal work on their behalf in the pre-war period.
As the major political survivor from this era, as a
skillful builder of political machines, and most of
all as the beneficiary of an anti-Vichy reaction,
Gueye was the dominant Senegalese political figure
in 1946. In the 1946 elections for the French
National Assembly he used his strength to impose
Senghor as his candidate for the seat reserved for
"subjects". Although younger students in Paris and
militants in the Senegalese section of the SFIO objected that Senghor was too "colonial" in his out-
look, the two men won a sweeping triumph in the
elections.[25]

As much as any political figure in Africa,
Senghor showed the ambivalence that French assimilation policies could produce among Africans.[26]
Born in 1906 to a prosperous Serer peanut trader in
a small village, Senghor could call upon his early

132

life in "the bush" to show the Senegalese peasants
that he was one of them, although his father had had
him baptised a Catholic. However, after his schooling in Senegal, where he almost committed himself to
the priesthood, Senghor in 1928 went to France for
further education, where among his close friends was
de Gaulle's future right-hand man and successor as
president, Georges Pompidou. During the 1930s
Senghor pursued a French academic career, gaining a
reputation as a poet and developing his arguments
for the distinctiveness of African culture which
later emerged as his concept of "Negritude".
     There were several ironies in this. Senghor,
the champion of African culture, had only returned
to Senegal for two brief visits between 1928 and
1946, remaining for the most part in a French intellectual millieu. The man who maintained that the
distinctiveness of African culture lay in its emphasis on emotion, on warm feeling rather than on
the cold rationality of Europe, argued his case in
the brilliantly rational manner of a French intellectual. The very fact of his having to create an intellectual defence of an abstract and idealized
African culture suggests the extent to which this
had in fact been replaced in his soul by the culture
of France. It can also be said that even while he
rose to political power in Senegal, he was so busy
trying to recapture a rarefied abstraction of
"African culture" that he neglected such mundane
questions as whether Senegalese peasants might enjoy
more material well-being if they were less dependent
on France and the sale of their peanut crop for a
living.
     Yet despite his rarefied intellectual concerns,
much of Senghor's strength from 1946 onward derived
from the fact that he could still maintain a rapport
with the ordinary Senegalese peasant. His campaign
style in 1946 contrasted sharply with that of Gueye.
The city-bred Gueye always campaigned fastidiously
dressed in a suit and tie. Senghor campaigned
through the bush in a khaki shirt and trousers, and
dipped food with his hand out of the same calabash
as the peasants.[27] His appeals too were decidedly
"populist"; he contrasted the assimilated, the
"wearers of false collars", with the peasants, and
at one time even took a hard, radical line on independence for the African territories:

> "[I wish to assure] the Whites of our un-
> shakeable will to attain our independence...
> we are ready, if necessary and in the last

resort, to gain liberty by any means, even violent ones."[28]

This, coupled with his espousal of African culture and later of African federation, was enough to earn him, ironically, the reputation of being anti-French, although never to the point where the administration attempted the repressive tactics against him or his party that they used in the Ivory Coast against Houphouet-Boigny.

By 1948, Senghor had decided to break with Lamine Gueye and the French Socialists. Already in 1946 Gueye's control of the SFIO nominations in Senegal had kept him unwillingly away from the founding conference of the Rassemblement Democratique Africaine in Bamako, whose militant African and Communist orientation frightened the SFIO.[29] In 1948 he broke with both the SFIO and Gueye, charging that the former was not interested in African problems, and that the latter had made the AOF section of the SFIO a personal machine.[30] Within Senegal, he then formed the Bloc Democratique Senegalaise (BDS) which in varying forms was to dominate Senegalese politics thereafter.

Senghor's background helped him to cast a wide appeal during this period. He could claim to be a "man of the bush" in a way denied the urban-bred Gueye. At the same time his educational achievement helped make him acceptable to the educated elements in Senegalese society, as well as suggesting that he could deal with the French on an equal footing. His Catholicism was a handicap in a predominantly Muslim culture, but he offset this quickly by recruiting an able young Murid economist, Mamadou Dia, as his lieutenant. This was a major factor in aligning the powerful Murid brotherhood behind Senghor's party. Most important, however, was the way Senghor concentrated on wooing influential groups with specific promises; the veterans by higher pensions, the chiefs by higher salaries and security of status, and the various regional and ethnic groups by places on the party executive.[31] The BDS became a catch-all coalition held together by patronage, a pattern it was to retain.

There were some costs to this system of coalition-building, however. The party leaders could only hold their supporters together by a series of specific and limited payoffs. This precluded their making any broader over-arching appeal such as nationalism that would transcend local interests; and it also precluded their reaching past the

leaders of these groups and appealing directly to
the rank-and-file. Furthermore, since the rewards
they could offer for support were in short supply,
they had constantly to be deciding which groups to
allocate resources to, and how to placate those who
lost out in this distribution. This all contributed
to the development of the competing clans which came
to characterize Senegalese politics. These "clans",
which though they might be based on ethnicity,
were frequently interest groups devoid of any emotional attachment, inevitably were in conflict with
each other over the allocation of resources.[32] For
better or worse, this meant that there would be no
mass popular movement supporting a single leader and
single goal, as happened in Guinea or Tanzania. The
way in which Senghor chose initially to construct
his party, in short, ensured that he would remain a
brokerage leader.

The BDS need not have evolved in this way, however. Rather than allowing it to become a somewhat
amorphous party tied together largely by a system of
alliances among local notables and by specific patronage appeals, Senghor and Dia might have capital-
ized on the clearly discernable anti-French, anti-
colonial sentiment of the time to make a stronger
direct appeal to urban workers and to ordinary farmers. Such a campaign could have been built on a
more or less discreet anti-French appeal for "Equality or Independence", and could have been used to
build up cadres independent of the marabouts. Since
apart from their limited influence with the French
government in Paris the leaders of the BDS had
little largesse to distribute, this non-material appeal would not have cost them many supporters, and
would likely have gained them a great number. There
were, to be sure, two risks: first, that the marabout would resent being bypassed, and would see a
threat to their position implicit in a mass popular
party; and second, that the French would undertake a
campaign of repression against such a party, bringing the marabouts into line by appealing to their
economic interest in the French market for peanuts,
and setting up a more malleable "administration
party". The first of these risks, although real,
probably could have been contained by a moderately
skillful effort at dividing the marabouts and blur-
ring any goals of social change. The second likely
would not have materialized for two reasons: first,
the French were more concerned with the
pro-Communist tendencies of the rival RDA, and likely would have seen even a nationalistic Senghor as

a lesser evil; and second, they would have had a difficult time finding a tame yet electorally viable alternative. Lamine Gueye's socialists were too strongly identified as a "citizen" party to have much chance of attracting voters in the "bush" and there was nobody else in sight.

Senghor, however, had no interest in mobilizing popular support; rather, his preference was to balance off the different forces in the Senegalese polity. Thus he was quick to incorporate radical critics into the BDS, since he feared that their opinions could spread among other opinion leaders and their strength could thus surge up dramatically.[33] Even the Senegalese branch of the RDA was lured into the BDS, and in 1956 several young intellectuals were parachuted into key party posts, from which they proceeded to try to turn the BDS into a mass-based party.[34] The older "notables" protested, but Senghor and Dia for the time being backed the "young Turks" as the BDS was transformed. Its name too changed, first to Bloc Populaire Senegalaise, and then to Union Progressiste Senegalaise, which it retained until 1976.

But this tentative "radicalization" soon was aborted by events outside Senegal. The Loi-Cadre of 1956 and the subsequent balkanization of French West Africa into largely autonomous territories, though anathema to Senghor's dream of a grand federation, was a possible step toward independence for individual territories (though the French refused to acknowledge this). De Gaulle, on coming to power in 1958, chose to restrict the African territories' choice in the constitutional referendum to whether they would accept or reject membership in a new French Community, with no recognition of the territories' right to independence. Senghor, who in the 1957 territorial elections had insisted on the Africans' right to decide their own destiny and threatened non-violent resistance if necessary to achieve this end,[35] regarded this draft as "worse than that of 1946"[36] and wrote to Georges Pompidou that he would have to campaign for a "No" vote. Already at a conference in Cotonou in July the young radicals had brushed aside his attempted compromise formula of "the right to independence within a federal system" in favour of an unconditional demand for independence, and they had been joined by Lamine Gueye.[37] Then de Gaulle on his grand tour through Africa encountered a reception in Dakar even more hostile than that which Sékou Touré had arranged in Guinea, with masses of militants supporting the "No" vote, while Senghor discreetly stayed at his retreat in Normandy.

While they might not influence the young urban militants, the French could still influence Senegal's main power brokers, the marabouts. The former Governor-General of the AOF and now Overseas Minister, Bernard Cornut-Gentille, visited Senegal in late August, and in 48 hours, by skillful use of "charm, threats and promises", convinced the major marabouts to support a "Yes" vote.[38] The fact that France paid a price well over the world level of Senegalese peanuts undoubtedly was his major talking point.

Faced with the strong probability that this combination of maraboutic support plus French administration of the vote would result in a triumph for the "Yes" vote for the new French Community, Senghor and Mamadou Dia prudently retreated. Returning quickly to Senegal, Senghor managed to steer through the UPS executive a motion which was a masterpiece of double-talk: "Yes to African unity, yes to independence, and yes to association with France!" With this endorsement from the UPS, the "Yes" vote won overwhelmingly, 870,362 to 21,901 "No".[39]

But the costs of this victory were high. Many of the "young Turks" who had begun to build local party branches and to undercut the power of the marabouts and clan leaders left to form opposition movements. The UPS slowed down Africanization, since it was reluctant to replace Frenchmen with Senegalese who were its political opponents.[40] More generally the UPS reverted to being a "cadre" party reliant upon local notables, and lost the talents of those who might have pointed the way to a more balanced and less dependent economy. Not all the "young Turks" left at this time; a number stayed on, attracted by the seemingly more progressive attitudes of Senghor's second-in-command, Mamadou Dia. But enough had pulled out to reduce Dia's base of support within the UPS so that when a crisis came between him and Senghor four years later, he was heavily outnumbered.

Meanwhile, Senghor was trying to salvage a federation of parts of French West Africa in the face of French opposition. Not content with thrusting Sékou Touré's Guinea into an ill-prepared independence for its temerity in voting "no" to continued association with France, the French sought to isolate its dangerous contagion of independence. The best way to isolate it was to keep the other territories divided, weak and dependent on French beneficence.

Furthermore, Houphouet-Boigny had proved himself France's most loyal supporter, and Houphouet wanted no truck with any African federation. This convergence of interests led the French government to subvert the grouping that Senghor first put together as a nuclear federation, the territories of Dahomey, Upper Volta, Soudan and Senegal. The combined pressures of the French government and of Houphouet-Boigny, specifically a threat to encourage an uprising of war veterans in Upper Volta, led Maurice Yameogo to reconsider; in Dahomey the desire for French aid to build port facilities in Cotonou outweighed the commitment to a federation.[41] The result was that the Mali Federation (named after the ancient empire) was launched in 1959 with only two members, the smaller but more developed and richer Senegal and the more populous but far poorer Soudan.

The two partners had almost diametrically opposed bases of support. Senghor's UPS was based on the marabouts, upheld the highly inegalitarian order that the French had imposed, and was opposed by the young intellectuals who sought more widespread rural mobilization. The Union Soudanaise, which had come to power in opposition to the chiefs and the French administration through mobilizing its own party cadres, sought to transform Soudanese society and to reduce dependence on France, and was opposed by the remnant of traditional chiefs, and their followers.

The French, after first trying unsuccessfully to ignore the new federation,[42] soon realized that short of direct military intervention, they could not replace the governments of either Soudan or Senegal. After some hesitation, they allowed the Mali Federation to accede to national sovereignty, while still remaining within the "one and indivisible" French Community and the franc zone, and receiving French aid.[43]

However, the French were soon able to help the differences between the two partners break up the Federation. The Union Soudanaise envisioned a tightly structured, mobilizing polity, and apparently were planning to take advantage of the lack of tight discipline in the UPS to replace Senghor with Lamine Gueye as President of the Federation at the congress which was to meet on August 27 in Dakar. Gueye would provide a respectable cover behind which the Soudanaise militants could run the Federation their own way.[44]

French intelligence at this point played a decisive role, by intercepting a message from the Soudanese commander of the army to Soudanese units

to be present in Dakar by August 27. They promptly
passed this information to their Senegalese friends.
The Senegalese quickly used the police to take control of all key government buildings, and to arrest
and expel the Soudanese. Senghor's own actions had
thus killed his dream of federation. The decisive
factor seems to have been that if he had allowed the
federation to continue he personally would have lost
power, and worse yet, seen either his old rival
Gueye or the young radicals ascend to supremacy.
Faced with this choice, he chose his own survival.

Senegal was thus independent and on its own,
though still closely tied to France through aid and
defence agreements. Rid of a partner which could
support his challengers on the left, and reassured
by the support of the marabouts in the crisis,
Senghor was in a more secure political position than
he had enjoyed for some time. But now that Senegal
had attained independence, new choices had to be
made, and a rift over the direction of the new state
began to divide Senghor and Mamadou Dia.

The two men had worked out a division of labour
over the years which seemed satisfactory. While
Senghor struggled to achieve a federation and to
maintain ties with France, Dia busied himself with
economic development and internal administration,
areas which held little appeal to the poet president.[45] Those radicals who had not left the UPS for
the Parti du Regroupement African-Senegal and the
Parti Africain de l'Independence gathered around Dia
to work for economic developments which would mobilize ordinary peasants into self-help projects
through co-operatives and through animators chosen
from within the villages. They also established an
Office of Agriculture Commercialization which bought
peanuts from and sold seeds and other necessities
directly to the peasants.[46] All of these actions
threatened the established intermediaries who comprised the UPS power bases, and they began to object. Perhaps to overcome this resistance, Dia
tried with only limited success to rally the
marabouts[47] and to proclaim the need for a Muslim
country like Senegal to have a Muslim president.[48]
However, he did not win much support from the marabouts, and without them he lacked widespread
strength in the country. In December 1962, the
Assembly prepared to vote censure on the Prime
Minister, whether at Senghor's instigation or merely
with his acquiescence is not clear. Dia tried to
win the police and army to allow him to appeal to
the party, but the army leaders proclaimed their

loyality to Senghor. Dia was arrested, and subsequently tried for treason and imprisoned.

With Dia's departure the economic reforms slowed down, although they were not dropped completely, and control over many of the co-ops and other "reform" institutions fell into the hands of the marabouts.[49] Senegal embarked on a long period of economic lassitude, from which it was aroused only by the riots of 1968.

THE POLITICS OF ACCOMMODATION

Could things have evolved differently? Although it would have been more difficult and somewhat riskier for Senghor and the UPS to have pursued the program of reform advanced by Mamadou Dia, it seems possible that it could have been done. If Senghor had supported Dia, as he had earlier supported the infusion of young radicals into the BDS, the marabouts and major traders would have had a difficult time organizing an opposition which could have ousted them. Individual marabouts could have been bought off, reforms could have been presented as small individual steps rather than as parts of a grand design, and even the French could probably have been placated by Senghor's continuing professions of attachment to France.

But to suggest all this is to suggest the need for a leader of a different disposition than Leopold Senghor. It suggests the need for a leader who had a long-term goal of reducing Senegal's economic dependence, and more important, one who sought to achieve this goal by creating in ordinary farmers the belief that by their own actions they could alter their lives. Senghor may not have opposed such goals; but they were not of central concern to him. His main interest was to reconcile what he saw as African communal and humanist values with the technological values of Europe; but the level at which he proposed to attempt this was far removed from the day-to-day, mundane questions of determining the peanut price or of building factories in Senegal. At this practical level, Senghor appeared to be very much a pragmatist, moving back and forth among different interests in accordance with his perception of their strength in the Senegalese polity. He cultivated the marabouts, but allowed Dia to carry forward his economic program, which would undermine them; he fought for the Mali federation, but decided to end it when it seemed likely

140

to terminate his personal career. On the referendum,
in 1958, he hesitated, weighing up his principles
and the beliefs he had professed in independence
against the risks of losing to a combination of the
French administration and the marabouts, and ultimately decided to store away his principles for
another day.

What I am suggesting, in short, is that
Senghor's personal attitudes made a considerable
difference. He could have moved Senegal in a much
more "radical" direction just after independence.
Instead he chose to ditch Dia and embark on a more
conservative path. Once again, whatever his beliefs
at a spiritual level, in practical politics he proved a cautious broker, swaying delicately back and
forth between conflicting interests, but making no
effort to reach beyond these interests to create a
new synthesis.

After Mamadou Dia's fall from grace in 1962,
Senegal for the remainder of the 1960s and the 1970s
pursued a classic "accommodationist" course.
Senghor might still occasionally refer to his
"socialist" goals, and in 1976 he gained admission
for the UPS (re-born as the Parti Socialiste) to the
Socialist International, but the practice in running
Senegal's economy was more and more clearly peripheral capitalist. Senghor himself guarded his personal position by a skillful brokerage style, balancing the demands of the marabouts against those of
the young radicals, and acting occasionally to assuage regional feelings of neglect. Some opponents
were drawn back into the UPS; the "young Turks" who
formed the PRA during the 1958 referendum to support independence were enticed back with three portfolios in the government. Milcent and Sordet claim
Senghor regarded these portfolios -- social affairs,
national education and cultural affairs -- as important[50] but it is worth noting that he did not let
the radicals near any economic post. Other opponents were elevated out of politics; the noted historian Cheikh Anta Diop, whose short-lived Bloc des
Masses Senegalaises (BMS) had in 1962-63 posed some
electoral threat to the government, occupied a research post at the government-sponsored Institute
Fondamental d'Afrique Noire (IFAN) as did Aboulaye
Ly, formerly of the PRA.

The most serious shock to this rather delicate
process of neutralizing opposition came in May 1968.
It began as a student strike (inspired by the
Parisian students' actions) focusing on the need for
"Senegalization" of the predominantly French-

controlled University of Dakar, but containing overtones of a wider protest against the neo-colonial
situation of the country. The government responded
forcefully, ringing the campus with police and ordering all educational institutions closed. The students responded by calling on the Senegalese workers to stage a general strike, and the government-
approved Union of Senegalese Workers called for such
a strike to take place May 31. On May 30, the government arrested 40 trade unionists, and then alleged that the unions had planned a <u>coup</u> to seize
power. However, four days later the arrested union
leaders were released in exchange for calling off
the strike, which had closed down Dakar, and seen
the burning of many governmental and foreign technicians' cars, despite the presence of army helicop-
ters and armoured cars with machine guns. A week
later, Senghor announced that minimum wages were to
be raised 15% (half of what had been demanded earlier by the unions), social security was to be improved, and firms would be obliged to submit plans
for "Senegalization" of staff. The University received less concessions; at first the President said
it would need to remain closed for a year, but in
September it was partially re-opened, with some
"Senegalization" of faculty and curricula.[51]

The 1968 strikes came from a cumulation of
smouldering grievances. The general stagnation of
the Senegalese economy throughout the 1960s (per
capita Gross Domestic Product had had a zero growth
rate from 1960 to 1965, and a negative rate of 2.2%
from 1965 to 1970[52]) meant that numbers of rural
Senegalese had come to Dakar in an unsuccessful
search for work. Even among those who were employed, wages were not keeping up with the cost of living; it was estimated that the purchasing power of
the minimum wage for unskilled labour in 1968 was
only 88% of what it had been in 1961.[53] Then too,
the sight of so many "petits blancs" occupying jobs
that Senegalese felt they could fill was a standing
irritation. Still, it is a noteworthy comment on
the close ties between Senegal and France that the
contagion of the French student uprising was the
factor that ignited the Senegalese discontents.

Equally noteworthy is the fact that the disturbances were confined to Dakar. Here the power
of the marabouts was shown clearly. The chief Murid
marabout, Falilou M'Backé, publicly called on the
workers to refrain from striking, and in up-country
towns very few did in fact go out. The government's
forceful response, followed by conciliation, also

142

likely reduced the risk that further disturbances would occur.

In the countryside a more far severe yet less visible crisis was brewing. The peanut, as we have already noted, maintained both a rural patron-client system and an expanding urban-centred bureaucracy. Yet the price for peasant producers remained low throughout the 1960s and after 1967 the government even attempted to transfer further marketing costs to them.[54] Government agencies set up ostensibly to help the peasants, such as a national co-operative office, became more and more obviously a means of controlling the peasants by pushing them further into debt and dictating their choice of crops and methods of production. By 1970 increasing numbers of peasants were resisting these exactions by a variety of means, including the fearsome threat of growing millet for their own consumption rather than peanuts for export -- and some marabouts were encouraging them in this! The government realized action was imperative if the peasants were to remain safely apolitical, so debts were forgiven, cash payments on delivery of peanuts were re-instituted, and then in 1974 the producer price for peanuts was nearly doubled, from $83 to $155 a ton. Had the peasants known that the world price that year was more than $500 a ton, they might still have felt short-changed; but they did not know, and thus the danger of a politicized peasantry was temporarily averted.

However, the long-term problem of who should benefit by how much from the peasants' crops remained unresolved. The various agencies set up by the central bureaucracy, including the National Co-operative Office (ONCAD) and regional organizations for development, stressed the marketing of cash crops, even when these were not as profitable as crops grown for the peasants' own consumption.[55] The more sophisticated peasants came rightly to suspect that these organizations were more concerned with extracting a surplus to support the bureaucrats than with meeting the peasants' needs for local food crops. However, with all the weight of government and foreign aid agencies against the peasants, it was only rarely that the latter could exercise much control over development schemes, and that only through constant struggle.[56] For the most part, the conflict over who should benefit from rural agriculture was fought between the marabouts and other rural patrons, and the bureaucrats, with the latter holding the edge.

However, here Senghor's government faced a dilemma. If it allowed the bureaucrats to "modernize" agriculture by moving to large-scale mechanized farms run by an agricultural elite, it would both dispossess many people from their farms and destroy the personal links between rural client-cultivators and their traditional patrons. The result would be a very volatile and discontented rural proletariat.[57] On the other hand, if it insisted on protecting the power of the marabouts and other rural patrons, it would have to curb the power of the bureaucrats, many of whom had been brought into government to curb their dangerously radical tendencies. By the time Senghor retired, this dilemma had not quite reached a crisis point, but it still loomed as a problem which could force major changes in the political base of support for the regime.

As if anticipating an increasing level of political conflict as a result of both the urban and rural dilemmas, Senghor in the mid-1970s began to provide a safety valve by partially opening the political system. In that up to that time his main work had been "the relatively delicate elimination or incorporation of organized opposition"[58] his announcement in 1976 that the constitution would be revised to establish three political parties to represent the three main ideological tendencies he saw as important in Senegal, marked a major reversal of policy. But perhaps not; this was still "democracy on a leash", with the three slots so defined as to make it very difficult to assemble a coalition that might oust the President. His own Parti Socialiste was given the preferred "social democratic" slot; a rather urban-oriented coalition led by the lawyer Abdoulaye Wade received the more conservative "liberal democratic" slot, despite its avowed preference for a "socialist" designation; while the "Marxist-Leninist" slot, with its overtones of atheism (electorally anathema in a Muslim country) was bestowed on a re-legalized splinter of the banned Marxist party, the PAI. There was no place in this spectrum for what might have been a serious challenger to the Parti Socialiste, the radical nationalist (but non-Marxist) grouping around Cheikh Anta Diop, the Rassemblement National Democratique. There was thus some outlet for opposition, but not in a form that could sweep Senghor's party away. It came as no surprise to any citizens or observers that in the national elections of 1978 Senghor's party won all but 17 of the 100 seats on a similar split of the popular vote with Wade's PDS,[59] with the PAI winning only 0.3%

Nevertheless, Senegal's government remained a remarkably open one by comparison with most others in black Africa. Opposition newspapers circulated freely in the larger centres, and though in 1979 the government imposed a rule requiring that they clear their contents 48 hours before they went on sale, the two most severe critics of the government simply planned to circumvent the law by going to a comic book format.[60]

Senghor's motive in opening up the system was unclear. Perhaps he felt Senegal would be a healthier society when opposition was open and above-board, or possibly he may have decided "Après moi, le déluge". The man being groomed as his successor, Abdou Diouf, was a technocrat with no significant personal base of his own, and it was possible that Senghor was prepared to allow a challenge to Diouf through the electoral system to succeed, bringing to power a safely bourgeois individual like Abdoulaye Wade, or possibly even a radical nationalist like Diop. In any case, Senghor himself decided he could safely leave office, and on December 31, 1980, he resigned as President of Senegal, allowing Abdou Diouf to succeed him as President.

SENGHOR'S LEGACY: HOPELESS BUT NOT SERIOUS?

What were the major features of the situation that Senghor left to his successor? On the positive side, the regions and ethnic groups of Senegal seemed to get along with each other reasonably well. There were, to be sure, frequent rumblings of discontent from the isolated Casamance region in the south, but there seemed little danger of secessionist movements or a civil war anywhere. Nor did class discontent seem so widespread that a violent uprising could spread to the countryside, although Dakar remained vulnerable in economic hard times. Equally important, there was not the pervasive sense of fear that one finds in, say, Cameroun or Malawi, nor the acute sense of national incapacity to make a viable society that pervaded Ghana by the late 1970s. The polity remained relatively open and tolerant, with little sense of foreboding that things would suddenly get much less pleasant. Yet economically and socially, Senghor's regime had largely failed to make the lives of Senegal's people better, and politically it was heading into an impasse. The economic failure was indicated by a negative growth rate of

-0.4% over the years 1960-1978[61] with most of this
regression concentrated in the 1970s and coupled
with an inflation rate of 8% for the years 1970-78.[62]
Meanwhile Senegal's external debt had risen to 30%
of GNP by 1978.[63]   It is true that by the most readily available indicator of the diffusion of well-
being, life expectancy at birth, Senegal had increased by five years, from 37 years in 1960 to 42 in
1978, but among the 25 low-income African states, 19
had increased their peoples' life expectancies by
more than this, and only one (Ethiopia) by less.[64]
     This failure of the economy to provide more
wealth seems to go back largely to Senegal's continuing dependence on a single export crop. Other factors certainly contributed; the increases in world
petroleum prices in the 1970s raised Senegal's expenditures on oil to about the same level as her earnings from peanuts, about $250 million.[65]   But with
even her industry, which was largely centred around
crushing peanuts for their oil, dependent upon the
size and value of the peanut crop, Senegal was inevitably hit hard by either crop shortfalls or slumps
in world prices. Yet the scale of peanut growing
meant that there was a substantial body of individuals -- the marabouts and their followers in the
rural areas, and business executives, factory workers, transporters and others in the cities -- with
a strong vested interest in continuing this situation.
     How far Senegal could have diversified, either
by creating new export crops as in the Ivory Coast
or by aiming at a more self-reliant, internally or-
iented economy as in Tanzania, is open to question.
The physical environment precluded much of the diversity which sustained the Ivory Coast boom, while
the strength of export-oriented interests and a shortage of competent managerial and technical personnel would probably have made an attempt at self-
reliance as disastrous as Guinea's. Senegal's options, in short, were very restricted, no matter
what goals a government wanted to pursue.
     The narrow economic base, and in particular the
limited amount of processing and manufacturing, limited the range of opportunities for the ordinary man
to develop new skills and find an improved place for
himself in the cities. In the rural areas the continuing power of the marabouts and their efforts to
keep farmers producing peanuts similarly limited
opportunities, particularly for farmers to create a
more egalitarian social structure through cooperative efforts. The government always avoided a

direct confrontation with the marabouts, although
one key social change would likely undermine their
control over the long run. The proportion of school-
age children in primary school had increased greatly
from 1960 to 1977, from 27% to 47%, and the proportion in secondary schools had nearly quadrupled,
from 3% to 11%.[66] However, for this increased level
of education to produce more questioning of the
marabouts' role was a very long, slow process, and
it could lead equally readily to questioning of a
government which was unable to provide the jobs
school leavers thought they should have.

A further problem which was coming to a head
was that of providing sufficient payoffs to keep the
various elites and sub-elites contented with the
system. In order to win these groups' support rather than coercing them into acquiescence, the government had to provide jobs for school leavers,
maintain incomes for the marabouts and generally distribute the wealth to growing numbers of claimants.
But since the pool of wealth was not expanding, especially when drought cut back the peanut crop, the
government was having to choose between raising producer prices for peanuts to satisfy the marabouts
and their followers, or expanding the bureaucracy to
soak up the urban dwellers who wanted jobs. As the
country's international indebtedness rose, and the
domestic budget continued to run a deficit, the end
of the government's ability to provide payoffs for
everyone came nearer.

But given Senegal's natural endowments and the
colonial heritage, were there any policies that
might have led the country out of this morass? Can
we say that Senghor played a role in shaping present-
day Senegal, or was he merely a figurehead presiding
over a territory controlled by inexorable forces?

First, did Senghor seem to have any ability to
influence the Senegalese? Did he have some support
among the people, or was his survival for twenty
years as president of an independent state a fluke?
I think it is fair to suggest that his "French
connection" and particularly the presence of French
troops just outside Dakar helped safeguard him in
times of tension like 1968, by discouraging the
Senegalese army from any thoughts of ousting him.
But the French have never let sentiment interfere
with their commitments to their interests, and a
leader who has turned his people against him cannot
do much to protect French interests, as the Abbé
Youlou in Congo-Brazzaville and Maurice Yameogo in
Upper Volta learned to their cost. French support,

in other words, would likely not have been maintained if Senghor had lost his hold on the Senegalese.

But who in Senegal supported him? We have
noted the various ways in which he skillfully absorbed different elites into the ruling party and the
government -- for example, the young intellectuals
in the mid-1950s and again in the post-Dia period
(and perhaps again with Diouf's ascendency), and the
marabouts through judicious manipulation of the peanut prices. Among the elites, in short, he was the
consummate broker, allocating resources in response
to the perceived strength of competing claimants.

Yet by itself this was not enough to account
for his continuing strength, which was evidenced by
the 1978 election results in which he won some 82%
of the vote against Abdoulaye Wade.[67] While the
election results were certainly influenced by government pressure and handicaps imposed on the opposition parties, still they were not crudely rigged
in the manner of Western Nigeria's infamous 1965
election, and probably represented an indication
that Senghor was preferred as leader to any available alternative. Part of this acceptability, of
course, derives simply from the fact that Senghor
had been around long enough to become a part of the
landscape, a fixed and familiar feature, although
this certainly does not guarantee acceptability.
More important, I suggest, is the residual loyalty
to the "little Serer" as the man who first spoke for
the rural people, and vicariously gave pride to
Africans through his intellectual achievements.
Even though, as one observer noted, he addressed his
countrymen in a style and on matters far over their
heads,[68] this may have helped more than hurt the regard in which they held him, even though it would
prevent their doing what he was asking. Again, in
the face of subsequent failure to deliver much material well-being, this by itself was not enough to
guarantee survival; but it did contribute a share.

Could Senghor have done more to improve the
lives of ordinary Senegalese, given the constraints
within which he had to operate? I think he could,
at least if he had started in the pre-independence
period to travel along a different path. The strategy that might have worked more successfully than
accommodation would have been one involving more
participation by peasant farmers, a grass-roots socialism. The first step would have been to assert
Senegalese nationalism in the early 1950s as a means
of building a mass party not so reliant upon the
marabouts and other local notables. Once such a

party was securely established, it could have encouraged the development of rural organizations that could by-pass the marabouts. This approach was tried sporadically in the late 1950s and again in the 1960s but with the government susceptible to maraboutic pressure, these experiments were quickly dropped when the rural elites protested. Such an approach could have foundered, to be sure, upon either the self-seeking and corruption of the rural organizers, or upon a perceived need to impose it by force. Yet it could at least have been tried, and would certainly have been more in accord with Senghor's professed socialist beliefs than the economic strategy he in fact pursued.

Was Senghor then merely a hypocrite in preaching socialism while binding Senegal tightly into a neo-colonial trap? This seems to be too harsh a judgment. I think the problem was that he was thinking on two separate planes, the rarefied philosophical plane of "African culture" as an abstract entity, and the day-to-day level of practical affairs. On this latter plane he was blocked by his own values. He was not, as we noted earlier, terribly interested in the mundane problems of economic development. He had a deep-seated dislike of demagoguery and of over-simplification, which led to his refusal to "talk down" to his people.[69] This attitude also led him to distrust the political process, and to prefer dealing with problems through functional and technocratic means rather than by encouraging political participation.[70] Finally, the depth of his assimilation into French culture was such that he was not capable of suspecting France could harm Senegal's development.

The tragedy of Leopold Senghor, then, was that for all his vision of a distinctive African culture, he failed to grasp the means for its attainment. He could not bring his abstractions down to the level of everyday economic and social structures and actions.

NOTES

1. His satirical film Xala, about a rich Senegalese businessman's sexual impotence, was banned in Senegal because of its portrayal of the collusion between the Senegalese bourgeoisie and the French. Le Mandat also is sharply critical of the behaviour of Senegal's bourgeoisie.

2. For Senghor's philosophy, the most

comprehensive study from a political scientist's
viewpoint is I. L. Markowitz, Leopold Sedar Senghor
and the Politics of Negritude (Atheneum, New York,
1969).
3. Michael Crowder, Senegal: A Study in French
Assimilation Policy (Oxford University Press, London,
1962), p. 10.
4. Ibid., p. 15.
5. West Africa, July 19, 1978, p. 1331.
6. Donal Cruise O'Brien, Saints and Politicians, (Cambridge University Press, London, 1975),
pp. 130-31.
7. Calculated from United Nations, Yearbook of
International Trade Statistics, 1978.
8. For production up to 1973, see O'Brien,
Saints, p. 144; for 1977-1978, see West Africa, July
10, 1978, p. 1329.
9. Donal Cruise O'Brien, "Ruling Class and
Peasantry in Senegal 1960-1976; The Politics of a
Monocrop Economy", in Rita O'Brien (ed), The Political Economy of Underdevelopment: Dependence in
Senegal (Sage , Beverly Hills, 1979), pp. 222-23.
10. Calculated from United Nations Yearbooks of
International Trade Statistics, 1965 to 1978.
11. Donal Cruise O'Brien, "Class, community,
nation: dimensions of political loyalty in Senegal",
in D. R. Smock and K. Bentsi-Enchill, The Search for
National Integration in Africa (Free Press, New York,
1976), p. 255.
12. For a detailed study of the brotherhoods
see Lucy C. Behrman, Muslim Brotherhoods and Politics in Senegal (Harvard University Press, Cambridge,
Mass, 1970).
13. O'Brien, "Ruling Class and Peasantry",
p. 223.
14. Lucy C. Behrman, "Muslim Politics and Development in Senegal", Journal of Modern African
Studies, 15, 2 (June 1977), p. 268.
15. Behrman, Muslim Brotherhoods, p. 109.
16. Ibid., p. 118.
17. Ibid., pp. 127-28.
18. Kenneth Robinson, "Senegal", in Kenneth
Robinson and W.J.M. Mackenzie, (eds) Five Elections
in Africa (Clarendon Press, Oxford, 1960), pp. 283-
83.
19. Leopold Senghor, "Some Thoughts on Africa:
a continent in development", International Affairs
(London), 38 (April 1962), p. 195.
20. Christian Coulon, "Political Elites in
Senegal", Mawazo, 2, 3 (June 1970), p. 22.
21. Ibid., p. 18.

22. Donal Cruise O'Brien, "Senegal" in John
Dunn (ed), West African States: Failure and Promise
(Cambridge University Press, Cambridge, 1978),
p. 246.
23. Ibid.
24. See O'Brien, "Ruling Class and Peasantry",
pp. 209-11, for a summary of the role of the French
army in Senegalese politics.
25. See Ernest Milcent and Monique Sordet,
Leopold Sedar Senghor et la naissance de l'Afrique
moderne (Seghers, Paris, 1969), p. 87: also Ruth
Schacter Morgenthau, Political Parties in French-
Speaking West Africa, Clarendon Press, Oxford, 1974),
pp. 137-38.
26. This sketch of Senghor's career is based
upon Milcent and Sordet's biography.
27. See Coulon, "Political Elites in Senegal,
2" Mawazo, 2, 4 (December 1970), p. 32; Morgenthau,
Political Parties, p. 138.
28. Cited in Milcent and Sordet, Senghor, p. 94.
29. Ibid., pp. 98-99.
30. Ibid., pp. 115-16.
31. Morgenthau, Political Parties, pp. 148-49.
32. For a good discussion of the role of clans,
see Clement Cottingham, "Political Consolidation and
Centre-Local Relations in Senegal", Canadian Journal of African Studies IV, 1 (Winter 1970),
pp. 101-120.
33. Milcent and Sordet, Senghor, pp. 139-43.
34. Morgenthau, Political Parties, pp. 158-61.
35. Robinson, in Five Elections, p. 383. Note
that this is a retreat from Senghor's earlier warning that the resistance would be violent.
36. In Le Monde, cited in Milcent and Sordet,
Senghor, p. 176.
37. Ibid., pp. 171-75.
38. Ibid., p. 183.
39. Ibid., p. 185.
40. Morgenthau, Political Parties, p. 164.
41. Milcent and Sordet, Senghor, p. 193.
42. Ibid., pp. 195-96.
43. See William Foltz, From French West Africa
to the Mali Federation (Yale University Press, New
Haven, 1965), pp. 116-17.
44. The most detailed account of this break-up
is ibid., pp. 168-79.
45. See Milcent and Sordet, Senghor: for the
break with Dia, p. 216, and for Senghor's attitude
toward development planning, p. 224.
46. Coulon, "Political Elites in Senegal, 2",
p. 35.

47. Behrman, Muslim Brotherhoods, pp. 99-103.
48. Milcent and Sordet, Senghor, p. 216.
49. Coulon, "Political Elites, 2", pp. 35-36.
50. Milcent and Sordet, Senghor, p. 221.
51. For details of the riots and subsequent events, see West Africa, June 8, 1968, p. 674; June 22, 1968, p. 730; and July 27, 1968, p. 861.
52. Data taken from World Bank, World Tables, 1976, Comparative Economic Data, p. 394.
53. Maureen Mackintosh, "The Political Economy of Industrial Wages in Senegal", in Rita O'Brien, Political Economy of Underdevelopment, p. 159.
54. I have drawn the following analysis largely from Jonathan S. Barker, "Stability and Stagnation: The State in Senegal", Canadian Journal of African Studies, 11, 1 (1977), p. 38. See also Edward J. Schumacher, Politics, Bureaucracy and Rural Development in Senegal (University of California Press, Berkeley, 1974).
55. See Adrian Adams, "The Senegal River Valley: What kind of Change?", Review of African Political Economy, 10 (September-December 1977), p. 58.
56. Adams' article provides an excellent case study of the struggle between a local peasants' association and one central government organization for regional development. Ibid., pp. 33-59.
57. Barker, using Senegal as an illustration, has pointed out the dilemma facing any essentially status-quo-maintaining government which nevertheless wishes to provide some "development". In supporting "development" such a government necessarily undermines its existing base of support, Jonathan S. Barker, "The Paradox of Development: Reflections on a Study of Local-Central Political Relations in Senegal", in Michael Lofchie (ed), The State of the Nations (University of California Press, Berkeley, 1971), pp. 47-63.
58. D. O'Brien, in Dunn, West African States, p. 179.
59. West Africa, March 6, 1968, p. 421.
60. See Africa Confidential, June 6, 1979, p. 7.
61. World Bank, World Development Report, 1980, Table 1.
62. Ibid.
63. Ibid., Table 15.
64. Ibid., Table 21.
65. West Africa, January 19, 1981, p. 104.
66. World Development Report, 1980, Table 23.
67. West Africa, March 6, 1978, p. 421.

68. Markowitz, Leopold Senghor, p. 33.

69. R. A. Mortimer, "From federalism to francophonia: Senghor's African policy", African Studies Review, 15, 2 (September 1972), p. 303; also Markowitz, Leopold Senghor, pp. 32-34.

70. Mortimer, p. 33.

Chapter Eight

TANZANIA: STRUGGLING AGAINST GOOD INTENTIONS?

At Tanganyika's independence on December 9,
1961, climbers placed a torch on the peak of Mount
Kilimanjaro, to cast symbolic rays of hope beyond
the country's borders. Few would have predicted
then that Tanzania would capture the attention not
just of Africa, but of much of the world, for its
efforts to create through persuasion a rural-based
socialism. To be sure, its 39-year-old leader,
Julius Nyerere, had already shown a strong concern
for equity among his people, a Gandhian commitment
to non-violence, and an ability to reach his countrymen unsurpassed by any other African leader. Still,
as a poor backwater in British East Africa,
Tanganyika seemed to have little choice but to work
within the economic, social and political structures
it had inherited.
     However, in the succeeding two decades, Tanzania
(as it was re-named in 1964) embarked on one of the
most ambitious experiments in Africa, an attempt to
produce a co-operative and self-sufficient society
based on the values of equality and popular participation. The odds against such an experiment succeeding were long; it sought a major transformation of
the values of all Tanzanians, and it contained within itself almost insoluble dilemmas. That it has
lasted this long is primarily due to the leadership
of Julius Nyerere, whose persuasive abilities and
personal commitment have inspired both ordinary
people and party and state officials to follow his
teachings, even against their own material interests.
But Nyerere's own actions have not been free from
ambiguities and contradictions. He has stressed
that changes are meaningless unless people can be
persuaded to adopt them voluntarily, yet in 1973-76,
he used massive force to move millions of people
from their ancestral homesteads into villages. He

has argued the need for co-operatives, and yet in 1969 he banned the most successful of Tanzania's co-operative village associations, and in 1976 he abolished the whole independent co-operative movement. He has placed great emphasis on grass-roots participation, yet in the 1970s he put local development plans and even the running of the new villages, under the direction of officials appointed by the central government. In short, there has been a constant struggle within Tanzania between Nyerere's ideals and many of the actions he and his subordinates felt compelled to take.

Two fundamental dilemmas lie at the root of this struggle. Nyerere's personal dilemma, which he shares with any other leader committed to a peaceful transformation of his society, is that he must persuade his people to accept a vision of a new world that he knows is best for them; yet because this vision involves uprooting existing values and structures, most people will not accept it until they can be convinced that it works. Thus a leader is faced with the choice either of forcing a transformation of structures and leaving the populace hostile to the new values which must accompany these structures, or of waiting indefinitely for people to be won, a few at a time, to the new society, so that he will be long dead before the transformation is accomplished. The other dilemma is that the administrative hierarchy beneath him are subject to an "organizational imperative" of justifying their own positions by taking the initiative in formulating and choosing government courses of action. Nyerere's calls for ordinary people to participate directly themselves in working out the policies that affect their well-being may appeal to an altruistic streak in administrators, but it also runs directly counter to their raison d'etre. Without organized grass-roots movements capable of compelling administrators to allow popular participation in policy-making, this goal depends entirely upon the latter's self-denial, a rather frail reed on which to rest a major goal.

However, despite all the pressures working against the pursuit of this participant socialism -- Nyerere's own impatience to realize his vision, the bureaucrats' desire to establish their control, and a series of economic blows inflicted by climate, oil prices and the world economic recession -- the experiment still continued as the world entered the 1980s. In this chapter I will examine the crucial points in the Tanzanian experiment, the extent to which Nyerere succeeded in exercising leadership at these key junctures, and the major on-going conflicts within Tanzania.

THE MAKING OF A MASS MOVEMENT

Tanganyika was a backwater under colonial rule. The coast had been involved in trade with Asia long before the Portuguese established their presence in the 16th century, but until Germany acquired the territory as a colony in 1885, none of its outside contacts had uprooted existing political or social structures. The vigorous period of Germany colonization ended quickly with the First World War, and in the inter-war period Britain, as the Mandate power, tended to neglect Tanganyika in comparison with its own richer colonies of Kenya and Uganda. There was little to tempt European settlers, even apart from the barriers imposed by its status as a Trust Territory. Most of the territory suffered from low and uncertain rainfall, and partly in consequence of this, it was estimated at independence that only 3.7% of the total land area was arable, compared to 22% in Uganda.[1] A few climatically favoured areas in the north produced sisal, cotton and coffee as export crops, but the per capita value of these crops was again below that of its richer neighbours (see Table 8.1). Nor were other forces for social mobilization, such as education, as far advanced as in Kenya and Uganda. Moreover, while there were few European settlers, there were a large number of Asians who had entered East Africa since the late 19th century and pre-empted most retail business activity, as well as those higher civil service and professional jobs not held by Europeans.

Colonial Tanganyika thus lacked the substantial pool of upwardly mobile, articulate Africans who provided the driving force behind most West African nationalist movements. However, this also meant that there was not an embryonic African bourgeoisie entrenching itself to siphon off the major share of benefits the state could provide after independence. The situation posed severe difficulties for a nationalist movement, yet at the same time left open a wide range of potential directions.

Three further features which eased the problems facing any widespread anti-colonial movement should be noted. The lack of any large centralized kingdoms, or even of any single ethnic group comprising more than an eighth of the total population, spared

Table 8.1: Some comparative indicators of social mobilization, 1955.

Country	Population ('000,000)	Value of exports per capita	School enrolment (pct. of 5-19 age group)	Radio receivers per '000,000 population
Tanganyika	8.5	$11.70	12%	887
Kenya	6.4	$15.41[b]	24%	3,461
Uganda	5.9		23%	4,240
Ethiopia	15[a]	$ 4.05	3%	1,000
Ghana	4.6	$52.53	26%	8,874
Ivory Coast	2.9	$60.57[c]	10%	...
Senegal	2.2	$54.29[c,d]	10%	44,984
Guinea	2.6	11.43[c]	5%	...

a: 1951 estimate. b: only combined data for Kenya and Uganda available. c: 1956 figures. d: includes re-exports from Mauritania and Soudan.

Sources: Population, school enrolments and radio receivers from UNESCO Statistical Yearbook, 1963 Tables 1, 9 and 39, exports per capita from United Nations, Yearbook of International Trade Statistics, 1956, Vol. 1, except Ivory Coast, Senegal and Guinea, taken from Elliot Berg, "The Economic Basis of Political Choice in French West Africa", American Political Science Review, 54, 2 (1960), p. 400.

Tanzania the bitter ethnic conflicts for control of the state that racked such neighbouring territories as Kenya, Uganda and Burundi. Second, an indigenous language, Swahili, had spread from the coast throughout the territory as a lingua franca. A mixture of Bantu and Arabic languages with eclectic borrowings from English and elsewhere, Swahili was not only free from any taint of identification with the colonial powers, but it also was free from being identified with any particular domestic ethnic group, and thus could not be feared as a vehicle for establishing an ethnic hegemony. Being in widespread popular use, it also offered a more egalitarian means of national integration than a colonial language such as English, which was largely confined to a formally educated elite.[2]

Finally, the territory's status as a Mandate under the League of Nations after World War I, and then as a Trust Territory under the United Nations after World War II, provided some restraint on the willingness of the colonial power to repress nationalist movements. In particular, the triennial inspections of the United Nations Trusteeship Council from 1948 onward gave Tanganyika Africans a chance to articulate their grievances against Britain, and amplified and disseminated these grievances.[3] Anticolonial sentiments could be expressed more safely in Tanganyika than in the white settler-dominated British colonies of Kenya to the north and the Central African Federation to the south.

These features, particularly the lack of a substantial African bourgeoisie and the lack of a fierce ethnic struggle for power, at least kept open the possibility of building an integrated and egalitarian society. However, they also offered substantial barriers to social changes requiring mass participation. The fact that most Tanzanians were close to the borderline of subsistence could produce an extreme caution about taking any risks in trying to transform society, and a leader faced with this attitude might well decide that accommodation with existing colonial patterns was the best course to follow. Then too, the Asians' high visibility as competitors to aspiring Africans could easily lead to a racial scapegoating for all the country's problems, a risk that might well tempt a leader to try to reduce popular participation.

The colonial administration itself was the object of several African grievances widespread enough to provide the basis for a strong national movement. The most pervasive were those arising out of colonial officials' attempts to "improve" agriculture. Such attempts to safeguard Africans' food supplies as the requirement that they plant a certain amount of cassava, and tie-ridge parts of their fields as a soil conservation measure, were well-intentioned but not well-suited to the soil and labour conditions of much of Tanganyika. The compulsory slaughter of "excess" cattle to reduce pressure on rangelands ran up against a "supra-rational" glorification of cattle among a number of tribes.[4] Most serious of

158

all was the threat to their possession of the land
implied in the Meru Land Case, where Africans were
dispossessed from an area they had bought back from
European ownership in order that the administration
could consolidate the land in each race's hands.[5]
All these factors produced widespread concern and
anger in the rural areas.

The chiefs, as has so often been the case in
colonial regimes, were frequently inhibited from
acting in their traditional roles as spokesmen for
their people. While many continued to see themselves as having a responsibility for the well-being
of their people, they were dependent upon the colonial administration for their salaries provided in
lieu of collecting tributes from their people.
(Often, however, they would still collect the tribute as well.)[6] Some chiefs enjoyed both the cash
benefits and the power this situation gave them, and
worked willingly to impose colonial regulations upon
their people. Most often, while they might disagree
with the regulations, they felt themselves too dependent upon the colonial administrators to resist.
The result was that many people became somewhat disillusioned with their chiefs, and began to look
elsewhere for spokesmen and protectors.

However, there was little opportunity for any
spokesmen to bring people's grievances to the colonial regime through established channels. The first
African unofficial members of Tanganyika's Legislative Council, both chiefs, were first appointed in
1945, where they shared the unofficial side with
seven Europeans and three Asians. Not until 1958
was there any election of African representatives to
the territorial assembly. Nor did Africans have any
effective voice through the civil service; in the
policy-making administrative class, there were no
Africans appointed until 1955.[7] The only way for
Africans to make their grievances heard would be
through extra-constitutional channels, such as a
mass movement.

The need for such a movement was given additional impetus in the early 1950s when the British
Conservative government attempted to spread the idea
of "multi-racialism" through East and Central
Africa. The application of this idea in the Central
African Federation was rightly seen by most Africans
as a thinly-disguised means of preserving European
dominance, even without a white Rhodesian leader
spelling it out as "the partnership of rider and
horse". Nowhere was such an approach more untenable
than in Tanganyika, where ten million Africans

coexisted with 100,000 Asians and only 22,000
Europeans.[8] The threat of both European and Asian
domination over such an overwhelmingly African
country was the surest way of uniting the small educated minority of Africans and the mass of rural
farmers in opposition, particularly when the British
tried to introduce multi-racial representation in
the local councils after 1951.[9] As Pratt observed,
by 1957 "[o]pposition to multiracialism became the
cause...which united the rural African and the educated and politically active town dweller."[10]

This set of grievances - agricultural regulations, the threat to land tenure, and the threat of
European and Asian domination - created the potential for a number of possible mass African movements.
The most likely possibility would have been a junc-
ture of aspiring town dwellers with the more prosperous rural farmers under the banner of African
nationalism, demanding stepped-up access for
Africans into the privileged positions held by
Europeans and Asians. This would entail accelerated
educational programmes to allow Africans access to
"European" positions in the civil service, financial
help to buy out Asian businesses, and in the rural
areas a continuation of the "focal points" approach
of helping the most "progressive" and prosperous
farmers, begun by the colonial administration in
1956.[11] Such a movement, in short, would bring little economic or political change beyond giving a few
Africans a share of power, and thus would be widely
acceptable both in Britain and in Tanganyika.

Another possibility would have been a more militant movement demanding massive changes on both
racial and class lines. To gain widespread support,
a militant movement would have had to attack the
Europeans as the root of Africans' problems and the
chiefs as their stooges, and for good measure the
Asians too as exploiters. Such a movement would
have had to seek complete African control over the
institutions of Tanganyika, including private ones
such as the banks. It seems unlikely that any
British administration would have allowed such a
movement to function legally, but it was not clear
how far they would go to wipe it out. Given the
depth of Tanganyikan grievances, and the lack of
institutions through which the British could continue to rule in the face of these grievances, it
seems possible that a militant party could have
built up enough support to challenge British rule,
but the struggle would have been long and costly.

There were, in other words, two major

160

dimensions along which alternative developments were possible. On the economic dimension, the choice lay between a non-egalitarian, "bourgeois" movement seeking a minimum of restructuring, and a radical movement seeking economic equality among Africans as well as control by Africans over the economy. On the social dimension, there was a continuum of possibilities from the improbable growth of a racially tolerant atmosphere uniting Tanganyikans of all races, to the more easily attained situation of a violent racial attack upon all Europeans and Asians.

There were three principal groups who could provide the cadres to produce any of these developments; the secondary school leavers in salaried or business jobs, the recent university graduates, and the rural co-operative leaders. The earliest of these, and the one which provided the largest number of early workers for TANU, was the group of aspiring Africans with some formal education who had found niches in clerical work, teaching, or running small businesses. Most of these were politically neutered through being civil servants, but there were enough outside the civil service's restraints to take active roles when their original perception of specific personal grievances widened to a more general anti-colonial view. They had had a means of contact since 1929 in the Tanganyikan African Association (TAA), under Governor Sir Donald Cameron to aid their self-improvement, and it was this organization which provided the womb in which TANU gestated until its birth in 1954.

But the TAA, partly because of its large civil service component, and partly because its members had to come to nationalism by a series of personal experiences, was after World War II more of a social organization than a political one. The spark that transformed it came from a much smaller group, the first university-trained Africans who had come to their anti-colonial commitment by a more intellectual process. How small this group was is indicated by the fact that at Makerere College, Uganda, the only East African post-secondary institution, there were only 41 Tanganyikans studying for degrees or diplomas in 1950. By 1954, when the first two degrees were awarded, the total number enrolled had risen to 113. However, their skills and their commitment magnified their influence. In Dar es Salaam in 1950, in order to present African views to a Constitutional Committee set by Governor Twining, four Makerere graduates aided by a half-dozen ex-servicemen were able to take over control of the

Dar TAA branch and turn it into a vehicle for
nationalist views.[14] Julius Nyerere himself, as the
first Tanganyikan African to gain an overseas degree
(an Edinburgh M.A. in 1952) was automatically part
of this small group who were looked to as the
"obvious" leaders for any African movement.

Neither of these groups could be assured of
reaching the 98% of Africans who lived outside the
towns. Farmers, as we have already noted, were
aroused over a number of problems, most notably the
multiplicity of agriculture regulations which forced
them into extra work for no apparent benefit.
Another of their concerns, resentment over what they
perceived as cheating by Asian produce buyers, had
begun to give rise to a major organizing vehicle for
rural areas, the co-operative movement; by 1953 the
co-operatives had some 157,700 members, or approximately 6-8% of the adult male farming population.[15]
Paul Bomani, the architect of the most powerful
co-op grouping, the Victoria Federation of Co-
operative Unions, rose from this base to a key role
in TANU, and many other TANU cadres entered through
the co-operative movement. Again, however we should
note that the co-operatives tended to be dominated
by the most successful farmers, and frequently were
used by these for their own benefit to the exclusion
of other members.[16]

Finally, mention should be made of the various
tribal unions, which had developed largely as local
protests against agricultural regulations. The Meru
Land Case, already mentioned, gave rise to the Meru
Citizens' Union, which carried its protest to the
United Nations in 1952, and then affiliated itself
to the TAA. Other tribal unions had sprung up among
the Chagga, the Sukuma, and other ethnic groups and
provided a further rural base for the TAA as they
came under its umbrella.[17] Most of the leaders of
these unions were from the same strata as the TAA
cadres, and frequently were active in both before
their organizations joined the TAA; on the other
hand, they were often in opposition to the chiefs
and other traditional authorities, whom they regarded as too tightly subordinated to the British.

In summary, the evolving pattern of Tanganyikan
nationalism was one of relatively prosperous and
successful Africans forging links between their own
grievances and those of the rural populace. All of
the "available" groups of individuals who could
provide leadership for a broad-based nationalist
movement were inclined toward a non-egalitarian,
bourgeois society which could easily come to terms

162

with British economic interests once the interests of a small advantaged group of Africans were catered for. That this was not the path ultimately followed by TANU requires an explanation, one which shows how some counter-force could override the material self-interest of these groups.

NYERERE'S STRENGTHS: MORAL VISION AND TACTICAL SKILL

The counter-weight to elite self-interest came largely from the moral commitment and persuasiveness of Julius Nyerere. When he first began to attract contemporaries' attention at Makerere College in the early 1940s, Nyerere did not seem to his fellow students the man who would one day reach most Tanzanians as their "Mwalimu" (teacher). While he was a brilliant debater who could express ideas more clearly than most and who was ahead of his peers in developing a comprehensive political vision of what Tanganyika should be, this slight, self-effacing "lone-wolf" must have seemed far too scholarly to succeed in the practical give-and-take of the political world.[18] In fact, although at Makerere he studied the subjects he was later to teach -- biology and English -- his greatest interest was in philosophy, and particularly in John Stuart Mill's ideas on representative government and on the subjection of women.[19] This passionate interest in philosophy and in teaching turned out to be one of his greatest political assets. The interest in philosophy contributed to his detachment and lack of concern with personal aggrandizement, while his passion for teaching helped him perfect his ability to instruct and persuade his countrymen. Then, too, his personal qualities helped him build a close rapport with all those who came in contact with him. He showed a genuine interest in others' accomplishments and problems, balancing his shy reserve with a warmth and affectionate humour, both in personal relations and in large gatherings, and he tempered his commitment to ultimate goals with a pragmatic view of how quickly they could be attained.

While Nyerere's abilities and personality made him the most likely potential leader of a nationalist movement, his "availability" at the right time was also important. While he was in Edinburgh from 1949 to 1952, some of his Makerere colleagues had tried to turn the TAA into a pressure group for African political representation and a champion of popular African interests such as the Meru Land Case.

163

However, the colonial government's shrewd use of job transfers had taken the steam out of the Dar es Salaam head office, so that in 1953 Nyerere was persuaded by his old friends to take over the TAA presidency to restore the organization's effectiveness. It is a comment on Nyerere's conciliating ability that the incumbent TAA president he defeated, Abdul Sykes, remained an active member of the TAA and became a founding member of TANU.

After Governor Edward Twining banned civil service participation in the TAA in August 1953, Nyerere and his friends began to plan a more effective mass political movement based on the model of Nkrumah's Convention Peoples Party. On July 7, 1954, they used the TAA annual meeting to announce the birth of the Tanganyikan African National Union, and unanimously elected Nyerere president of TANU.

While the fact that Nyerere himself had provided much of the spark that created the first mass political movement made it understandable that he should become its first leader, there had been other potential nationalist leaders who had either eliminated themselves or arrived on the scene too late. Chief David Kidaha Makwaia of Sukumaland, for example, had been the most prominent critic of British policies from his first appointment to the Legislative Council in 1945. However, he had no interest in any African political organization, and after 1951 lost the trust of the young intellectuals by supporting both multi-racialism and curbs on African political activity.[20] Rashidi Kawawa, who was to become Nyerere's most loyal and important lieutenant, and Paul Bomani, the major force behind the rural co-operatives, also had largely eliminated themselves as potential leaders. Kawawa, as a social worker, was a civil servant and thus restricted from direct participation in the TAA, and in any case his commitment in 1953-54 was to the civil servants' trade union, although he did what he could to support TANU from its formative phase. Bomani had concentrated on building the co-operatives, and was in England for most of 1954 while the TAA was being transformed into TANU.

Another talented young teacher who could have appealed to the young militants was Oscar Kambona. However, it was not until August, 1954, after Nyerere had already been acclaimed president of TANU, that Kambona accepted the challenge of one of his pupils to "do something" to back up his denunciations of the colonial regime.[21] Kambona promptly resigned his teaching post and offered Nyerere his

164

services as an organizer, confident that he could collect enough membership dues to provide himself with a salary. His confidence was backed by tremendous energy and the insight of reaching the peasants through their chiefs and elders. With Nyerere's first trip to the Trusteeship Council in New York in 1955 to dramatize TANU's role as the spokesman for Africans,[22] membership soared to 100,000 and TANU was firmly launched.

Though Nyerere's views on Tanganyika's social goals differed from those of his colleagues even in 1954 -- for example, he proposed freezing all wages and salaries until the rural masses' living standards had been improved[23] -- for its first five years TANU could subordinate all other goals to the task of winning political power. Some leaders, including Kambona, wanted a racial policy that would have denied full participation to Europeans and Asians, a sharp contrast to Nyerere's call for a society where all were treated equally regardless of race. Most who thought about the matter likely would have supported a market economy, including both unequal incomes based on skills and training, and competition among individuals to advance themselves, though most had probably not thought beyond replacing Europeans and Asians with Africans and trying to get more revenue for African producers. Despite these differences, however, the core of TANU militants could all agree that their first priority was to wrest political control from the British.

The colonial administration's attempts to suppress TANU greatly helped its phenomenal growth as the nationalist movement. Governor Twining tried a two-pronged attack, harassing TANU and supporting a rival "multi-racial" party. However, the harassment took relatively mild forms, such as forbidding civil servants to become members of TANU, and even where TANU branches were banned, as in Sukumaland, "there was no provision against being a TANU member, against attending TANU meetings outside Sukumaland, or even, at first, against gathering together in groups for purposes of discussion". Nyerere and his lieutenants remained free to travel about the country to build their party. The only organized opposition to TANU, the administration's United Tanganyika Party, never had a chance against it. The white settlers were too small a group to carry much weight, Asians were ambivalent because they too had suffered discrimination at the hands of Europeans, and Africans were thoroughly convinced that the UTP's "multi-racialism" was another name for

165

European domination.

TANU spread like a Serengeti grass-fire. From 10,000 members six months after its founding, it reached 100,000 after Nyerere's 1955 appearance at the United Nations, and 1,250,000 by the time the 1960 Constitutional Conference settled the details of independence.[25] To Africans, Nyerere and TANU embodied a diverse range of hopes, such as an end to onerous rural agricultural regulations, protection against threats to Africans' land tenure and against Europeans and Asians being injected into local councils, and opportunities for educated Africans to take over choice European jobs. This mixture of hopes was enough to allow TANU to sweep all the seats in the 1958 and 1959 elections, and from then until independence on December 9, 1961, it had to share with the British responsibility for governing Tanganyika.

By the 1958 elections, Nyerere had established himself as the unchallengeable leader of TANU. Part of this pre-eminence was attributable to his role and to the administration's behaviour. The fact that he was the person who went to the United Nations Trusteeship Council in 1955 and 1956 to present the Africans' case against the British administration suggested that his power was comparable to that of the colonial rulers, and his stature was further enhanced by the fact that Governor Twining became concerned enough to publish a leaflet in Tanganyika refuting Nyerere's assertions.[26] Yet at the same time, unlike many other educated Africans Nyerere retained a close rapport with ordinary Tanganyikans, both through his ability to explain TANU's goals in homely but persuasive terms, and also through the fact that when he wanted time to think, he could go happily to his family homestead and there live like an ordinary peasant. His simple, ascetic life-style and his obviously selfless dedication to ordinary Tanganyikans' welfare won him a universal reputation as a "good" man, while the positive results shown by his shrewd sense of strategy and tactics strengthened his position as a leader.

Two episodes in 1958 showed the hold Nyerere had gained over his followers. In January 1958 TANU's National Conference had to decide whether it was to participate in or to boycott the forthcoming elections, which were to be for three equal blocs of seats based on race. Nyerere had been strongly denouncing this "multi-racialism" as grossly iniquitous, and most delegates clearly preferred the emotional satisfaction of a boycott. However, Nyerere had concluded that a boycott would be counter-productive because it would leave the administration's United Tanganyika Party in control, and in turn this would either entrench "multi-racialism" or bring about violence. In a masterfully persuasive speech closing the debate, Nyerere managed to swing the conference to a policy of participating in the elections.[27]

A few months later, he had his only brush with jail when the government charged him with criminal libel. Nyerere, feeling strongly that the accusations he had levelled needed to be made, was fully prepared to take the martyrdom of becoming a "Prison Graduate". However, before sentence was passed, a new Governor, Sir Richard Turnbull, arrived and Nyerere decided to give him a chance to see whether they could work together. He therefore paid a fine rather than go to jail, risking charges of cowardice from his followers, but sparing the British a potentially violent situation.[28]

SEARCHING FOR SOCIALISM

Until he became Prime Minister in 1960, Nyerere had been able to promote a goal on which almost every Tanganyikan could agree: winning political independence. Now, with independence clearly in sight, it was necessary to consider what kinds of social and economic structures an independent country should try to build. This situation was one faced by all African leaders as their territories arrived at independence; and to this point, there was little to suggest that Tanzania would choose a path markedly different from that of other states.

Nevertheless, Nyerere had already given some hints that he might try to lead the country in a direction that few other African leaders had ever considered. He had at least since 1954 emphasized the desirability of equality, and in particular had stressed how all the high incomes of civil servants, teachers and other functionaries were extracted from the peasant's meagre surplus. The influence of John Stuart Mill showed in his belief that participation in the political process was important for individuals' self-development. What he had not yet worked out was the means for realizing these values of equality and participation. The 1960s saw him gradually evolving policies by which his country might achieve these goals, while the 1970s were to demonstrate just how severe were the barriers to making these policies work.

Within weeks of Tanganyika's becoming independent, Nyerere startled observers by handing over the Prime Minister's post to Rashidi Kawawa, and devoting himself to working out a TANU philosophy for the post-independence period. His goals were the creation of a non-exploitive, egalitarian society, and a party whose leaders would remain open to criticism and control by the people. To this end, he devoted 1962 to revitalizing TANU as a "two-way, all-weather road" from the smallest village to the national executive, meanwhile pondering how to achieve effective popular participation in a state overwhelmingly dominated by a single party. There was a further advantage to being out of government office in this first flush of Tanganyikan independence. The government sought to demonstrate African political control by deportations, by advancing Africans over Europeans and Asians in the civil service, by bringing in a Preventive Detention Act, and by other actions which seemed both high-handed and racist, actions which Nyerere would have had qualms about taking.[29] TANU was thus able to satisfy its activists, while Nyerere managed to distance himself from its "excesses", until December 1962, when a republican constitution was introduced and he was overwhelmingly elected President.

Despite Nyerere's efforts at re-building TANU as a effective instrument of mass mobilization, its ability to rouse and direct the population was still feeble. This was shown starkly in January 1964, when the army's two battalions mutinied. While the troops were not seeking to overthrow the government, but only to remove their British officers and win better pay, there was no sign of any part of TANU's organization rallying to defend its leaders or to contain the mutineers. Only the intervention of 60 British marines put an end to the mutiny.[30] Nyerere learned from this humiliation the need to ensure that the army was committed to the regime, and subsequently took steps to rebuild it from personnel who were loyal to TANU. However, since there was no certain guarantee that an organized group of armed men could be counted on to obey civilian rulers in all circumstances, the army remained a vaguely menacing background shadow.

Another crisis at the same time as the mutiny showed Nyerere's penchant for acting by himself without consultation. Shortly before the Tanganyika Army had mutinied, an African uprising on the offshore sultanate of Zanzibar had replaced the

British-backed Arab government with an odd mixture
of African nationalists and Marxist radicals. The
latter had encouraged China, the Soviet Union and
the East European states to establish their presence,
and Nyerere saw a serious danger that the Cold War
would be fought out on his doorstep. In April 1964,
he managed to contain this danger by the expedient
of persuading the Zanzibari leaders to merge with
Tanganyika into the United Republic of Tanzania,
even though in practice Zanzibar has remained a separate state within Tanzania.[31]

A more long-term concern for Nyerere was the
problem of how to devise a political system which
would allow ordinary Tanzanians some say in who was
governing them. In the last elections before independence, TANU had been unopposed in 58 out of 71
seats, with the result that most citizens had no
chance even to cast a ballot. Nyerere was concerned
with this lack of any popular participation, and in
1965 set up a commission to consider how a de facto
one-party state could be made democratic. The commission proposed a system whereby two or more candidates from within TANU should be allowed to contest
each parliamentary seat, with the entire electorate
choosing among them. While there was thus a considerable restriction on the electors' freedom of
choice through TANU's power to decide who would be
allowed to contest, they could at least vote out a
candidate or member who was particularly unpopular.
This system was implemented in 1965, and followed in
subsequent elections.[32]

Meanwhile, on the economic front, the gap between urban and rural dwellers continued to grow,
with the urban dwellers' incomes increasing in real
terms by 65% from 1960 to 1968, while farmers' incomes stayed almost constant. Attempts to improve
rural living standards through co-operative villages
foundered, in part because the more efficient farmers saw more benefit in working as independent family units[33] and also in some cases because the
people chosen to take part were simply incompetent.[34]
But the urban areas were not building any solid base
for prosperity either; Western private investors
were not tumbling over each other out of a desire to
set up businesses in Tanzania, Western governments
were rather niggardly with aid, and neither the
Soviet Union or China offered much useful help, with
the one significant exception of China's financing
of the TanZam railway.[35] If Tanzania were to make a
major economic leap forward, she would have to do it
herself.

Nyerere's approach to resolving these political and economic problems crystallized into the Arusha Declaration of 1967, which has remained Tanzania's fundamental guideline ever since. The principal point made in this document was that Tanzania had neither any reason nor the right to expect help from other countries in her attempts to achieve economic development, and thus must rely entirely upon her own resources. Since these did not include money or high technology, but did include plenty of labour power and land, it followed that the country's emphasis should be on rural development, employing technology that ordinary people could utilize, and aiming at meeting basic needs through hard work. At the same time, Nyerere recognized the influence that national economic institutions could have over the choices open in the rural areas by nationalizing the "commanding heights" represented by the banks, insurance companies, and major food processing and exporting firms. He followed the Arusha Declaration with two further indications of his general philosophy, "Education for Self-Reliance" and "Socialism and Rural Development"[36] and undertook a number of concrete steps to encourage co-operative rural enterprises.

Meanwhile, the search for equality started at the top, with a strict "Leadership Code" presented to the same TANU convention that endorsed the Arusha Declaration and the popular nationalizations of foreign firms. The Leadership Code was far less appealing to the party and government elites; it prohibited high- and middle-level government officials and TANU office-holders from "capitalist" practices such as owning shares in private companies or even owning houses for rent, a practice which had been the major source of wealth for many officials. Nevertheless, Nyerere managed to persuade the conference to accept the code, and despite widespread unhappiness, it seems to have been reasonably effective.[37]

This rather ascetic approach to leadership had been foreshadowed in a revealing incident a year earlier, when students at the University protested to Nyerere against a requirement that they should do two years' National Service at only 40% of the salary they might otherwise earn, or some $1,000 a year. Declaring that if Tanzania could give every farmer an income of $1,000 a year, it would have produced "a terrific revolution", Nyerere raged that everyone was being paid too much "except the poor peasant", and then announced that he was slashing his own salary by 20% from that moment, and that the students must go home to their villages.[38] It was not until six months later that the expelled students were re-admitted, and then only after their parents had indicated that they would work for the nation.

In the years after the Leadership Code, a variety of policies curbed the growth of a privileged elite. These included growing restrictions on luxury imports, including eventually an almost total ban on the importation of private automobiles, a school admission plan which largely eliminated the advantages civil servants in the capital enjoyed in gaining secondary school places for their children,[39] and direct restrictions on higher incomes so that by 1977 the ratio of the highest income in the public sector to the minimum wage had fallen from 50:1 at independence to 9:1.[40] Other policies curbed the advantages of an elite more indirectly, notably the replacement of English by Swahili in much government business, a move which widened the base from which administrators could be recruited, and ensured that they could not communicate among themselves in a private language. These policies were made more palatable to aspiring civil servants by the expansion of the civil service and consequent rapid promotions, but nevertheless, the senior civil servants in Tanzania were far less well off than their counterparts in neighbouring states such as Kenya or Uganda.

The other side of the drive for equality was the effort to make life better for ordinary farmers. Here Nyerere's desire for an egalitarian society merged with his goals of participation and self-reliance, to produce in the 1960s the philosophy of the ujamaa villages. These villages were to be based on the "traditional socialism" that Nyerere claimed was familiar to all Tanzanians: the family unit, based upon the principles of mutual respect, shared property, and a willingness of all members to work for the common good. What Nyerere proposed[41] was to extend this communal approach beyond the bounds of the individual family to embrace an entire village. In this way, he argued, everyone would be better off, because the joint efforts of all the villagers would increase total productivity, and at the same time, would avoid the growth of great inequalities among rural dwellers that would appear if some men were able to hire the labour of others for their personal gain. Such villages, he insisted, could not be forced on people, since they depended upon a "willingness to co-operate"; government could only "explain, encourage and participate" in their creation.[42] However, Nyerere did see other benefits in villagization besides the development of a socialist morality. Bringing people from their isolated homesteads into villages would enable them to obtain schools, dispensaries, clean water supplies, and other basic services more readily, as well as facilitate their education in socialist principles.

Nyerere had always spent much of his time as President travelling around the countryside, answering questions at a town meeting about government policies, pitching in to dig a field or harvest a crop, or even spending eight days in a march through the countryside to inspire support for the Arusha Delcaration.[43] Many of his actions tried to encourage people to decide for themselves what should be done, rather than simply following government orders. Yet at the same time, other actions indicated a supreme confidence that he had the right answers. The manner in which the Arusha Declaration itself evolved was a classic illustration of this; not even his own Cabinet or the major organs of TANU, let alone the rank-and-file of the party, had any direct part in preparing it. Nyerere simply presented it to the Cabinet and to the party and then argued it through.[44] A further element in his framework of values which was to have tragic repercussions was his over-riding concern with equality and his fear of letting some individuals establish themselves as a privileged elite. This was to lead to the destruction of an association which seemed to embody most of the virtues Nyerere sought to inculcate in his countrymen.

The prototype for Nyerere's _ujamaa_ villages was the Ruvuma Development Association, a co-operative venture begun by a number of TANU activists in 1963 in a town near the Mozambique border. The association during the 1960s gradually expanded to embrace a number of villages with a widening range of economic activities, including a flour mill, sawmill, and road transport company. Each community started from a nucleus of a single lineage, and rigorously screened all new applicants for membership. Individuals who were elected to managerial roles still had to contribute a full share of manual labour, and while families lived and ate as separate units, each village would have weekly communal meals and meetings, at which members would discuss the week's activities, and any slackers would be singled out for public criticism. So successful was

the RDA that one of its founders was sent to TANU
headquarters in 1969 and there put in charge of the
Party's ujamaa village programme, while Nyerere drew
much of the inspiration for Socialism and Rural
Development from the association's visible success.[45] The RDA, despite such problems as a too-
heavy reliance upon expatriates and upon imported
capital goods, did seem to be a fairly encouraging
indicator that the ujamaa ideals of equality,
co-operation and self-reliance could produce an increased well-being for its participants.

However, in October 1969, President Nyerere,
exercising powers vested in him under the Societies
Ordinance (ironically, the act that had been used by
the British to proscribe TANU in the 1950s) declared
the Ruvuma Development Association an illegal society and ordered it wound up,[46] an order immediately
enforced by gun-toting soldiers who appeared at the
society's offices. The banning of the RDA signalled
two major turns in government policy. First, it
signalled a turn toward centralizing control over
developmental activities under the party and the
state, a pattern which was to become increasingly
prominent over the next few years. Second, it signalled the beginning of a much greater reliance on
force than previously, a reliance which was soon to
culminate in the massive "villagization" programme.

How we should interpret Nyerere's destruction
of an association which seemingly epitomized his
ujamaa goal is a matter of controversy. There can
be no question that he was aware of what the RDA
was doing, nor that he himself approved of its banning, since no one other than the president had the
power to ban an organization under the Societies
Ordinance. What can be debated, I think, is the
extent to which Nyerere himself thought the RDA was
a threat to his values. It could be argued that he
decided to ban it not because he personally disapproved of the extent that it was building up a
position for itself outside the TANU structure
(while RDA members considered themselves loyal members of TANU, they had little use for the party officials in their district) but because he felt he
had to placate party officials who had decided for
their own self-esteem or power that the RDA had to
go. However, given the way Nyerere had managed to
force the party officials to swallow such bitter
medicine as the Leadership Code, I find this argument a little hard to believe. Two other more plausible arguments are, first that Nyerere saw the RDA
as turning into a new privileged elite group,

through both its selectivity in choosing members and
its growing affluence, or second, that he did not
really want an autonomous organization that might
not pursue the goals that he, the President, had
decided were necessary. Events in the next few
years suggested that the last may have been the key
factor.

THE END OF PERSUASION?

By 1973 it was clear that attempts to transform
the rural areas by persuasion would take a very long
time. One official estimated that in early 1974
only some 2.5 million people were living in villages
and that figure included some who had always been
village-dwellers.[47] It also included some who had
already been forced into villages, such as the
people of Dodoma region, who had been compulsorily
uprooted in 1971 in the first of a number of military style "Operations".[48] In 1973 Nyerere openly
abandoned the reliance on persuasion for rural
transformation, announcing to the TANU conference
that it was time to force people to move in order to
save them from a continuing "life of death". To
meet a deadline of moving all Tanzanians by 1976,
district administrators set up a series of district
"Operations" involving lorry-loads of people being
dumped into new sites on which minimal preparation
had been done, and that entirely by government officials rather than the people who would have to
live with the results. Some houses and crops were
burned to ensure that people would not run back to
their old homesteads, and while the numbers of
people actually abused may have been small[49] their
misfortunes had a powerful demonstration effect.[50]
In total, some 11 million people were incorporated
into new villages from 1973 to 1977, although perhaps less than half this number were physically
uprooted. Whatever the numbers, it was the largest
mass movement in Africa's history.[51]
The forced villagization programme brought to
the fore the question of what goals Nyerere and TANU
were really pursuing. Was the motive for villagization, as Nyerere claimed, to enable the government
to provide services such as schooling and health
care which it could not manage while people were
widely scattered? Or was the real motive, as
critics insisted, to bring the peasants under government control so that the dominant "bureaucratic
bourgeoisie" could extract a larger share of their

174

surplus production? The government's arguments did
sound somewhat implausible, to be sure; although
Nyerere claimed villagization had made universal
primary education attainable by the end of 1977,[52]
it did seem hard to accept that the government really wanted to have to cope with the increased expectations stirred by villagization when it could bare-
ly afford existing levels of social services.[53] On
the other hand, bringing the peasants together in
villages and broadening schooling would increase
political consciousness, and thus facilitate the
peasants' organizing to defend themselves. Two further factors may have entered the government's cal-
culations. More production could have been achieved
without villagization, but only by encouraging the
growth of an affluent stratum of farmers, something
Nyerere sought hard to avoid. Furthermore, locating
peasants in villages would leave large tracts of
unoccupied land that could then be filled by state
farms.[54] In view of other actions Nyerere took at
this time, the most plausible argument seems to be
that he saw villagization as a key step toward a
more collective mode of living which would promote
rural equality.

Despite the short-run problems, villagization
seems generally to have been accepted by rural dwellers. Certainly the increase in votes against
Nyerere, from 3% in 1970 to 6.7% in 1975, though
most marked in regions where villagization had been
carried out heavy-handedly, was not of such a magnitude as to suggest seething discontent.[55] In 1978,
I was assured by many individuals, including some
with no ties to the regime, that people had come to
see the benefits of villagization as outweighing
the problems. One high government official told me
that just after his home area was moved, he was
shocked on a visit to discover that for the first
time in his experience, people were bitterly hostile
toward Nyerere. When he told this to the President,
Nyerere's reply was "Just wait six months and then
go back and talk to them again." Sceptical, he
returned home a few months later, and was surprised
to discover, just as Nyerere had predicted, that his
people now saw benefits such as shorter walks for
water and readier access to a road as outweighing
the initial disruption.

Two other actions Nyerere took in the rural
areas at this time were responses to the failure of
TANU to live up to his expectations as a grass-
roots vehicle for disseminating co-operative socialism. Nyerere seems to have assumed that popular

175

opinion in TANU was favourable to socialism, and
that the job of central authorities was simply to
guide people toward the best ways of achieving this
agreed-upon goal. In fact, however, at the lowest
levels of the party, the ten-house cell and the
branch, where all party workers were volunteers,
there was a widespread tendency for shopkeepers,
well-to-do farmers and other comparatively privileged individuals to emerge as the party's local
leaders.[56] Such local notables frequently opposed
activities such as co-operative shops that ran contrary to their interests, and made sure that agricultural and marketing co-operatives were run so as
to channel most benefits to themselves. The higher
echelons of the party thus faced a dilemma. If they
tried to impose more egalitarian values from above,
they undercut local participation. However, to wait
for the local cells to embrace socialism voluntarily
would be like waiting for bankers to foreswear
usury. Even in districts which were too poor to
have many notables whose economic interests ran
against TANU policy, those individuals chosen to
lead cells or branches were simply too little ahead
of their neighbours in political consciousness to
be able to inculcate TANU's values.

The central government's response to this dominance of local party branches by a privileged
stratum was to reduce the opportunities for local
participation. The major step was the "decentralization" of major government departments begun in
1972.[57] Numbers of the most able and committed
civil servants went out into the field to oversee
district and regional development, taking direct
control of developmental budgets with them rather
than leaving it in Dar es Salaam. However, in this
process "elected district councils have had their
operating responsibilities substantially reduced".[58]
In 1976 came a further step in the same direction,
the closure of the (locally run) marketing
co-operatives.[59] In both the district councils and
the co-ops, rich farmers had been disproportionately
influential, and terminating the powers of these
bodies could thus be seen as a step toward preventing the growth of greater economic disparities.
However, it also served to tighten central government and party control over the rural areas, and to
reduce the opportunities for any grass-roots participation.

These moves toward tighter control over the
rural areas were linked to the most severe economic
crisis Tanzania had faced since independence. In

1973 and 1974 the countryside was gripped by
drought, with the result that grain production dropped from 1,439,000 tons in 1972 to 1,031,000 tons in
1974 (see Table 8.2). Export crops, and thus export

Table 8.2: Tanzanian food production, cost of living
and import data in 1970s.

Year	Cereal output ('000 metric tons)		Pro-ducer price maize, per ton	Con-sumer price index	Imports Maize Amount ('000 tons)	Value ($'000,000)	
	All cereals	Maize				Maize	All im-ports
1972	1,469	881	36.40	100.0	116.0	7.8	402.9
1973	1,439	888	40.60	110.3	3.5	.4	504.2
1974	1,031	550	46.20	131.9	253.5	49.3	752.8
1975	1,463	825	60.50	166.4	230.6	38.8	693.3
1976	1,518	897	90.10	177.9	155.6	7.9	642.7
1977	1,625	968	100.50	198.3	.....	....	774.0
1978	1,786	1,041	114.60	221.0	.....	....	1,186.5
1979	1,609	900	......	251.4	.....	....	1,087.5
1980	1,430	800	......	327.5	.....	....	1,248.0

Sources: Cereal production from Food and Agriculture
Organization, Production Yearbooks; producer price
for maize calculated from Hyden, Beyond Ujamaa,
p. 143; consumer price index and total imports from
International Monetary Fund, International Financial
Statistics (with price index recalculated to make
1972 the base year); maize imports, United Nations,
Yearbooks of International Trade Statistics.

earnings, meanwhile just held their own,[60] with the
result that the huge imports of food necessary to
offset the shortfall were enough by themselves to
seriously upset Tanzania's rather delicate balance
of payments. When to this was added the upsurge in
world oil prices after 1973, the over-all effect was
disastrous; from an import bill of $318 million and
a modest balance-of-trade deficit of $67 million in
1970, by 1975 the import bill had reached $691

million and the balance-of-trade deficit $356 million.[61] This meant that the foreign exchange reserves that Tanzania had laboriously accumulated in the 1960s were nearly exhausted, and all imports, even essential parts for factories, transport and agriculture, had to be scrutinized carefully.

To what extent did villagization contribute to this crisis? It seems probable that in the short run it contributed substantially; the big drop in grain production, and particularly in maize, came in 1974, at the height of the forced moves to new areas. Thereafter grain production moved steadily upward until by 1978 it reached a new peak, equalling on a per capita basis the 1972 crop, despite a relentless 3% annual growth in population. The key factor here seems to have been a major increase in prices paid to producers. The price for maize rose from 0.33 shillings per kilogram in 1973-74 to 0.85 shillings in 1977-78, an increase of 157%. Wheat, rice and cotton prices all rose by more than 100%.[62] A further effect of these increases was to raise average rural incomes from 53% of average urban incomes back to their old ratio of 77%.[63]

However, the striving for equality seems to have had other less beneficial effects. To prevent the growth of a rural business elite of small millers and shop-keepers, the government gave the National Milling Corporation a monopoly over the milling and wholesale distribution of cereal grains, and even tried to ban local private shop-keepers in favour of village co-operatives. (This latter order was rescinded after a few months.) The NMC became a particularly severe drain on government funds, borrowing by 1980 more than twice as much as it was paying out to farmers and losing a great deal of grain through poor storage.[64] It was not alone, however; most of the 300-odd state-run companies, as agronomist Rene Dumont noted in a scathing 1979 report, were "overstaffed, under-equipped, poorly run and heavily spendthrift". While some of their problems could be blamed on shortages of materials and of transport caused by the foreign exchange crises, there was also, as former Finance Minister Edwin Mtei remarked, "an almost general go-slow" among Tanzanian workers,[65] a problem exacerbated by the practice introduced in the 1970s of workers' participation in the management of companies.[66]

Still, despite these problems, by 1978 the worst of the crises seemed to have been overcome; Tanzania was still running a serious balance-of-payments deficit (because the government was forced to remove import restrictions prematurely, the deficit had leaped from $149 million in 1976 and $213 million in 1977 to $691 million in 1978), but food production had recovered and the other disruptions arising from villagization seemed to have been accommodated. Then two further blows were heaped on top of the rising cost of imported oil, the slumping terms of trade, and the continuing drains of the state companies: the war with Uganda, and another severe drought in 1980.

The war launched in late 1978 to end Idi Amin's reign of terror in Uganda was clearly one of the most justifiable wars in history, but it dealt Tanzania's shaky economy a costly blow. By the time Tanzania's troops left in 1981, the total cost had come to some $500 million, of which $300 million represented foreign exchange for arms and ammunition.[67] Since this represented more than half Tanzania's export earnings, while oil imports also consumed more than half these earnings, a shortage of foreign exchange again loomed. Then the 1980 drought reduced grain production by some 350,000 tons from the 1978 output (Table 8.2), sending Tanzania cap in hand for food aid and long term loans. A number of side effects began to appear. Inflation intensified, with the official consumer price index rising from 133 in 1978 to 197 in 1980 and 228 in the first quarter of 1981.[68] Corruption, which had hitherto been kept fairly effectively under control, began to gnaw away at all levels of officialdom, with damaging effects on popular morale. As Tanzania entered the 1980s, it was problematic whether the experiment in self-reliant socialism would continue, or for that matter, whether Nyerere himself would survive.

These gloomy facts, however, should not be allowed to blot out Tanzania's real accomplishments. By comparison with most other African states, Tanzania had fared relatively well. Her per capita annual rate of economic growth from 1960 to 1979, at 2.3%, placed her thirteenth among the 37 states listed by the World Bank.[69] The literacy rate of 66% in 1976 was one of the highest in Africa, and even food production to 1979 was above average for African states.[70] Furthermore, Tanzania had done more than almost any other state to distribute benefits such as health care and education down to the ordinary farmer in the bush, and had also had more success than almost any other state in convincing its elites that this was right. At the same time, the government was among the most open to criticism

of its short-comings. "There's a grass-roots feeling," noted one correspondent, "that one can always
appeal to authority" against abuses of power,[71] and
another observed that in Dar es Salaam in 1981 maga-
zines and books were being published questioning
whether Tanzania was on the right track.[72] Furthermore, in 1975 and 1980, despite the severity of the
crises faced by the regime and the country, the
presidential and legislative elections were held on
schedule. In each, the voters removed a substantial
proportion of the sitting legislators, including
three and two Ministers, respectively.[73]

    The great failure of Tanzania so far has been
the failure of self-reliance. The fact that foreign
aid, totalling some $500 million in 1980, had become
the main source of the development budget,[74] marked
an abandonment of the major tenet of the Arusha
Declaration. Even in the earlier crisis of 1973-75
Nyerere had expressed concern over the slide back
into structural dependency upon the Western industrialized states.[75] The political risk he faced from
this was that he could lose the moral claim to be
able to ask his countrymen to continue to bear
material hardships for the sake of their autonomous
development. In 1980 he still appeared able to make
this claim on them, but his power to persuade could
not survive too many more years of crisis.

IS THE GRAIL BEYOND REACH?

    After two decades of independence, there are
few of the optimists, so numerous in the 1960s, who
regarded Tanzania as the prototype of the brave new
African world, the egalitarian, self-reliant society
whose citizens would eschew the temptations of an
individualist, materialist consumer society in favour of sharing with and supporting each other. The
critics, both "radical" and "conservative", are in
the ascendant, presenting from diametrically opposed
premises their explanations of where Tanzania took
wrong turnings. Before considering their critiques,
however, let us summarize the goals that Nyerere set
out to pursue.

    Over the years Nyerere developed three princi-
pal goals: first, building a non-racial society in
which an individual's race (or other fixed attributes such as ethnicity or religion) would be irrelevant to his role in Tanzania; second, broadening
popular participation in all decision-making processes, in order to increase people's control over

their own fate; and third, creating an egalitarian and co-operative economic order aiming at satisfying basic needs for all collectively, rather than satisfying individual desires for personal luxuries.

These goals, however, were not only hard to achieve, but to some extent they were in conflict with each other. Thus allowing people to participate in determining the shape of their community implies that there must be a significant scope for local initiatives and a concomitant restraint upon central direction. It also implies that these initiatives may run in different directions, and that some communities may in consequence deviate from Nyerere's concept of socialism, or oppose his nonracial attitude. Similarly, Nyerere's goal of nonracial society ran contrary to the deeply felt emotions of most Africans. Furthermore, the Asians, who stood to benefit most from this goal, were often in the forefront of opposition to his socialist values. Finally, though Nyerere might proclaim fervently that equality and co-operation were the basis of pre-colonial African society, the acquisitiveness which he sought to prevent had taken firm root during the colonial era, and was constantly reinforced by Tanzania's external economic links. Restraining acquisitiveness might require not just the development of a widespread commitment to alternative goals, but the imposition by a central authority of severe restrictions on individuals' choices of actions, which would undercut the principle of people developing through learning to make their own choices.

Julius Nyerere's constant questioning and uncertainty about the best means to achieve these contradictory goals has been both the greatest strength and the greatest weakness of the Tanzanian experiment. More single-minded ideologues could have produced a "final solution" to the Asian problem, or achieved a form of socialism in which all shared equally in misery, as the Khmer Rouge demonstrated in Kampuchea. Yet at the same time Nyerere's lack of certainty about how to achieve his goals made it easier for his subordinates, particularly in the government bureaucracy, to pursue different goals without clearly violating his over-all vision, or at least to provide a different balance among the goals than he might have favoured.

The goal in which Nyerere has achieved the clearest success, and in the process has turned around the attitudes of many of his supporters, has been in building a non-racial society. To be sure, the Asians are hardly loved by ordinary Tanzanians, and because they are painfully aware of their vulnerability, they do seem particularly prone to be involved in black market dealings and other acts which undermine the state, which in turn creates more suspicion of their position.[76] Europeans too are still regarded with some suspicion, although there does not seem to be the festering bitterness that can manifest itself in, say, Kenya. Yet both Asian and European candidates have won elections against African opponents since TANU began holding competitive constituency elections in 1965, and after the first years of independence, there has been little public sniping at racial targets. Nor have intra-African ethnic conflicts emerged; TANU has always taken great pains to prevent any appeals to ethnicity or religion in politics, and this seems to have had the desired effect. Overall, given the basic attitudes on which he had to build, Nyerere has done as well as might be expected of any leader in coping with racial and ethnic pressures.

The extent to which Nyerere has succeeded in building a participant and co-operative socialist society is much more controversial. Radical critics[77] generally contend that the goal of co-operative grass-roots socialism might have been feasible, at least if it had relied upon an explicit class appeal to the less privileged sectors of rural society, but that it was sabotaged by a "bureaucratic bourgeoisie" who concentrated their efforts only upon those parts of Nyerere's programme that enhanced their own power. Thus they encouraged the nationalization of industries because this increased the number of lucrative jobs open to them, and supported the villagization programme and other changes in the rural areas only so far as these allowed the central government to extract more wealth from the peasants to support a growing bureaucracy. On the other hand, they opposed schemes in which the peasants decided for themselves how to run their own affairs, such as the Ruvuma Development Association.

Conservative critics, by contrast, see the whole idea of co-operative socialism as fundamentally misconceived.[78] Peoples' acquisitive tendencies are too strong to be overridden by idealistic appeals to help each other even at some personal sacrifice, at least beyond the immediate family. At the grass-roots level, this tendency is shown when successful farmers prefer to concentrate on their own crops rather than work in a ujamaa village, and conversely when those who do re-settle look to government hand-outs rather than producing their own food and shelter. At a managerial level, whether in rural co-operatives or in the nationalized industries, the same attitude is shown by managers' concern with obtaining "perks" for themselves while neglecting the efficient running of their businesses. The government's continuing pressure against these self-seeking attitudes has simply resulted in the more efficient farmers no longer producing the food the country needs, and in gross inefficiency in the nationalized industries.

How far is each of these critiques justified? Let us look again at two crucial sectors, the government and party bureaucracy, and the rural peasants.

Among government and party elites, there has clearly been a substantial acceptance of the goal of equality. We noted earlier that the differential between the top salaries of public officials and the minimum wage had been sharply reduced.[79] Furthermore, such rewards of high status as private cars have been reduced by rules which allow the import of cars only for official purposes, and while managers can still enjoy the use of a car as part of their job, I am told that they are inhibited from using these cars excessively for private purposes by the fear that their workers will protest, leading to the loss of both job and car.[80] Also, it has been top civil servants who have developed and carried out the policies that have severely curtailed the luxury goods they might otherwise enjoy, who have reduced the opportunities for their children to gain access to secondary schools vis-a-vis the children of less privileged parents[81] and who have provided the impetus for change in the rural areas against the resistance of local entrenched interests.[82] The idealistic readiness to subordinate personal interests to a general good that one scholar had found characteristic of the younger and newly recruited civil servants in the early 1960s[83] seems to have persisted even after Arusha imposed more serious sacrifices.

The elite's willingness to encourage popular participation has been far less marked than its support for equality.[84] Both government "experts" in technical fields, and TANU officials in matters of ideology, could claim "superior" knowledge as a justification for imposing their own decisions, sometimes to the extent of consciously emulating their colonial predecessors.[85] This tendency was reinforced by the fact that many farmers seemed to take short-sighted views of the benefits from government plans, and often those with whom the experts dealt at the local level were not strongly committed to TANU's goals. Against this attitude, the only feasible check was an insistence from the top down that the experts must work <u>with</u> the people; but Nyerere and his senior colleagues themselves were frequently torn between their desire to encourage participation and an equally strong desire to get the results they <u>knew</u> would be best for people in the long run, and to get these results quickly. This ambivalence meant that officials in the field could interpret their directions as justifying a "top-down" approach.[86]Nor were peasants likely to protest against this approach; even apart from the barriers of lack of knowledge and a sense of powerlessness against government, many appeared to prefer being forced to carry out development projects rather than having to take initiatives voluntarily.[87]

In the rural areas, we have already noted that richer individuals in economically strategic positions tended to take control of both TANU branches and co-operatives, and that Nyerere dealt with this problem by sacrificing participation to the goal of equality.[88] Perhaps this problem is too deeply rooted in human nature to ever be contained effectively. One study of the breakdown of a <u>ujamaa</u> community in the 1960s suggested that the main obstacle to an equal sharing of the community's farming profits was that the more efficient farmers wanted the larger share of the profits that their skill produced, and to get this greater income preferred to hire their own labour rather than work communally.[89] A later study noted a decline in co-operation even among neighbours and within extended families as the spread of cash crops allowed a demand for a greater range of material goods to develop. Each farmer was too busy with his own farm to help his brothers or neighbours, and the more skillful were able to afford more wives and hired labourers, widening the economic gap between themselves and the less skillful.[90]

Yet the Ruvuma Development Association suggested that the co-operative ideal could succeed under the right conditions. Perhaps its fate suggests that even the most idealistic leader is driven by his own "power imperatives" to override his most cherished goals, or more cynically, idealistic goals are quite acceptable for public display just so long as they do not jeopardize the leader's hold on power. Clearly there are strong pressures in

Tanzania hostile to any autonomous local development, and thus to any meaningful grass-roots participation. However, it may be premature to say that centralizing forces have gained the ascendancy to such a degree that the goal of participation is dead, even though it seems further away than it did in the 1960s. One might say of Nyerere's "participation", as of Leopold Senghor's "democracy", that it is "participation on a leash", a limited participation liable to be curbed from above, yet at the same time giving some opportunity for people to develop their own skills.

This brings us to two further threats to Nyerere's goals. We have noted that one weakness of TANU at the local level has been the lack of commitment of its local leaders to its goals, with the consequence that changes in both economic relationships and in the extent of popular participation have been minimal. As TANU (or Chama Cha Mapinduzi --CCM--as it has been known since 1977) control becomes more pervasive, the party offers increasing attractions to those who want power or prestige within Tanzanian society, and is thus likely to attract even more individuals who are seeking material or psychological gratification rather than any "public interest" goal. If not countered, this can bring about three results: first, that the party's capacity to promote change is reduced even further as the opportunists take over (just as the CPP died in Ghana); second, as it becomes less idealistic and more an organization of self-seekers, people regard it more and more as an alien force; and third, as people turn away from the party, the restraints on self-seeking among its activists are reduced. The final result would be one more self-seeking oligarchy clinging to power solely for the "sweets of office" that power brings.

The second threat flows from this first. As the government loses its popular appeal, it has to rely increasingly on force to survive. The more idealistic military officers are likely to regard it as having abandoned the values of TANU, while the more cynical will think that if the politicians are able to serve their own interests, the army should be able to do likewise. Already in 1978 I had the feeling that the military was largely a law unto itself in Tanzania, and while keeping it busy in Uganda during 1980-81 was a short-term means of giving it a useful role, in the long run I can see no way of stopping it from staging a <u>coup</u> unless the government can harness it to some popular public purpose.

Whether Nyerere or a successor can succeed in retaining and expanding TANU's idealistic commitments is problematic. There is a glacial inevitability about the forces within the bureaucracy and the party which lead to experts pushing their own solutions at the expense of popular participation, and to opportunists seeking to fill elective posts for their personal benefit rather than for the benefit of all. The economic problems of Tanzania have not helped either. While Tanzania has done well for the "man in the bush", so that by 1980 he was "fed and cared for...as well as his Kenyan brother"[91] there was an air of austerity after two decades of independence which made it seem less materially well off than its booming capitalist neighbour, and thus left the impression that socialism did not offer as satisfactory an approach to development.

On the side of hope is the fact that the regime is still among the most willing in Africa to admit and examine the reasons for its mistakes. Nyerere has, for example, punished police who used torture, and expelled CCM officials for incompetence as well as for corruption. However, whether this openness is enough to stop the CCM sliding down an increasingly coercive path of centralized control remains to be seen. Are the conservative critics right in claiming that what Nyerere professes to be trying to do is too deeply contrary to human nature to succeed? If Nyerere himself has had to compromise his ideals, what chance is there that less committed individuals can live up to them?

Certainly Nyerere is trying to overcome some very strongly entrenched human desires -- and he has succeeded this far beyond what anyone could reasonably expect. Still more remarkably, he has managed to instill new attitudes and new patterns of behaviour with a minimal use of force, relying instead on the power of reason and persuasion. Even if ultimately he fails to achieve a lasting transformation of Tanzania, he will have to go down as the most remarkable leader in African history. Given a territory where people had to struggle for the necessities of life, and lacking the trauma of a violent struggle for independence that might have jolted people into accepting a unifying ideology, one would have to be impressed by any leader who could hold the territory together by peaceful means. For a leader not only to succeed in creating a strong sense of nationhood under these circumstances,

but to incorporate in this sense of nationhood a
commitment to idealistic values which require people
to overcome some of their most basic selfish instincts, is leadership of the highest order.

NOTES

1.   United Nations, FAO Production Yearbook,
Vol. 30 (1976), Table 1.
2.   For a discussion of the importance of
Swahili, see Henry Bienen, Tanzania: Party
Transformation and Economic Development, rev. ed.
(Princeton University Press, Princeton, 1970),
pp. 43-49.
3.   H. W. Stephens, The Political Transforma-
tion of Tanganyika, 1920-1967 (Praeger, New York,
1968), p. 95.
4.   G. Andrew Maguire, Towards "Uhuru" in
Tanzania: The Politics of Participation (Cambridge
University Press, Cambridge, 1969), pp. 30-31.
5.   Judith Listowel, The Making of Tanganyika
(New York: 1965), pp. 214-15.   See also Kirilo
Japhet and Earle Seaton, The Meru Land Case (East
African Publishing House, Nairobi, 1967).
6.   Maguire, Towards Uhuru, p. 124-25
7.   R. Cranford Pratt, The Critical Phase in
Tanzania, 1954-1968 (Cambridge University Press,
Cambridge, 1976), p. 92.
8.   Ibid., p. 12.   Pratt's figures are for 1961,
but it is unlikely that the number of Europeans had
dropped significantly since the early 1950s.
9.   Ibid., p. 29.
10.   Ibid., p. 35.
11.   Andrew Coulson, "Agricultural Policies in
Mainland Tanzania" Review of African Political
Economy, 10 (September-December 1977), pp. 78-79.
12.   Pratt, The Critical Phase, pp. 22-23.
13.   Listowel, Tanganyika, p. 180.
14.   Ibid., pp. 186-91.
15.   Stephens, Political Transformation, p. 38.
16.   Coulson, "Agricultural Policies", p. 86,
provides several illustrations of this tendency,
albeit from a later period when equality was supposed
to be more entrenched as government policy.
17.   Bienen, Tanzania, pp. 24-26.
18.   Listowel, Tanganyika, pp. 182-85.
19.   William E. Smith, We Must Run While They
Walk (Random House, New York, 1971), p. 55.
20.   See Listowel, Tanganyika, pp. 138-39, and
Maguire, Towards Uhuru, pp. 52-57, for two different

interpretations of when Chief Makwaia lost the support of the young men.

21. Listowel, Tanganyika, p. 231.
22. Ibid., p. 232.
23. Ibid., p. 228.
24. Maguire, Towards Uhuru, p. 181.
25. Listowel, Tanganyika, pp. 232, 392.
26. John Hatch, Two African Statesmen: Kaunda of Zambia and Nyerere of Tanzania (Secker and Warburg, London, 1976), p. 112.
27. Ibid., pp. 120-21.
28. See Listowel, Tanganyika, pp. 332-33; Smith, We Must Run, pp. 91-92.
29. See Listowel, pp. 409-10; Pratt, The Critical Phase, p. 123.
30. Pratt, The Critical Phase, pp. 178-79; Smith, We Must Run, pp. 150-61.
31. Pratt, pp. 137-39; Smith, pp. 121-47.
32. The electoral system has been commented on from a wide variety of perspectives. See, for example, Ruth Schacter Morgenthau, "African Elections: Tanzania's Contribution", Africa Report, X, 11 (December 1965), pp. 12-16; John Saul, "The Nature of Tanzania's Political System: Issues Raised by the 1965 and 1970 Elections", Journal of Commonwealth Political Studies, X, 2 (July, 1972), pp. 113-29, and X, 3 (November 1972), pp. 198-221; and Denis Martin, "The 1975 Elections; the disturbing 6 per cent", in Guy Hermet et al., Elections Without Choice (Macmillan, London, 1978), pp. 108-128.
33. See especially David Feldman, "Rural Socialism in Tanzania," in Colin Leys (ed.) Politics and Change in Developing Countries (Cambridge University Press, Cambridge, 1969), pp. 85-111.
34. See especially James L. Brain, "Is Transformation Possible? Styles of Settlement in Post-Independence Tanzania", African Affairs 76 (April 1977), pp. 231-45, for a devastating description of the effect of planning blunders, bureaucracy and bad farmers.
35. Pratt, The Critical Phase, pp. 160, 161-65.
36. "Education for Self-Reliance" is dated March, 1967; "Socialism and Rural Development" is dated September, 1967.
37. Pratt, The Critical Phase, pp. 160, 161-65. Several expatriate government employees told me in 1978 that the guidelines generally had been well enforced.
38. See ibid., pp. 233-34; Smith, We Must Run, pp. 26-32.

39. Pratt, pp. 222-23.

40. Julius K. Nyerere, "The Arusha Declaration Ten Years After" (Dar es Salaam, 1977), p. 16.

41. As spelled out in "Socialism and Rural Development", passim.

42. Ibid., p. 21.

43. Smith, We Must Run, pp. 6-14, 245-51, provides excellent illustrations of Nyerere's style when he was visiting rural areas.

44. Pratt, The Critical Phase, pp. 237-38; C.R.S. Muzo, "Party leadership and socialist transformation" in The Party: Essays on TANU (University of Dar es Salaam, Studies in Political Science, No. 6, 1976), p. 7.

45. Robert Martin, Personal Freedom and the Law in Tanzania (Oxford University Press, Nairobi, 1974), p. 34. Brain, "Is Transformation Possible?", pp. 239-45, has an excellent description of how the Ruvuma Development Association worked.

46. Martin, Personal Freedom, p. 35.

47. J. V. Mwapachu, "Operation Planned Villages in Rural Tanzania: A Revolutionary Strategy for Development", African Review 6, 1 (1976), p. 3.

48. Frances Hill, "Operation Dodoma, 1969-71", in Andrew Coulson (ed.) African Socialism in Practice: The Tanzanian Experience, (Spokesman Books, Nottingham, 1979), pp. 106-13. Rob Martin has pointed out (personal conversation) the alarming connotations of the continuously used term "Operation", which in military parlance refers to an action aimed at overcoming and destroying an enemy.

49. See Nyerere, "Arusha Ten Years After", p. 10. One Tanzanian official working in the President's office at that time gave me an estimate of 100,000 people who had undergone some kind of abuse by government personnel.

50. Mwapachu, "Operation Planned Villages", p. 8, noted that people in his district moved "voluntarily" before the government officials arrived for fear that the house-burning that had occurred in neighbouring districts should be applied against them.

51. Nyerere, "Arusha Ten Years After", p. 42, says 11 million were moved. Martin, "The 1975 Elections", p. 117, suggests a figure of 7 - 8 million, while Goren Hyden, Beyond Ujamaa in Tanzania (University of California, Berkeley, 1980), p. 130, suggests that only 5 million actually changed their location.

52. Nyerere, "Arusha Ten Years After", p. 42.

53. Coulson, "Agricultural Policies", pp. 94-95.

54. A. B. Amey and D. Leonard, "Public policy, class and inequality in Kenya and Tanzania", _Africa Today_, 26, 4 (1979), pp. 25-26.

55. See Martin, "The 1975 Elections", pp. 117-120. The official vote totals are generally regarded as reasonably reliable.

56. _The Party, passim_: Joel and Rachel Samoff, "The Local Politics of Under-development", _African Review_, 6, 1 (1976), pp. 80-94.

57. See Julius Nyerere, _Decentralization_ (Government Printer, Dar es Salaam, 1972).

58. Joel Samoff, "The bureaucracy and the bourgeoisie: decentralization and class structure in Tanzania", _Comparative Studies in Society and History_, 25, 1 (1979), p. 36.

59. Phil Raikes, "Rural differentiation and class formation in Tanzania" _Journal of Peasant Studies_, 5, 3 (1978), p. 313.

60. See Joel Samoff, "Crises and Socialism in Tanzania", _Journal of Modern African Studies_, 19, 2 (1981), p. 296.

61. See John Briggs, "Villagization and the 1974-6 Economic Crisis in Tanzania", _Journal of Modern African Studies_ 17, 4 (1979), p. 697.

62. Samoff, "Crises and Socialism", p. 297.

63. Richard N. Blue and James H. Weaver, _A Critical Assessment of the Tanzanian Model of Development_ (Agricultural Development Council, New York, 1977), pp. 5-6.

64. See _Africa Contemporary Record_, 12, (1979-80), p. B326; Hugh Winsor, "Good Life for Peasants Usurped by New Elite", _Globe and Mail_ (Toronto) September 1, 1981.

65. See Jean-Pierre Langellier, "Tanzania's Socialist 'choice': peasant power", _The Guardian Weekly_, November 9, 1980.

66. For a discussion of the problems caused by worker participation, see R. H. Baguma, "Inefficiency, Irresponsiveness and Irresponsibility in the Public Services -- Is Mwongozo to Blame?", _African Review_, 5, 2 (1975), pp. 195-200. See also Nyerere, "Arusha Ten Years After", pp. 35-36.

67. Langellier, "Peasant power".

68. International Monetary Fund, _International Financial Statistics_, XXXV, 6 (June 1982), pp. 392-93.

69. World Bank, _World Development Report_, 1981, Table 1.

70. Ibid.

71. Jean-Pierre Langellier, "Tanzania --

Africa's conscience", The Guardian Weekly, November 16, 1980.
72. Hugh Winsor, "A land of broken dreams because its President tried to jump too high", Globe and Mail, October 24, 1981.
73. For the outcome of the 1975 election, see Martin, "The 1975 Elections", p. 110; for 1980, Africa Report, January-February 1981, p. 32.
74. Hugh Winsor, "Decay and hunger in once-bright land", Globe and Mail, August 29, 1981.
75. Quoted in Martin, "The 1975 Elections", p. 114.
76. Thus in 1980, the Minister of Commerce called explicitly upon non-African Tanzanians "to observe the principles of socialism more closely". Quoted in Langellier, "Africa's conscience".
77. Among the best-known of the numerous radical criticisms are Issa Shivji, Class Struggles in Tanzania (Heinemann, London, 1976); Andrew Coulson (ed), African Socialism in Practice: The Tanzanian Experience (Spokesman Books, Nottingham, 1979); Michaela von Freyhold, Ujamaa Villages in Tanzania (Heinemann, London, 1979); and Frances Moore Lappe and A. Beccar-Varela, Mozambique and Tanzania: Asking the Big Questions (Institute for Food and Development Policy, San Francisco, 1980).
78. There have been surprisingly few conservative intellectual critiques of Tanzanian policies. The one which attracted the most attention was Michael Lofchie, "Agrarian Crisis and Economic Liberalisation in Tanzania", Journal of Modern African Studies, 16, 3 (1978), pp. 451-75. See also Shiva Naipaul's biting traveller's account, North of South (Andre Deutsch, London, 1978).
79. See above, p. 171
80. This raises neatly the dilemma of interpretation: do we stress the fact that managers still get a car, or that they must be satisfied with one tied to the job rather than privately owned?
81. Pratt, The Critical Phase, pp. 222-24. For more evidence that the "bureaucratic bourgeoisie" have shown considerable altruism, see his "Reflections of a democratic socialist", in B. U. Mwansasu and R. C. Pratt (eds), Towards Socialism in Tanzania (University of Toronto Press, Toronto, 1979), pp. 212-15.
82. See especially the various essays in The Party.
83. Raymond F. Hopkins, Political Roles in a New State (Yale University Press, New Haven, 1971),

Ch. 4.

84.   Lappe, Asking the Big Questions provides the most vehement critique from this perspective.

85.   See M. V. Freyhold, "The Problem of Rural Development and the Politics of Ujamaa Vijijini in Handeni", African Review 6, 2 (1976), p. 134, citing David Brokensha. For an illustration of the "technocratic" approach, see Gerhard Tschanneral, "Rural Water Supply in Tanzania: Is 'Politics' or "Technique' in Command?", ibid., pp. 165-94

86.   This is the main thrust of Jannik Boesen, Birgit Madsen and Tony Moody, Ujamaa--Socialism from Above, Uppsala: (Scandinavian Institute of African Studies, 1977).

87.   See Clyde Ingle, "Compulsion and Rural Development in Tanzania", Canadian Journal of African Studies, IV, 2 (Winter 1970), pp. 77-100.

88.   See above, pp. 175-76.

89.   Feldman, "Rural Socialism", pp. 98-110. Cf. the breakdown of a Nigerian communal society, albeit with very different motivations, described by Stanley Barrett in The Rise and Fall of an African Utopia (Wilfred Laurier University Press, Waterloo, 1977).

90.   J. H. Kontor, "Economic Imperatives for a Socialist Development in the Rural Economy of the Nyakyma (Tanzania)", Cultures et Développement, 3 (1978), pp. 418-21.

91.   Langellier, "Tanzania--Africa's Conscience" Guardian Weekly, November 16, 1980, 14.

Chapter Nine

THE REPUBLIC OF GUINEA: THE DEATH OF A DREAM?

No ex-colony in Africa has displayed greater contradictions and paradoxes than the Republic of Guinea and its leader, Ahmed Sékou Touré. In 1958, Guinea shot into prominence when Touré challenged the new French constitution with the assertion that "we prefer poverty in freedom to riches in servitude", and was swiftly cast into independence by a vengeful Charles de Gaulle. Over the years, however, increasing numbers of Africans came to see Touré's Parti Democratique de Guinée as imposing, along with growing poverty, an even more terrible servitude than any the French had brought. At independence, when the French government sought to cripple the new state by withdrawing all its personnel and equipment, the PDG provided a lesson in how well-organized party cadres could provide at least the basic functions of a modern state. But again, over the years the constantly recurring deterioration and failure of organizations showed how limited were the possibilities of major structural transformations when the country lacked men and women who were both competent and dedicated to the professed ideals of the PDG.

Other contradictions abounded. The founders of the PDG had believed that the party and its ideology should be supreme over any individuals. Yet even before independence, one man had largely gained control as the interpreter of the ideology and the final source of authority in the party.[1] The party also earnestly tried to achieve mass participation both in party operations and in economic development projects, but at the same time it slid more brutally than most parties into mass repression, instigated and directed from the top. And yet Guinea was not just another case of a new African state which had fallen under the control of a self-serving authoritarian elite. The leaders of such regimes, as they spiralled down the paths of repression and economic collapse, usually lost any semblance of popular support long before their almost inevitable overthrow. Yet Sékou Touré as of mid-1982 had headed an independent African state for 24 years, longer than any other post-colonial African ruler, and despite the failures of his regime he could still draw enthusiastic support from huge crowds throughout the country.

Much of the explanation for these paradoxes can be found in the personality of Sékou Touré. This has contributed more than any other single factor to the kind of hold he developed over the people of Guinea, to the choice of policies pursued by the government, and to the kind of organization that the PDG became. The characteristic which first brought him to prominence and gave him wide support among the people was his courage and readiness to defy the Europeans, whether these were French colonialist, American or Russian. Then too, his fierce nationalism and insistence on the value of a basic "African" culture (despite his contemptuous dismissal of "African socialism" as a reactionary dream) appealed to ordinary Africans smarting under the scorn of the évolués. Touré's very lack of formal education (he had been expelled from secondary school as a student strike leader) and his youthfulness (he was only 30 when he became secretary-general of the PDG in 1952) helped his appeal to the "man in the street" against the older, more educated and more francophile Guinean politicians who had appeared after World War II. Coupled with his dynamic style, his forceful oratory, a skill in organizing urban workers and a reputation for personal integrity despite his frequent tactical shifts, these qualities gave him a powerful appeal to Guineans, especially in the early years of independence when the country represented a bold but beleaguered outpost surrounded by the forces of imperialism. Young, handsome and dynamic, Sékou Touré was one of the few African nationalist leaders who were genuinely charismatic.

The dark side of these strengths became apparent only later in Touré's career. His paranoia about enemies seeking to overthrow both him and the Revolution grew over the years as conditions in Guinea worsened, and as attempted <u>coups</u> masterminded by the French and Portugese did in <u>fact</u> take place. This paranoia as well as a deeply-rooted intolerance of challenges to his power led to his readiness to kill alleged enemies, and made many people suffer

for his beliefs. Finally, while he could be flex-
ible in many ways, he developed a stubborn commitment to ensuring that Guineans controlled all important facets of their society, whatever the cost in
terms of efficiency and well-being.

The results of Touré's regime since independence have been dismal by most conventional indicators of economic and social development. In per
capita GNP, it recorded only a 0.4% increase per
year from 1960 to 1976, a record considerably worse
than the average 1.7% increase recorded by the 37
African states listed by the World Bank, and also
poorer than any of its six neighbours except
Senegal.[2] A further indicator of a poor economic
performance was the fact that consumer demand for
many essential items could only be met by the thriving black market which ran parallel to the shambles
of the "official" economy.[3] Even more disturbing in
the light of Guinea's professed commitment to an
egalitarian society is its record in distributing
benefits in health and education, as compared to the
other two richest and avowedly inegalitarian ex-
French colonies, Senegal and the Ivory Coast. As
Table 6.1 (p. 98) showed, Guinea had little more
success in lowering its over-all death rate than
either of these two states, and it provided far
less educational opportunities even at the primary
level than did either of the other two. Particularly surprising in view of Sékou Touré's commitment to
the emancipation of women was the fact that less
than a fifth of school-age females were actually
enrolled in school in 1975.

The most significant comment on the Guinean
regime since independence is that made by Guineans
with their feet. The number of Guineans who have
fled to neighbouring countries, variously estimated
at between one and two million, is far too large to
be accounted for by the intelligentsia, traders and
others who were special targets of the regime: a
very large proportion were ordinary farmers and
their families, people who do not normally uproot
themselves and go to a strange territory. These
were the people on whose behalf the regime professed
to act.

Yet somehow the regime managed to survive these
failures. Its ability to repress opponents certainly contributed to this, but other factors were also
necessary. The strength of the party organization
and its ability to direct large numbers of people in
the pursuit of the regime's goals was important;
even more important was the ability of its ideology

to offer intangible benefits such as national pride. Finally, a leader who personally symbolized the defiance that succeeded in throwing off the strongly disliked yokes of colonial rule and of autocratic chieftaincy was able to call for a long time upon reserves of respect and admiration, no matter what he might subsequently do.

The clearest way to analyse these contradictory tendencies in Guinea's political evolution is to start with a chronological examination of Guinea's political evolution since World War II. I will concentrate on, first, the rise of the PDG and of Sékou Touré as its leader; second, the break with France in 1958 and its consequences; and third, the erosion of revolutionary idealism after independence, and the slide into repression, up to the government's near-abandonment in 1977 of its revolutionary goals.

THE FIGHT AGAINST FRANCE

The 1945 elections to the French Constituent Assembly marked the first occasion on which African "subjects" as distinct from citizens of France were able to vote. In Guinea, Yacine Diallo, a middle aged Ponty graduate and teacher, won the "African" seat largely on the basis of superior organization by his predominantly Fula political group. Like Houphouet-Boigny, he gained popular support at home for being one of the Africans who had achieved the abolition of forced labour and the indigenat, the system of harsh laws arbitrarily applied to Africans.[4] But unlike the Ivorian leader, he did not manage to build his coalition of supporters into an overwhelmingly strong political structure.

Meanwhile, in early 1946 the minority of Ponty graduates who had been influenced by Marxism through the Groupes d'Etudes Communistes created the Parti Progressiste de Guinée, with Madeira Keita as its first general secretary. Later that year the PPG joined with a number of delegates from ethnic groups, including Sékou Touré for the Union du Mandé, to represent Guinea at the founding of the Rassemblement Democratique Africaine in Bamako. However, the Socialists feared the RDA meeting would be Communist-dominated and stayed away. Thus Yacine Diallo, who had joined the socialists, declined the chance to participate as the leading Guinean spokesman. The next year the Guinea section of the RDA, the Parti Democratique de Guinea, was formed on the initiative of Madeira Keita and

196

Ray Autra.

The RDA, it will be recalled, was allied in Paris with the Communist Party of France, which imparted its organizational skills as well as its beliefs. However, the 1947 expulsion of the Communists from the French government led to a campaign by the colonial authorities against the RDA. In Guinea this took the form of pressure on the leaders of the PDG's constituent ethnic groups to withdraw their support, and also of direct attacks on the more militant members of the PDG. The lower level civil servants such as Sékou Touré were summarily fired, but were able to remain in Guinea. Ponty graduates were not so often fired, but they could be transferred to other French territories. The PDG's general secretary, Madeira Keita, first was posted to Dahomey in 1950 and then on his return in 1952, to the Soudan, with the probable connivance of Touré, who by that time had succeeded him as general secretary of the PDG. The other key PDG founder, Ray Autra, was sentenced in 1950 to two years in jail on trumped-up charges, and then in 1953 was posted to the Soudan, not to return until 1957.

While the PDG was severely weakened by the administration's attacks, it managed to keep its position as the major party of opposition to French rule. Until Touré gained the post of general secretary in 1952, the PDG remained largely a party of intellectuals, with only a weak mass base.[6] In its major electoral test, the elections to the French National Assembly in 1951, Touré won only 14.3% of the popular vote.[7] Yacine Diallo and two other candidates running for the SFIO and the Independents d'Outre-Mer used a combination of their own coalition-building skills and French repression of RDA campaigners to capture all three of Guinea's seats. However, the fact that the French concentrated their repression on the RDA helped underline its role as the chief nationalist party.

After 1951, the PDG immensely strengthened its position, while the French abandoned their hostility toward it. The PDG's strength increased in two major areas. In the cities, Touré's past as head of the Confederation General des Travailleurs (CGT) allowed the PDG to lead the fight to force the French to provide better wages and working conditions for Africans. This struggle had its major triumph in September-November 1953, when as a result of a bitter two-month general strike the minimum hourly wage was raised by 20%.[8] This success brought a great upsurge of support for the unions, whose total membership rose from 4,600 in 1953 to 44,000 in 1955.[9] It also marked Sékou Touré as a man who could fight the French and win. In the countryside, the fight was directed against the chiefs, who in most areas outside the traditional Fula chiefdoms had been largely discredited through being used as tools of the French administration, and also through their own eagerness to exploit their positions for personal advantage.[10] Here was a latent source of discontent waiting to be tapped; and the PDG's Marxist hostility to "exploiters" encouraged the party to tap it. In the coastal district, where traditional loyalties to chiefs had been eroding for years, and in the forest zone of the southeast, where the chiefs had always been weak, the PDG drew strong support. In the Mandingo area Touré's claim that he was descended from the 19th century warrior Samory, who had successfully resisted French colonialization for years, provided an additional powerful appeal. Only the Fula chiefdoms of the Futa Jallon, where the chiefs were still widely respected, offered much resistance to the PDG's spread, and even here the traditional "serf" villages provided a toehold for the PDG's attacks on the "feudal" abuses by the chiefs.

For their part, the French were becoming reconciled to the PDG as the most likely ruling party when self-government arrived. The RDA's disengagement from the French Communist Party in 1951 helped, although the Guineans' continuing links through the Communist-dominated CGT and the Marxist sympathies of many Guinean leaders still worried them. But in 1955-56 this fear too was partially quelled when Touré and other union leaders set up a separate African trade union federation.[11] Meanwhile, Touré himself had developed a close personal link with the liberal Governor-General of French West Africa, Bernard Cornut-Gentille, and had moderated the PDG's public stand, avoiding all talk of independence and emphasizing a continuing fondness for France once a more equal relationship was achieved.[12]

By 1956 when the French loi-cadre allowed the Territorial Assemblies to become elected legislatures controlling their territories' internal affairs, the PDG was firmly established as the dominant party. Sékou Touré and Saifoulaye Diallo won two of the three seats to the French National Assembly in 1956, winning 62% of the vote (the third seat was won by the head of the conservative pro-chief Bloc Africain de Guinée). In March 1957, the party won 56 of 60 seats in the Territorial Assembly elections and prepared to form the new government.[13] As yet there was no talk of independence, at least from the party leadership. Then came the collapse of the French Fourth Republic in 1958 and General de Gaulle's referendum on his tailor-made constitution. Like the Senegalese leaders, the Guineans seem to have wanted only to be assured that they could opt for independence at a later date, and not necessarily to take it immediately. However, de Gaulle was determined to show the world that unlike the Fourth Republic politicians, he would make no compromises; the African political leaders would associate with France on his terms or not at all.

When he arrived in Conakry on August 25, the huge crowd which came out to hear him and Touré was strongly anti-French and fervently pro-Touré. De Gaulle's attitude was blunt; Guinea could choose independence at the referendum by voting "No" and would have to bear the consequences, or it could vote "Yes" and be locked into permanent association with France. Touré, a man every bit as proud and stubborn as de Gaulle, drew wild cheers from the crowd with his passionate rejoinder, "We prefer poverty in freedom to riches in servitude". The insulted French President left the platform and Conakry in a huff, and refused ever again to see Sékou Touré. A few days later Touré announced that the PDG would ask Guineans for a "No" vote. The opposition parties joined in supporting this, and on September 28, by 1,134,324 votes to 56,981, Guineans rejected the French Community.[14]

The French response was swift. To make an example of Guinea, de Gaulle immediately ordered the withdrawal of all French officials and the termination of all French aid. In Conakry and elsewhere, departing French officials carried de Gaulle's pique to more elementary levels by destroying files, tearing out telephones, and smashing furniture. When on October 2 Guinea proclaimed itself independent, with Sékou Touré as President, it faced the task of building a new nation literally from scratch.

FREEDOM IN POVERTY?

Guinean policies since independence appear to have had four main objectives: to maintain Sékou Touré in power; to establish the control of the PDG under Touré's direction over all facets of Guinean life; to enable Guineans to determine their own pattern of both economic and cultural expression;

and to develop the economy so that it can underpin the regime. At independence, the regime started with a balance sheet on which great political assets were matched by substantial economic and social liabilities. Politically, the PDG was a well-organized and disciplined party whose cadres were capable of taking over a good number of the functions, such as tax collection and maintenance of order, jeopardized by the precipitate withdrawal of the French. Moreover, Guinea began independence with a great burst of popular enthusiasm for showing that Africans could do great things once they were freed from foreign control. Internationally, while France's allies held back from aiding Guinea both out of concern with its apparent "Communistic" tendencies and out of a sense of solidarity with the French, the Soviet bloc was quick to offer aid and personnel. Within Africa, while the other governments of French West Africa officially disapproved, Guinea's readiness to defy France made Touré a hero to most of the educated youth and many others besides. Ghana, still the only independent black African ex-colony, provided Guinea with an immediate loan of $28 million.

Guinea's economy also had one major asset in its huge bauxite reserves, variously estimated at 3.5 to 8 billion tons. Two major mines were already in production, and a third was underway. Furthermore, at independence Guinea had substantial exports of bananas, coffee, palm kernels and other agricultural crops, with bananas and coffee providing about 80% of export receipts in 1957. On the other hand, despite the continuous assertions of French governors that Guinea could be the "granary of West Africa" it was importing some 10,000 tons of rice each year, out of a total consumption of 250,000 tons.[15] More generally, it suffered from French under-investment, at least compared to Senegal and the Ivory Coast.[16]

A final asset worth noting is that the PDG had managed to reduce, even if not eliminate, ethnic tensions by its persistent policy of denying the significance of ethnicity when all Africans were struggling for their dignity. Although the Fulas still held somewhat aloof, they accepted the new order, despite predictions that they would make trouble after the PDG declared independence.[17] A number of policies aimed at breaking down ethnic fears, such as locating party officials outside their home regions, coupled with a careful balancing of different groups, helped prevent any outbreak of "tribal" conflict.

200

The major liability facing the PDG at independence was that Guinea was still heavily dependent on
France, both economically and administratively.
French trading firms controlled the currency, and
French officials provided most of the high-level administrative and technical skills in both government
and the private sector. There were only about 30
Guineans who occupied senior level posts in the public sector, and none in the private sector.[18] Nor
were there large numbers of Guineans who had sufficient training to take over high-level roles calling
for formally taught skills, There were about a
dozen university-level graduates in all fields and
some 2,500 students enrolled in secondary schools,[19]
a sharp increase from the 540 of ten years earlier.
The pool of Guineans who could cope with such basic
needs as bookkeeping, let alone with more sophisticated problems, was very small.

All this meant that for Guinea to choose any
course other than close links with France would be
difficult. If the French stayed, they could be expected to keep Guinea closely aligned with France in
trade, in diplomacy, and in its cultural aspirations.
But if they went, the lack of Guinean cadres to take
their place meant that many services and activities
that Guinea had come to expect would no longer function efficiently, if indeed they functioned at all.

The three years following independence saw the
economic patterns set which were to persist for two
decades. Touré and the PDG leadership attempted to
build a centrally-controlled economy which would
free Guinea from its subordination to France and the
other industrialized states, and would prevent the
growth of a class of private exploiters within the
country. In the process, however, they created a
"New Class" of party and state exploiters more ruthless, if less efficient, than their predecessors,
and failed even to mitigate the effects of this new
exploitation by providing a "trickle down" kind of
prosperity.

In the commercial sector, the first major step
toward building a socialist economy was the attempt
in 1959 to break the monopoly of the French trading
houses by banning private wholesale trading and setting up a state agency to handle imports of necessities and much of the export of cash crops.[20] To prevent the private firms from evading restrictions and
repatriating their profits, it was necessary also to
control the currency, which was accomplished in March
1960 by replacing the CFA franc with an inconvertible
Guinean one, and establishing a Bank of Guinea.[21]

The French trading companies, which had been the
major distributors of manufactured consumer goods
throughout Guinea, responded by closing most of
their local branches. In order to distribute goods,
the government was thus forced to set up a domestic
agency. In 1961 it broke this into 17 specialized
agencies, each responsible for an area such as construction, motor vehicles, or furniture.[22] After
some vacillations over the role to be left to the
private sector, in 1964 further rules curtailed the
number of private merchants and set up a commission
to allocate merchandise and control prices.[23] State
control over the economy was by this time nearly
total, at least in theory. While private industries
still survived, their existence was precarious because of their need for permits to import essential
materials (for example, the brewery frequently lost
beer production because it could not get hops or
spare parts for its machines), because the government's "Guineanization" requirements often cost them
key expatriate workers or saddled them with poorly
trained Guineans, and (a condition more peculiar to
Guinea) because senior management, European or
Guinean, might find themselves jailed during a government round-up after an alleged plot.[24] Meanwhile
a number of state enterprises had been set up to provide commodities such as tomato paste, matches, and
textiles, largely financed by foreign loans. Most
of these were a serious drain on the economy, since
a failure to ensure adequate supplies of raw materials, improper maintenance of equipment, and too
frequently incompetent or dishonest managers, all
combined to ensure that they operated far below
their intended capacities. Since imports were not
available, the result was usually shortages of widely
used consumer goods.

One anomaly in this massive state take-over of
economic life was the continuation in private hands
of the great bauxite mines. These provided a steadily increasing proportion of the country's exports,
rising from 47% in 1964 to 71% in 1972, a factor
which undoubtedly was a major consideration in the
government's restraint. It did nationalize the
French company Bauxites de Midi in 1961 but soon
negotiated an agreement with Harvey Aluminum, Alcan
and other world aluminum producers, to allow them to
export the Boké bauxite at a rate of six million
tons a year, in return for which Guinea held 49% of
the shares and was to receive 65% of the profits.[25]
The other major mine, Fria, which converted most of
its bauxite into alumina and exported some 700,000

tons a year, remained under the management of private firms throughout, although here too Guinea cut itself in for 49% ownership and a 63% share of the profits as the result of a new agreement in 1973.[26]

The agricultural sector, from which 85% of Guineans make their living, also suffered seriously from the government's attempts to create a "socialist" economy. Two steps toward an egalitarian land distribution were taken in 1959 and 1961: the first declared all land to be in the public domain, a move which made available for redistribution all the lands abandoned by the French when they retreated in 1958, while the second required all land-holders to use within six months any land that they had left unproductive for three years, or see it revert to the state. In practice, this meant that the local Party chairman or his relatives gained preferred access to the land.[27]

Basically, these rules left ordinary peasant families' holdings undisturbed, and thus with little incentive to work in the co-operatives that the government tried to encourage. Furthermore, the co-operatives were undermined by their association with earlier forced cultivation of crops for the government, the fact that there was no tradition of co-operative farming or ownership of herds or equipment beyond the extended family, and the tendency of some local Party leaders to use co-operative goods and outputs for their own benefit. Given these problems, it was not surprising to find that membership had fallen from a peak of 60,000 in 1962 to 34,413 (about 4% of the total farming population) in 1964, or that the output of their two main products, bananas and coffee, fell from 55,000 and 14,000 tons respectively in 1960 to 37,000 and 7,000 tons in 1965.[28]

The saddest story of a good idea gone wrong, however, was the <u>investissement humain</u> programme started in 1959. The idea of this programme was that ordinary Guineans could provide many of the physical facilities they needed, such as schools, hospitals and roads, through their voluntary labour, thus freeing the financial resources of the central government to provide specialized equipment and skilled technical help. The programme started with a great burst of enthusiasm in 1959, but soon began to go sour. Partly this was because the government's lack of skilled personnel to guide local groups meant that these groups plunged into projects beyond their abilities, and thus became disillusioned. But the government also encouraged groups to build

schools, dispensaries and other needed community
facilities, and then could not provide the teachers,
dispensers, nurses and other personnel to operate
the facilities. More serious yet was the way the
programme became perverted from its original goal of
providing facilities that would improve social conditions to the quite different goal of providing
"housing for government functionaries and headquarters for party officials". Data provided by the
party itself shows the trend away from such amenities
as storehouses and toward works primarily of benefit
to the Party (Table 9.1).

Table 9.1: Accomplishments of the "investissement
humain" programme,1959-61

Construction	1959	1960	1961
Schoolrooms	335	741	572
Hospitals	--	1	--
Dispensaries	28	33	48
Maternity Clinics	--	1	--
Infirmaries	--	22	--
Party Headquarters	38	436	779
Mosques	28	118	214
Administrative Housing	81	147	185
Administrative Office Buildings	15	33	79
Storehouses	227	178	158
Airplane Hangars	--	19	74
Village Improvements	--	--	5
Total Projects	752	1,729	2,114

Source: Victor Dubois, "Reorganization of the
Guinean Economy" American Universities Field Staff
Reports, (West African Series) Vol. 6, 1, p. 14.

By 1961 the human investment programme had ceased to
be an outlet for the release of revolutionary enthusiasm and had turned into compulsory activities

indistinguishable from the forced labour of the colonial regime, with the youth movement of the PDG filling the role of the colonial police in bullying the populace into working.[30]

Government control over the prices of agricultural products and over the prices and supply of consumer goods was intended to ensure that "farmers receive adequate pay for their products and...that consumer goods are sold to them at reasonable prices".[31] However, the actual effect was very different. Since consumer goods in Guinea were in short supply because of the government's foreign exchange problems and the failure of domestic factories, few farmers saw much point in selling produce through the official channels. Two options were open to them. One was to withdraw from the cash crop economy and to concentrate on producing only supplies for one's own family. The other was to take advantage of Guinea's porous borders and smuggle one's produce to Guinea's hard-currency neighbours, there to exchange it for desirable consumer goods. While the volume of this contraband trade cannot be measured precisely, it was estimated at $10-15 million in the mid-1960s.[32]

Although the government undertook sporadic drives against smugglers, the contraband imports supported a black market in Guinea parallel to the legal state-run economy on a scale comparable to Eastern Europe. The black market, in fact, was probably the major factor in keeping Guineans from revolting against the perennial shortages of the official economy. But it created the rural bourgeoisie that state socialism was supposed to prevent[33] and it helped undermine both the state and the ideals of the PDG. At the same time, neither the black market nor the official market could provide sufficient food for all Guineans. Despite the PDG's efforts to encourage self-sufficiency, commercial imports of rice rose from 10,000 tons a year at the end of the colonial regime, to some 60,000 tons a year from 1967 to 1974,[34] using practically all the foreign exchange obtained from taxes on mineral exports.[35]

While ordinary people suffered, party and government officials prospered. Even in the early 1960s observers remarked on the luxury villas built by high government and party officials, both for their own enjoyment and to rent out for hard currency to foreign missions.[36] Although Touré himself retained a reputation for honesty, the visible corruption of many of his close associates made it difficult for the ordinary man to retain the idealism that had powered such programmes as "human investment".

The ultimate response to all these problems -- forced labour imposed by party militants, lack of fair prices for farm products and of goods to meet everyday needs, and a disillusionment with the ideals professed by the PDG -- was the vast exodus of ordinary farmers and their families to neighbouring states. Over the years an estimated 500,000 Guineans resettled in each of Senegal and the Ivory Coast, and as many again in other African states,[37] an ironic comment on the "benefits" of the revolution for the ordinary man.

Quite a number of exiles had more pressing reasons for leaving. For the intelligentsia and other conspicuous elites, the alternative to flight was often execution or imprisonment in one of Touré's purges after an alleged plot. There was no shortage of grievances among these elites; the teachers, civil servants and other intellectuals had been angered by their failure to receive as many high-level jobs as they had anticipated, by the anti-intellectual tone of the PDG, and by the decline in their living standards, while the traders had been even more severely hit by the restrictions on the private commercial sector.[38] Members of these groups in exile formed a series of groups aimed at overthrowing Touré's regime, but never were able to build an effective united front.[39]

Ineffectual as most of their organizations were, these exiles provided Touré with the continuing spectre of enemies on Guinea's borders waiting to destroy the "Revolution". From 1960 onward, successive "plots" involving the exiles, the French government, and various pro-French African states were "discovered" by the Guinean government, and provided convenient pretexts for Touré to liquidate domestic critics. We should not dismiss these allegations of French-inspired plots as totally groundless. Since the sinister Jacques Foccart was the chief African advisor to both de Gaulle and Pompidou, and successive French governments never showed any qualms about interfering in the internal affairs of their ex-colonies, there likely was French involvement in some of the plots against the regime. Nevertheless, it seems likely that most of the plots were carefully exaggerated by the Guinean government in order to liquidate opponents and strengthen its support at home.

The first discovery of a plot against Guinea erupted in April 1960 with the allegation that French nationals and Guineans had been conspiring to assassinate Touré. Ten Guineans died under torture in the round-up following this revelation. In November 1961 a "Teachers' Plot" aided by the Soviet Union was alleged after teachers had demanded equal pay for equal work, and criticized government policies. Several members of the Teachers' Union executive were jailed, including Ray Autra, who received ten years.[40] The Soviet Ambassador was summarily expelled. In 1965, following an attempt by some traders to form an opposition party (permitted under Guinea's constitution) a plot was discovered involving the government of the Ivory Coast and French ministers, which led to all those associated with the new party being imprisoned.[41] In 1969, following two officers' critical remarks against the Head of State at a party, a number of senior officers were arrested, along with such prominent political figures as Fodeba Keita, a very effective minister of defence, and Diawadou Barry, a pre-Independence opponent of Touré, on charges of working with French, Ivorien, and Senegalese agents to overthrow the regime. Keita and Barry were executed.

In 1970 came an event which showed some substance to the government's charges of external plots. On November 22, 1970, an invasion force including both Portuguese troops and Guinean exiles landed in Conakry. One group attacked and destroyed the headquarters of the PAIGC, but missed Amilcar Cabral, who was staying elsewhere that night. The other group seized control of two military barracks, but were driven back from the Presidential Palace where Touré was staying. Portuguese involvement in the invasion, in retaliation for Touré's harbouring the PAIGC guerrillas, was widely denounced, but Guinea soon managed to lose much of the sympathy it had gained by the savagery of the government's response. A series of mass public "trials" from which the accused persons were absent produced 91 death sentences. A number of the executions were public hangings, carried out in what the government called a "carnival atmosphere". In July 1971 eight of the top army officers were also sentenced to death for their alleged complicity in the invasion.[42]

Yet another "plot" was unveiled in 1976 with the arrest of a number of the more "pragmatic" wing of the PDG. A number of those involved were Fulas, and this prompted Touré to reverse his long-standing policy of denying the significance of ethnic affiliation in Guinean politics. Describing the conspiracy as a "Fula plot", he claimed the Fulas were "racialist" and that they sought to establish an exclusively Fula government. There were some grounds to his claim; Fulas had consistently provided a substantial share of both internal and exile opposition to Touré, and a number had been jailed or executed for their alleged complicity in various plots. This plot continued the tradition; among those jailed was Diallo Telli, the former Secretary of the OAU, who died mysteriously the next year while in prison.

By 1977, very few of Sékou Touré's close political associates had survived unscathed. Of the 71 ministers and secretaries of state he had appointed nine had been shot or hanged; eight had died in detention; 18 were doing hard labour for life, and another 20 had served prison terms and had subsequently been freed; five had escaped abroad; and only eleven had avoided condemnations.[45]

With a growing number of embittered exiles around his borders, the second largest ethnic group in the country thoroughly upset by his attacks on them, and most of the rest of the population driven into a mood of sullen indifference toward his revolution by economic hardship and the corruption of his elite, by 1977 Sékou Touré was in a very precarious position. He could probably continue to retain his position by purges and terror, although this would continue to create further families seeking vengeance until finally someone managed to kill him. What he could no longer hope to do was to rouse the population to the massive participation that had seemed possible in the first days of independence, and without this participation he could not achieve the goals of socialist communes, worker-run factories and other major transformations that he professed to want for Guinean society.

In 1977 came two major shifts in Touré's policies. First, in July he announced an amnesty for Guinea's political exiles, provided they were willing to be "rehabilitated", and also proclaimed a special investment code which would enable these exiles to start private businesses and to keep their funds in hard currency.[46] While this could have been merely a trap, or subject to one of Touré's capricious changes later, the second event made it likely that he would try to honour these promises. On August 27, 1977, thousands of market women marched on the presidential palace, protesting against a decree replacing their village markets with co-op stores, and more generally against the perpetual shortages of trade goods, the harassment by Touré's

"economic police", and the continued hardships
under the regime. The militia opened fire upon the
women, and several were killed.[47] This protest by
a group whom Touré had hitherto thought were among
his most devoted supporters severely shook him. The
economic police were disbanded, and contraband goods
began to appear freely in the markets, easing the
extreme shortages that had persisted so long.[48] At
the same time, Guinea increased its overtures to
Western investors to come and develop its mineral
resources, and sought to reduce its ties to the
Eastern European bloc. So far did he go in these
overtures that in 1979 a mini-summit of left-wing
heads of state held in Benin declined to invite him
to attend, on the grounds that he was becoming too
closely aligned with the Americans.

It is still too early to say that Guinea will
turn into a peripheral capitalist state or that the
transformation strategy has been abandoned for good,
and it is also too early to know whether Touré can
survive what appears to be an abandonment of the
major goals he has always professed to be fighting
for. Nevertheless, it seems unlikely that the PDG
can ever retain the widespread acquiescence that was
necessary for it originally to impose its transformationist schemes.

JUDGING THE REVOLUTION: WHO DID IT SERVE?

What did the "Guinean Revolution" do for the
people of Guinea? Judging it by the basic criterion
for a poor colony, whether it succeded in providing
more material well-being for most Guineans, it must
be considered a failure. We have already noted that
it failed to achieve economic growth, and that in
the general improvement of peoples' health and educational opportunities it lagged behind other states
with comparable resources. Similarly, in producing
food it fell increasingly behind needs, thus forcing
people into purchasing higher-priced imports. Material well-being for the ordinary man was further
undercut by the amounts drained away through corrupt officials, a condition encouraged by the
attempts to bring most of the economy under centralized control.

This economic failure had a pervasive effect in
undermining the regime's achievements in other areas,
notably its instilling of national pride and achieving a degree of ethnic integration by its over-
arching strategy. Guineans in 1958 were able to

take great pride in their country because of their readiness to do what other French Africans only dreamed of doing in saying "No" to de Gaulle's constitution. For several years thereafter, Touré was a hero to younger and more radical elements in all of Africa, and a reproach to the cowardice of their states' leaders. It took years of economic mismanagement and the bloodthirsty purges of critics to wipe off most of Touré's lustre outside Guinea, and within Guinea he still retained a good deal of popularity. Many young people who grew up under the PDG regime regarded their country with pride for its courage and innovation, and felt that this offset the material shortages.[49] On the other hand, the magnitude of the exodus from Guinea made it clear that not all Guineans felt this idealistic commitment to their country.

The PDG's greatest success, its ability to overcome the deep ethnic divisions that had plagued Guinea before independence, also came to be compromised in part by its economic failure, in that this failure stimulated the search for scapegoats.

Since the Guinean nationalist movement had to contend with the most deep-rooted ethnic antagonism in French West Africa, and started out as a collection of ethnically-based parties, the fact that by independence the PDG had managed to bring all ethnic groups, even the Fulas, into a unified movement still must rank as its finest achievement. Further, despite the fact that Fulas were prominent in all subsequent plots against the government, Touré and his ministers took great pains until 1976 both to deny the importance of tribal origins and to ensure that in party and government offices all tribes had a reasonably fair representation. It is hard to be sure what motivated the denunciation of the "Fula plot" in 1976, or to know how far it permanently damaged the hope of the government to create a state safe from being torn apart by "tribalism". We can say, however, that up to that time conflicts based on ethnic differences were less severe in Guinea than they were in most other West African states, and the PDG deserves most of the credit for this.

The darkest stain on the Guinean record, and one which may yet lead to bloody vengeance if Touré is ousted, is the government's treatment of its opponents. The PDG set one unenviable first in 1960 when it became the first government of an independent African state to kill opponents in its custody.[50] The hundreds of persons who were executed or died in prison, and the thousands who were jailed and tortured meant that a very large number of Guinean families have strong motives for revenge against the PDG leaders responsible. While Guinea has not seen the random killings by individual soldiers that marked Amin's regime in Uganda nor the systematic massacre of an entire elite that the Tutsi rulers of Burundi carried out against the Hutu, killing and torture as a means of terrorizing the population into acquiescence became firmly entrenched. Although there have not been any major purges reported since 1977, and in fact the regime has been releasing numbers of political prisoners since that time,[51] it could quickly return to repression if its current "liberalization" measures lead to more public challenges to its power.

Before dismissing the Guinean attempt at transformation as an unmitigated failure, we should note that however short of the intentions of its instigators the revolution fell, the intentions themselves did have a considerable effect upon Guinean society. The fact that Sékou Touré professed to be seeking an egalitarian transformation of society, a vanguard role for the PDG in this transformation, and the rooting out of all aspects of the colonial relationship, had a number of effects even though these goals were not achieved. The vanguard role for the PDG meant that the structure of opportunities lay through the party, and thus these opportunities were controlled by whoever first gained control of the PDG. It also provided an incentive for keeping the party functioning as an organization. Furthermore, anyone wishing to rise in the PDG had to at least pay lip service to its ideals, and while the gap between these ideals and the actual behaviour of the elite might induce cynicism among the masses, still the fact of having to profess the ideals publicly helped keep them alive, even if only as a measure of the regime's failure. Finally, anything that appeared to perpetuate colonial relationships, such as relying on the French for technical aid, was illegitimate, and support for such relations was evidence of a betrayal of the revolution. In all these respects post-independence Guinea was stamped in a very different mold than other francophone states, and thus even though the transformation strategy may eventually have been abandoned, the differences will persist for many years.

How "inevitable" was the course that Guinea
took during decolonization and independence? At
what point could it have evolved in different directions, and to what extent was the fact that it took
the directions it did attributable to the choices
of an individual leader, and to what extent to the
interaction of broader social forces? I will
examine the possibility that Guinea might have
taken different directions at a number of specific
points. Could another party have captured the anti-
colonial movement? Could another leader have taken
control of the PDG? Would events have gone differently if Guinea had voted "Yes" in 1958? Could
Touré have followed a different development strategy?
Could the strategy he did pursue have worked under
any attainable conditions? And when it became
apparent by the mid-1960s that it was not working,
could he have changed it radically? Finally how
has Touré managed to survive, despite his failure
to deliver on the promises of the "Revolution"? And
what has been the role of his ideology in his survival?

When we consider that in the Ivory Coast,
Senegal and most other states, parties with very
different programmes emerged as the dominant nationalist parties, our first question may be why a more
"moderate" party did not take the lead in advocating
African nationalism in Guinea and thus forestall the
PDG. The obvious possibility was a party built
around Yacine Diallo, who had shared with Houphouet-
Boigny and Senghor the credit for abolishing the
indigenat and forced labour in 1946. Like these two
leaders, Diallo was pro-French, a moderate in
economic affairs and tended to work through the
established traditional rulers. But the crucial
difference, I suggest, was that Diallo did not break
with the French socialists in the 1940s to create
an all-African movement. Like Lamine Gueye of
Senegal, he remained associated with the white
colonial rulers, and thus was out-flanked by a more
militantly African movement. His pro-chief orientation would also have been a handicap outside the
Fouta Jallon, but inland from Lower Guinea not likely a fatal one. It was his failure to capture and
articulate the anti-French sentiment which pervaded
all the French West African colonies at the time
that prevented his establishing an effective hegemony.

It might also have been conceivable for the

French to have crushed the PDG so thoroughly that a non-militant, pro-French party could have taken power, somewhat as their suppression of the Union des Populations du Cameroun opened the way for Amadou Ahidjo to become the president of Cameroun. I think this is a rather less plausible scenario than that of a moderately nationalist party pre-empting the stage, both because of the balance between the strength of the PDG and that of its opponents, and because of the restraints which the French imposed on themselves. Unlike the UPC, which was essentially confined to the Bamileke people of Cameroun, the PDG managed to transcend any identification with a specific ethnic group, and thus obtained supporters throughout the country. It was the administration-backed parties that tended to be identified with specific ethnic groups, and thus to restrict their own chances of making a successful electoral appeal. Furthermore, the French were not completely ruthless in their attacks against the PDG, even at the height of their concern over its Communist affiliations. While they transferred and fired Guineans who supported the PDG, they did not jail large numbers of them, and certainly did not execute them as Touré later was to execute his opponents. The effect of their persecution was to create martyrs, and thus to help enhance the PDG's legitimacy as the major opponent of the colonial regime, without destroying its effectiveness.

It was by no means inevitable, then, that the PDG should take over power in Guinea. The fact that the mobilized population were wage workers rather than small plantation owners made a situation more conducive to the PDG's type of appeal, but the rural masses who ultimately formed the voting backbone of the PDG could certainly have been guided toward different goals beyond getting rid of the French.

French repression was the critical factor, however, in allowing Sékou Touré to take the leadership of the PDG. The fact that the party's first general secretary, Madeira Keita, was shipped away from Guinea in 1950 just before the expanded franchise gave the PDG its chance to use its organizing abilities, and that most of the other more educated cadres were similarly either transferred to other territories or jailed left the way clear for Touré to take the job of general secretary in 1952. It is possible that Touré's work among the trade unions would have given him a powerful enough base that he could have taken over the leadership of the PDG in any event, or else set up a breakaway movement.

Whether a fight within the PDG would have hurt its
accession to power is unknowable, but it does seem
more likely that a more conservative party could
have made headway if the radical movement was split.

In any case, how much difference would a different leader have made to the PDG? I suspect that
if an intellectual like Madeira Keita, Ray Autra or
Saifoulaye Diallo had become leader, the party
would have been a more successful one in its
economic actions. A leader who had more assurance
that he belonged at the top, and was less paranoid
than Touré, would have been far less likely to turn
to coercion to keep revolutionary goals in sight.
Possibly also he might have been less doctrinaire
when it became apparent that the party's cadres did
not measure up to the job of restructuring Guinean
society.

The major fork in Guinea's evolutionary road
was its "No" vote in the 1958 referendum. Up to de
Gaulle's visit a month before the vote, and even
after, the decision to vote against the new French
constitution was by no means a certainty, and had
the General been more conciliatory on the right of
secession, or had Touré been more diplomatic in his
emphasis on this question, the PDG might well have
decided to stay within the French community.
Madagascar, with its bitter memories of the French
massacres of 1947, Senegal, with its still strong
party rivalries, and above all, the PDG's close RDA
affiliates in Mali, all were dubious about continuing the "French connection" but all voted "Yes".
To be sure, the Madagascar Social Democratic Party
under Philibert Tsirinana was far more conservative
and French-oriented than the PDG, and the
Senegalese leaders had to contend with the pressure
applied by the French through the marabouts, but
the Malien leaders of the Union Soudanaise-RDA were
no less radical than the PDG. While the US-RDA
leaders may have been a bit more restrained by the
fact that their pro-French rivals, the PSP, were
still stronger than any challengers to the PDG in
Guinea, and by the risk that the French might resort
to more blatant rigging of the results in a state
bordering Algeria, still I think the main reasons
why they chose to vote "Yes" were that they had no
direct personal confrontation with de Gaulle, and
that they had become more accustomed to using tact
and diplomacy rather than confrontation to get their
way.[52] Touré, who had by this time firmly established his personal ascendancy over the PDG and
especially its Directing Committee[53] was more used

to a confrontationist approach, and was impulsive
and stubborn by nature. Having in effect been
challenged by de Gaulle to take independence with
its consequences if he dared, his response was to
take the plunge.

Had Touré been less impetuous and swung the
PDG to a "Yes" vote, Guinea's history would have
been very different. The French would have remained
strong within both the public and private sectors,
and Guinea's economy would have remained linked
closely with that of France. Agricultural exports
would probably have been maintained at their existing levels, and possibly mineral development would
have proceeded faster, though French advisors
might well have blocked other Western investors
from any significant developments. Most of the
social changes, from investissement humain through
co-operatives to the civic brigades for youth[54]
would likely have been curtailed, as would the massive state investments in the industrial sector.
All of this would have meant continuing on a moderate level of economic well-being, though with only
limited potential for long-term development, and at
the cost of creating Guinean cadres firmly committed
by their jobs to maintaining the status quo. A
major cost would have been the psychological one
that Guineans would have continued to feel themselves dependent on European help, and that they had
not really rid themselves of colonialism. Then too,
without Guinea's example, the other French West
African states would undoubtedly have found it much
more difficult to move toward independence.

With hindsight, it can be suggested that this
might not have been a worse fate than what did
happen. The economic hardships of the first twenty
years of independence seem now to be diminishing
only because Guinea is finally entering the neo-
colonial economic relationship of exporting raw
materials in exchange for manufactured goods that it
could have had ever since 1958. Whether the psychological damage of continuing subordination would
have been worse than the loss of self-confidence in
their own abilities produced in Guineans by their
continuing economic failures is hard to answer, but
it seems likely that it would have been no more
serious.

Within the framework of "self-reliance" forced
upon it by the 1958 referendum result, was there
some other strategy that Guinea could have pursued
that would have brought better results? The strategy that was followed, such as it was, was first to

ensure the supremacy of politics over economics
(which meant in practice to ensure the control of
all activities by the PDG) and second, to establish
in Guinea the range and types of industrial activity appropriate to a "modern" state, but in a way
intended to ensure that these industries were controlled by, and operated for the benefit of, all
the people rather than individual private operators.
In practice this meant setting up large-scale,
state-owned factories using imported technology and
relying on high-volume production to cover their
substantial capital costs. The "peoples' role" in
this was largely to respond to exhortations for
improved productivity within a framework decided
from above.

The only departure from a very conventional,
"top-down" developmental strategy came in the rural
areas, first with the "human investment" programmes,
and later with the attempt to create "civic brigades" and colleges of rural education which were
to form nuclei for socialist communities.[55] It is
not clear how far these succeeded in drawing people
into active participant roles; but given the PDG's
tendency to be more "centralist" than "democratic",
it seems unlikely that there was much scope for
local decisions on such questions as whether to
grow crops for local consumption or commercial sale,
obtaining machinery and so on.

The kind of strategy that might have worked
would be a much more decentralized, "bottom-up" one
utilizing "alternate technologies" and the popular
enthusiasm generated at independence. However,
there was only about a year, in 1958-59, before
this enthusiasm flagged in the face of economic
hardships and political repression; and at this
time Guinea was desperately short of the trained
cadres who might have been able to make such a
strategy work. Further, at that time a rural-based,
low-technology approach was scarcely thinkable,
let alone fashionable: like all other African
leaders of the period, Touré held a vision of building Guinea's economy on high-technology industrialization, albeit while maintaining African cultural
roots. The readiness to accept such showpieces as
the huge printing press in Conakry, the Mamou canning factory and the Nzerekoré plywood factory, all
of which relied heavily upon imported machinery,
illustrates this attitude.[56] The path of a more
modest but genuinely "self-reliant" development, in
short, was just not open for consideration.

Might the central planning strategy chosen

by Touré at independence might have worked? And to
what extent were Touré's own shortcomings responsible for its failure? There were three major reasons
for the failure of the strategy. Two of these,
corruption both among the elite and at the grass
roots, and repression, helped to kill the popular
support that was a requisite for the PDG's approach.
But considerably more important in preventing industrial and agricultural improvement was poor planning, both in design and in implementation. This in
turn was attributable to several factors: the inadequacy of the cadres of both the party and the
administration for such a complex and sophisticated
task; the political constraints under which schemes
had to work, such as the lack of incentives for
farmers to provide inputs for factories, and the
uncertainties affecting managers; and the tendency
to think in terms of grandiose schemes, such as a
single giant canning factory or printing plant,
rather than on a more modest scale.

Some of these factors were clearly beyond any
leader's control, at least in the short run. There
was no way any scheme could turn a clerk or party
militant into a competent factory manager in a matter of weeks or months. Yet actions had to be
taken quickly; for example, French firms were taking
francs out of Guinea at a great rate just before
Guinea switched to an inconvertible currency. However, some factors were within the leader's control;
the size and nature of various development projects,
for example, and the political constraints under
which schemes operated. It is rather ironic, in
fact, that the same Sékou Touré who was both praised
and suspected for his flexibility, pragmatism and
readiness to compromise on such issues as dealing
with the French before independence, and with other
states afterwards,[57] should have imposed a doctrinaire programme of price controls on farmers' sale
of their produce. The leader, in other words, had
some responsibility for the poor planning which led
to his strategy's failure.

He also had some responsibility for the corruption which seriously undermined popular willingness
to sacrifice and struggle for the PDG's goals.
While the rapid swelling of the party's ranks with
opportunists when it appeared likely to win in 1956
inevitably created pressure for freedom for party
functionaries to line their own nests, Touré seemed
most reluctant to crack down on abuses at the top,
even though the elite's Mercedes and sumptuous
houses were clearly visible to everyone.[58] It was

217

not that he lacked any dedicated and hard-to-corrupt militants; at least until after independence, there were a number of such people in the party. But Touré seemed more concerned with preventing threats to his personal hold on power than with rooting out corruption among his ministers, and it has even been suggested that despite his reputation for honesty, that he has benefitted since 1960 from the proceeds of the nationalized diamond mines to the tune of some three million dollars a year.[59] With corruption firmly established at the top, it becomes very difficult to root it out among lower officials, with whom the ordinary man deals every day. Then too, corruption is further encouraged by the impossibility of working under the formal rules; for example, throughout most of the 1960s and 1970s, if it were not for the black market and smuggling there would simply have been no consumer goods available. Yet faced with corruption at all levels of government, it is asking a great deal of the ordinary man to expect him to sacrifice his personal well-being for some nebulous public goal.

Repression also contributed to the failure of the grand economic strategy, both through driving into exile many of the talented Guineans who might have helped make it work, and through inducing in those who stayed a self-protecting attitude which overrode their readiness to work for the state's goals. The "referendum honeymoon" had augured well, with the leaders of both the Bloc Africain de Guinée and the Democratie Socialiste de Guinée, the two main opposition parties, being taken into the government. But from the 1960 plot onward the spiral of repression--further plots--further repression moved steadily onward. This was part of a more general intolerance of dissent which contributed to the lack of corrective criticism when problems arose, an intolerance already apparent in dealing with party members even before independence.

Would it have been possible for Touré to change to a more "liberal" development strategy of reconciling foreign investors, and directing their activities toward building a sounder domestic economy? Specifically, in 1962-63, when the problems arising from setting up Guinea's own currency and banking and from channelling all imports and exports through huge state corporations had led to widespread smuggling and the growth of a tolerated private sector, could Guinea have moved toward reinstating private firms to carry on the country's wholesale and retail trade, instead of plunging in 1964 toward much tighter restrictions on private traders and more state trading corporations?

At that point, while Touré's reputation for unpredictability and caprice had not yet been so firmly established that foreign investors simply would not believe him, he might have succeeded in luring some trading firms into returning or entering the country. Until mining began to bring in foreign exchange, five or ten years ahead, he would also have had to offer incentives to farmers to provide produce for sale, which would require imports of popular consumer goods from the Western industrialized states. All of this would have required a substantial number of expatriates, though Guinea could have imposed some "Guineanization" rules for personnel and kept the Guinean currency or some other form of control over the foreign exchange situation.

The two major problems with such a "liberalization" strategy were, first, whether foreigners would respond favourably, and second, if they did, how Guineans would react. Guinea's major attraction was its minerals, which would take some time to provide economic benefits. Meanwhile, to stimulate the economy through agriculture would require the cooperation of both the farmers and a distribution network, and the latter in particular would involve letting both Guinean and foreign traders accumulate a good deal of wealth, as well as becoming powerful and influential figures largely free from political control. Since the foreigners at this stage would almost certainly be French and the Guineans would be those who had opposed the PDG, PDG militants would have been badly upset by what would appear to be a betrayal of the "Revolution".

Still, Touré might have managed such a shift in policy. The militants' disaffection could have been balanced by the relief of the women's movement and other ordinary people hit hard by the loss of consumer goods. Nor were the militants in a position to influence the army to stage a coup, or to capture control of the PDG, although they could embarrass Touré in the latter forum.

I think the main reason why this switch was not tried in 1962-63 was because of Touré's own concerns. His policy was to eliminate wherever possible the control exercised by the French over Guinea's economy, and liberalizing trade and encouraging French firms to re-enter would have run directly contrary to this goal. Even more important was his growing concern even at this stage with the "permanent plot"

he perceived against his regime and against his
personal hold on office. He had already found one
"plot" directed by the French in 1960, and had
killed the Guineans he had alleged to be involved
in it. It would be imprudent, or would undermine
the credibility of his plot claim to encourage
French agents to re-enter the country. Furthermore,
allowing Guinean traders to accumulate wealth could
also be dangerous, since wealth gave influence and
that influence could be used against the regime.
On security grounds then, a switch to a more liberal
policy was unlikely; but this was a conscious choice
after weighing various factors.

As of mid-1982, Sékou Touré was the longest-
ruling leader of an independent African state; only
Haile Selassie of Ethiopia and William Tubman of
Liberia had stayed in power longer during this
century. In view of the economic hardships Guineans
have suffered, the number of plots alleged against
him, and the exile communities who would dearly love
to remove him, his survival seems something of a
miracle. How has he managed to survive so long?

Terror clearly plays a substantial part in preventing his overthrow; anyone contemplating a coup,
or suspected of disloyalty, risks imprisonment,
torture and death. But despite the reliance on
stamping out "counter-revolutionary elements"
through as pervasive a system of informing as any
in Eastern Europe, Touré can also still inspire
considerable enthusiasm, particularly among his
major social bases of youth and women, who have both
gained socially from the regime's policies. More
broadly he has maintained a wide appeal as the
symbol of Guinean nationalism, first in the successful fight for independence from France, and then
against the continuing series of plots against
Guinean independence emanating from France, the
United States, the Soviet Union and the rest of the
sea of enemies that surround Guinea. While undoubtedly the frequent rapprochements with old adversa-
ries and the charges against Guineans who are too
coincidentally potential rivals to Touré weaken the
credibility of the government's claim to be surrounded by perennial plots, still events like
Portugal's 1970 invasion do give credence to the
government's claims.

Still more important in keeping Touré in power
is his astute use of ideology. The "permanent
plot", his killing of opponents, and the presence
of a huge community are explained not in terms of
Sékou Touré's personal desire for power, but as

220

costs of bringing about the revolution which will
ultimately make life better for all Guineans.
Obviously a "revolution" cannot please everyone,
and those who oppose Touré are those who stood to
benefit from the restoration of colonial relations
in economic matters, and who would prefer a non-
African culture to the "authentic" African one that
the PDG is developing. This claim that Touré is
the true bearer of the revolutionary ideology has
the further advantage that it enhances his image as
the pure and incorruptible leader, an image which
has survived despite the manifest evidence of personal self-aggrandisement among the elite around
him.

But this role as the bearer of the revolutionary ideology also raises a serious problem. To
shift, as he has been doing since 1978, toward the
neo-colonial relationship with Western corporations
that he has denounced in neighbouring states under-
cuts his credibility as no previous actions have
done. At the same time, the easing of repression
can also be seen as an admission of doubt in the
rightness of his previous course, as well as an
opportunity for others to challenge his rule. It is
hard to see at this stage how he can avoid relying
primarily upon force to maintain himself in power,
and even this approach leaves his future a precarious one.

The "Guinean Revolution" has to be judged, I
suggest, as a failure, and a considerable part of
the blame for that failure must rest with Sékou
Touré. The strategy he chose of massive industrialization, with a concomitant neglect of the rural
areas, was a questionable one for a country with
Guinea's pool of human skills, although in fairness,
very few people in 1958 were even talking about
alternative approaches more compatible with the
talents and resources available to a predominantly
rural country. More serious, however, were two
problems of human personality. The powers to be
used by many officials in running the economy and
society called for a good deal of self-restraint,
and reinforcing this, a structure which permitted
effective checks from below. However, many of the
individuals who came to exercise power appeared
notably lacking in self-restraint, particularly in
financial matters, and at the same time the tendency
to build the PDG into a highly-centralized, "top-
down" organization severely restricted the possibility of grass-roots curbs on official' use of their
power. This takes us squarely to the final problem,

Touré's own personality. Although he clearly was
able to exercise leadership up to and even after
independence, thereafter he slid steadily into the
spiral of coercion. To some extent he was driven
to this by events; undoubtedly some of the plots
against his regime were real, and too gentle an
approach might have been fatal not only to his
personal survival, but to any hope of Guinea's
staying free of a capitalist embrace. Still, it
seems pretty clear that his certainty that he knew
what was good for Guinea, and even more his personal insecurity and paranoia, were crucially important in his continuing attempts to tighten his grip
on the country by an ever-increasing use of force
and terror.

Yet despite both his failings and the pain he
inflicted on others, we can have some sympathy for
Sékou Touré. He was no General Amin or Emperor
Bokassa, pursuing primarily his personal gratification. Like Kwame Nkrumah and Julius Nyerere, he
had an inspiring vision of what he would like his
country to become, and like them he managed to
impart this vision to thousands of his countrymen,
even though it clearly would involve far more risks,
changes and sacrifices for all Guineans than would
the path of continuing subordination to France.
Far more than either Nkrumah or Nyerere, however,
he was ready to abandon persuasion for force, and
while this probably contributed to his survival, it
certainly ensured that the slim chance of being
able to achieve a socialist society was destroyed.

NOTES

1. See R.W. Johnson, "The P.D.G. and the Mamou
'deviation'", in C. Allen and R.W. Johnson (eds.),
African Perspectives (Cambridge Uiversity Press,
Cambridge, 1970), p. 363.
2. World Bank, World Development Indicators
(1978), Table I.
3. 'Ladipo Adamolekun, Sékou Touré's Guinea
(Methuen, London, 1976), p. 86.
4. Claude Riviere, Guinea: The Mobilization
of a People, trans. Virginia Thompson and Richard
Adloff (Cornell University Press, Ithaca, N.Y.,
1977), p. 62.
5. Ibid., p. 87.
6. Victor Dubois, "The Independence Movement
in Guinea: A Study in African Nationalism", unpublished Ph.D thesis, (Princeton University, Princeton,
N.J., 1962), pp. 99-100.

7. Riviere, Guinea, p. 67.
8. Ruth Schacter Morgenthau, Political Parties in French-Speaking West Africa (Clarendon Press, Oxford, 1964), p. 229.
9. Ibid.
10. See Jean Suret-Canale, "La Fin de la Chefferie en Guinée", Journal of African History, VII, 3 (1966), esp. pp. 479-80.
11. Riviere, Guinea, pp. 58-59.
12. Johnson, "The PDG", pp. 347-48. See also his later argument that Touré even in 1958 really did not want independence, but trapped himself by his own rhetoric into having either to retreat in complete humiliation or to plunge into the "No" vote in the referendum. "Guinea", in John Dunn (ed.), West African States (Cambridge University Press, Cambridge, 1978), pp. 39-40.
13. Morgenthau, Political Parties, p. 246.
14. Riviere, Guinea, pp. 81-82; Victor Dubois, "The Guinean Vote for Independence", American University Field Staff Reports, West Africa Series, V, 7, (1962), p. 5; Johnson, "Guinea", pp. 39-40.
15. Adamolekun, Touré's Guinea, pp. 42, 44.
16. Johnson, "Guinea", p. 46.
17. Dubois, "The Problems of Independence", AUFS Reports, V, 8 (1962), p. 10.
18. Adamolekun, Touré's Guinea, p. 50.
19. Ibid., pp. 45, 49.
20. Riviere, Guinea, pp. 103-06.
21. Ibid., pp. 106-07.
22. Ibid., pp. 107-10.
23. Ibid., p. 109.
24. Ibid., p. 194-97.
25. Ibid., p. 184.
26. Ibid., p. 186.
27. Ibid., p. 116.
28. Ibid., pp. 117-18. In 1958 the amounts had been 65,000 tons and 10,000 tons.
29. Victor Dubois, "Reorganization of the Guinean Economy", AUFS Reports, VI, 1 (1963), p. 14.
30. Ibid., esp. pp.. 13-14. See also Riviere, Guinea, p. 114, and David Hapgood, Africa: From Independence to Tomorrow (Atheneum, New York, 1965), pp. 149-150. Adamolekun, Touré's Guinea, p. 70, calls the programme "successful" but acknowledges a loss of mass enthusiasm.
31. Adamolekun, Touré's Guinea, p. 66.
32. Dubois, "The Decline of the Guinean Revolution", AUFS Reports, VIII, 8, (1965) p. 5. "Official" exports at this time were valued at about $50 million, with more than half this minerals.

33. Adamolekun, Touré's Guinea, p. 66.
34. Ibid., p. 88 citing Touré. See also
Lansana Diané, "Party - state - people", World
Marxist Review, (August 1976), p. 108.
35. Diané, ibid.
36. Dubois, "The Decline of the Guinean
Revolution", AUFS Reports, VIII, 9 (1965), p. 4.
37. "Deux million d'exiles", Jeune Afrique, 875
(14 octobre, 1977), p. 54.
38. Riviere, Guinea, pp. 122-23.
39. See Africa, 70 (June 1977), pp. 59-60.
40. Dubois, "The Rise of an Opposition to Sékou
Touré" AUFS Reports IX, 2 (1966) pp. 6-7.
41. Ibid., IX, 3 (1966), pp. 1-9; also Riviere,
Guinea, p. 129.
42. Riviere, ibid., pp. 136-137. See also
Jean-Paul Alata, "In an African Prison: a memoir"
trans. A. Foulke, Dissent, 24 (Fall 1977) pp. 418-24,
for a personal account by a French supporter of
Touré.
43. See Jeune Afrique, August 27, 1976, p. 24.
44. See. Ahmed Dumbuya, "National Integration in
Guinea and Sierra Leone", unpublished Ph.D thesis,
University of Washington, Seattle, 1974, pp. 266-67.
Dumbuya also notes earlier (p. 219) that by 1969
Malinké dominance over the government had been consolidated, leaving other ethnic groups effectively
excluded from power.
45. See Africa Confidential, 20, 7 (March 28,
1979), pp. 1-2.
46. See West Africa, August 1, 1977 pp. 1608-
1609.
47. Tamar Golan, "Returning to the Fold", West
Africa, May 1, 1978, p. 843.
48. Africa Confidential, 20, 7 (March 28, 1979),
p. 2.
49. This support from youth was indicated even
in one of the bitterly hostile attacks on Touré's
regime in Jeune Afrique. See Jacques Vignes, "La
double lecture", Jeune Afrique, October 14, 1977,
p. 39.
50. This action put it in the company of Moise
Tshombe's Katanga regime. Other early murders of
political opponents, such as those of Ben Barka of
Morocco and Félix-Roland Moumié of Cameroun, seem to
have been done by the French on behalf of these
countries's governments.
51. See Africa, 84 (August 1978), p. 38
52. See Morgenthau, Political Parties, p. 298.
53. Johnson, "The PDG", p. 354.
54. See Adamolekun, Touré's Guinea, pp. 66-68.

55. Ibid., pp. 66-69.
56. Riviere, Guinea, pp. 190-192.
57. See ibid., p. 89; also Johnson, "The PDG",
pp. 353-55.
58. See Dubois, "Reorganization of the Guinean
Economy" AUFS Reports, VI, 1 (1963), p. 19; also
"The Decline of the Guinean Revolution: The
Erosion of Public Morality", ibid., VIII, 9 (1965).
59. Cited in Riviere, Guinea, p. 182.

Chapter Ten

UGANDA: DOES RUTHLESSNESS PAY?

From its colonial reputation as the jewel of
East Africa, Uganda has come to symbolize the suf-
ferings imposed by tyranny, wanton bloodshed, and
the tearing apart of the very fabric of civilized
society. The effects of the casual and indiscriminate killings, the looting, and the hatreds unleashed by Idi· Amin's regime will linger for generations even if his successors devote all their
energies and skills to the time-consuming and complex task of rebuilding a sense of civic morality.
Amin's regime shows as dramatically as any in
Africa the consequences, as distinct from the policy choices, that can flow from a particular individual's behaviour as a leader, and thus raises most
acutely the questions of how inevitable or how for-
tuitous were the steps that brought him to power.
     The crumbling of restraints on violence under
Amin came as a surprise in Uganda. To be sure,
there had been a strong element of "violent
constitutionalism"[1] under his predecessor, Apolo
Milton Obote, but Obote had enjoyed some success in
reconciling many of the diverse claimants in
Uganda's political life, and even in resolving the
state's central problem, the non-integration of the
kingdom of Buganda. Some scholars have seen
Obote's actions as leading inevitably to Amin's
coup d'état,[2] but it seems to me that at least until
he had the military attack and destroy the Buganda
capital in May 1966, Obote might have returned to
a reconciling approach which would have forestalled
any coup.
     The questions I will deal with, then, concern
the possibility of different courses under both
Milton Obote and under Idi Amin. Was Amin's rise to
power inevitable, and once in power, could he have
acted differently and still survived? Were there

226

points at which Obote could have forestalled Amin's creation of a personal base within the army, or built himself an alternate base of support? Were Obote's conciliatory actions before 1966 merely tactical manoeuvres covering a dictatorial ambition, or was there a genuinely conciliatory side to him which was overwhelmed by events? Or was Uganda doomed to a violent denouement ever since the kingdom of Buganda abandoned any pan-Ugandan nationalist movement in the 1950's? Was there any way in which a nationalist movement at this time might have over-ridden the ethnic cleavages of Uganda, and thus allowed a leader to emerge with "heroic" stature and more scope for manoeuvre?

My contention is that while the turning inward of Buganda after the 1953 exiling of the king made the creation of a unified nationalist movement almost impossible, both by setting the Baganda apart from everyone else and by reducing the attractive-ness of independence as a goal, still there was some hope for a reconciliation after independence had been bestowed upon the country. While circumstances had deprived Obote of the opportunity to take a heroic stand against the colonial power that would give him moral authority over other claimants for leadership, he managed to compensate for this weak-ness by his ability to conciliate opposing interests. However, in reconciling people he was too obviously devious and calculating to win any affection from those with whom he dealt, and even more serious, he showed on several occasions that he was ready to subvert constitutional rules in order to gain per-sonal advantages. At the same time, he was not suf-ficiently ruthless to establish a tyrannical regime, with the result that the many people who distrusted him were not too terrified to challenge him, until finally he was ousted by a far more ruthless indivi-dual who lacked his partial commitment to accepted rules.

Perhaps the middle ground that Obote sought to occupy was untenable. If he had been less ready to act unconstitutionally, especially in 1966, he would likely have been ousted from office, and the deep fissures in Uganda's political life would likely have led to civil war; but if he had been a more ruthless leader, he might well have been borne down in a spiral of violence until he reached a stage of national bankruptcy similar to that of Sékou Touré. And yet there does seem a possibility that if he had acted a little less violently in dealing with Buganda in 1966, and tried less hard to press for

radical changes in 1969, he might once again have
succeeded in working out a national compromise. As
for Idi Amin, if he could have married his populist
instincts to a long-term strategy of economic development and political reconciliation, he could have
built an unshakeable popular base for himself. However, his paranoia and his Hobbesian view of life as
a war of each against all others, coupled with a
sense of inferiority and grievance against the educated elite, quickly drove him into the spiral of
terror that steadily intensified during the next
eight years. Some of his actions, we should note,
did build popular support, notably his public humil-
iations of Asians, Europeans and the Ugandan elite.
However, the most important lesson from Idi Amin's
rule is how effective a random and indiscriminate
form of terror can be in subduing a people, especially when coupled with a shrewd playing off of
personal and ethnic rivalries.

THE JEWEL OF EAST AFRICA

     Compared to most African states, Uganda started
independence with a prospering economy, a sophisticated indigenous elite and a strong commitment to
taking political action through constitutional procedures. Offsetting these advantages however, were
deep and bitter ethnic and racial divisions. Although land-locked and lacking any significant
mineral deposits, the country had built a solid base
of prosperity on its major export crops, cotton and
coffee. These crops, along with the major food
crops, were produced largely by African smallholders, with the richest areas lying around Lake
Victoria. The northern part of the country was much
drier and less productive, as reflected in the fact
that average annual cash income at independence was
$53 per year in Buganda, and only $14 in the western
and northern regions.[3] Like other primary producers,
Uganda was vulnerable to fluctuations in the prices
of its major products, and in the late 1950s both
cotton and coffee had dipped to just over three
quarters of their 1950 peaks.[4] Nevertheless, while
the slump in prices forced curtailment of some
development plans, Ugandans generally did not suffer
severely.
     Besides the broad peasant base for economic
property, Uganda had a further advantage, at least
compared to neighbouring Kenya: it did not have to
contend with an entrenched white settler minority.

228

The 11,000 Europeans were mostly missionaries, civil servants, and businessmen, and while many stayed in Uganda for years, they did not usually claim it as "home".

However, there was a serious racial conflict with the 72,000 Asians who dominated the small business sector, and provided many of the doctors, lawyers and artisans.[5] Unlike the Europeans, the Asians had usually lived in Africa since the turn of the century and could hardly return to India. Since they were the people who bought the peasants' produce, and provided most of the retail goods, they were in close daily contact with most Africans. Yet they were generally regarded as holding themselves aloof from the Africans, as cheating Africans in their business dealing, and preventing African businessmen from starting competing businesses, all of which made them universally hated.

Uganda in the pre-World War II period had been ahead of all other African colonies in the proportion of its children in school. In 1936 there had been some 273,000 pupils, 97% of them in the first three grades. Even in absolute numbers of children in school, Uganda surpassed all other colonies except Nigeria and the Belgian Congo, which had five and three times the population, respectively.[6] Only 40,000 of these children, it should be added, were in government-assisted schools, which suggested an enthusiasm for education but also a problem of standards. By the early 1950s, however, schooling opportunities in West Africa and Kenya had increased greatly, until not only Ghana but also Kenya were well ahead of Uganda at the primary level (Table 10.1). Nevertheless, Uganda was still second only to Ghana in its proportion of teachers in training, and the many years over which it had had a substantial educational system ensured that it was relatively well-endowed with educated men able to move into key roles.

These aggregate figures, however, concealed Uganda's major political problem: the regional discrepancies, and in particular the position of the Kingdom of Uganda, in relation to the rest of the country.

Buganda comprised about a sixth of Uganda's total population, twice as much as any other single ethnic group, but it included among its members at least half the educated elite and nearly half the agricultural wealth. Situated squarely in the centre of the country, in the rich area north of Lake Victoria, it had been a strongly centralized

monarchy when the British entered the territory. A
special agreement concluded between the British and
the King of Buganda, the Kabaka, in 1900, gave the
Ganda people the belief that they were still a
sovereign people, free to choose their own form of
government. While the first pan-Ugandan nationalist
politicians in the 1950s were Baganda, the Buganda
government, aware that it would ultimately be a
minority in a unitary Uganda, began to press vehe-
mently for secession, with the result that the
Kabaka was exiled in 1953. This martyrdom rallied
all the Baganda around the monarchy, and when the
Kabaka was returned in 1955 it was to a kingdom
which had developed a strongly inward-looking ethnic
nationalism. If the Baganda had been proportionately
stronger in Uganda, they might have been willing to
lead a territory-wide movement; as it was, their
rejection of any involvement with the development of
political parties in the rest of Uganda left a situation in which various fragments floated in search
of a unifying cause.

Table 10.1: Selected educational data for East and West
Africa, 1952

Country	Total population ('000)	Pupils in educational institutions (pct. of population in parentheses)			
	(year of last census)	Primary ('000)	Secondary	Teacher Training	Other Post-Secondary
Uganda	4,959 (1948)	273 (5.5%)	9,438 (0.19%)	2,575 (0.052%)	n.a.
Ghana	4,118 (1948)	419 (10.2%)	8,791 (0.21%)	2,426 (0.059%)	524
Kenya	5,406 (1948)	363 (6.7%)	7,734 (0.14%)	2,090 (0.039%)	292
Tanganyika	7,478 (1948)	227 (3.0%)	26,802 (0.36%)	970 (0.013%)	82
French W. Africa	17,362 (1951)	190 (1.17)	8,676 (0.05%)	1,677 (0.010%)	832*

*included 547 in France

Source: Lord Hailey, An African Survey, revised 1956 (Oxford,
London, 1957), pp. 143, 1258, 1260.

Although the symbols of the 1955 Agreement which brought back the Kabaka made it appear a victory for the Baganda, the reality was that in return for internal self-government, Buganda was to remain an integral part of Uganda and, equally subversive of the Kabaka's power, was to accept the principle that legislative and key executive offices were to be elective rather than appointed at the Kabaka's pleasure.[7] However, the massive grassroots support for the Kabaka following his return made these changes irrelevant for the time being. The Kabaka and his court kept tight control over all aspects of politics, to the extent that national parties trying to organize in Buganda found their members beaten and houses burned for affronting the principle that the Kabaka was the fount of all authority.[8]

This "opting out" by Buganda from national politics undercut the leaders of all the major political parties and left the country's politics badly fragmented. The first nationalist party, the Uganda National Congress, had been formed by a Ganda co-operative leader, Ignatius Musazi, in 1952, and had quickly formed branches in a number of sections of the country.[9] Three years later, a further party, the Democratic Party, strongly encouraged by Catholic missions, also spread out from Buganda, winning most of its support as the spokesman for Catholic interests. Since the Protestant-Catholic division had been Buganda's major source of conflict since the first missionary penetration, the DP leader, Benedicto Kiwanuka, could draw on pockets of dissidence even within the kingdom, as well as building substantial support elsewhere in Uganda along religious lines. However, when in 1962 his party had to confront a Ganda ethnic party mobilized in defence of the Kabaka's powers, the ethnic appeal overwhelmed religion.

Meanwhile, the UNC had split. First, in 1958 a younger group seeking a more militant approach had ousted Musazi, and then this group in turn divided essentially on Ganda versus non-Ganda lines. The Ganda group under Joseph Kiwanuka were left, like Musazi, without local roots in the wake of the Kabaka's opposition to political parties, and quickly withered away. The non-Ganda wing, led by Milton Obote, in 1960 concluded a merger with a Legislative Council grouping of non-Ganda members called the Uganda Peoples' Union, producing a new party which brought together most non-Ganda, apart from the DP's Catholic adherents. The new party took the name

231

Uganda Peoples' Congress (UPC) and chose Milton
Obote as its leader. The UPC's rise gives credence
to Ali Mazrui's contention that Buganda's combination of cultural leadership and intransigeant isolation served to integrate the rest of the country,
although by imposing what proved ultimately too
heavy a strain on the mechanisms of reconciliation.[10] The DP also was a party of national integration, in that it managed to override ethnic
cleavages in the name of religious solidarity.

MILTON OBOTE: THE RISE OF A CONCILIATOR

     Both the rise of Milton Obote to the leader-
ship of the UPC, and the UPC's opportunity to take
over the government of Uganda just before independence in 1962, were largely matters of luck.
Milton Obote, born in 1926 in the northern district
of Lango, had attended Makerere from 1947 to 1949,
which made him one of the more highly-educated of
his generation of Langi. Later he worked in the
more politically-charged atmosphere of Kenya for a
few years, becoming involved with Kenyatta's Kenya
African Union. He returned to his home district of
Lango in 1956, and began to work in the UNC. The
District Council, on which the UNC was strong, was
discontented with the failure of their representatives in the Legislative Council to articulate Lango
needs, and in 1957 they induced him to leave the
Legco to take a judgeship. Since the local founder
and chairman of the UNC branch was in jail at the
time, Obote's education, articulateness and participation in the UNC made him the next choice to fill
the vacant seat, and in March 1958 he took his seat
in the Legislative Council.[11] At the same time, he
became vice-president of the UNC, and when the party
expelled Musazi in early 1959, he emerged as
President-General, the post held by Musazi. This
was regarded by his colleagues as a figurehead post,
the real power supposedly resting with the chairman
and secretary-general, both Ganda.[12] But in August
1959 Obote and eleven supporters on the central
executive of the UNC suspended the chairman,
secretary-general and treasurer for, among other
things, inefficiency and acting without the author-
ization of the central executive.[13] The party
thereupon became two, with the chairman, Joseph
Kiwanuka, and his Baganda colleagues trying to build
support in their home soil, while Obote was left
firmly in control of the non-Ganda elements of the

party. Meanwhile the members of the Legislative
Council who were neither Baganda nor UNC had formed
the Uganda Peoples Union, and now with the UNC
cleansed of its Ganda elements, a merger was feasible. Since Obote had already distinguished himself
in the Legislature for the boldness of his attacks
on colonial government and his demands for independence, he was generally acceptable as the leader of
the new party, even though he could not claim any
clear precedence over others.

Obote's emergence as the leader of a potential
party of government was attributable initially to
his being in the right place at the right time to
gain national prominence, and then to his boldness
and skill in plotting the coup which gave him
control of the politically viable part of the UNC.
A further attribute, his skill at reconciling
widely divergent attitudes, was to show in the way
he overcame the most serious obstacle in his drive
for national power, the entrenched strength of the
Ganda establishment.

Once again, Obote had luck on his side.
Despite the 1955 Agreement, the Buganda government
still refused to be integrated into a national
state, holding out for near-sovereignty, and when
this was denied, attempting in December 1960 to
secede. The British managed to coerce Buganda out
of this attempt, but the Buganda government then
declared a boycott of the March 1961 national
elections to the Legislative Council, a boycott
which resulted in only 3% of Buganda's eligible
voters going to the polls. Both the UPC and the
Democratic Party campaigned in Buganda despite the
boycott, with the DP's Ganda leadership and appeal
to dissident elements giving it 20 of 21 Buganda
seats on this miniscule poll.[15] Since outside
Buganda the DP had won a respectable 474,000 votes
and 22 seats against 538,000 votes and 27 seats for
the UPC,[16] it had overall more seats and thus
Benedicto Kiwanuka was sworn in as Uganda's first
chief minister when internal self-government was
granted the following month. But this was a
Pyrrhic victory, because in campaigning and taking
Ganda seats, Kiwanuka was seen as a traitor to
Buganda. A purely Baganda ethnic party, the
Kabaka Yekka ("the Kabaka alone") was quickly
formed by the Ganda establishment, and swept 65 of
the 68 seats in elections to Buganda's own legislature. the Lukiiko, in February 1962. Meanwhile, in
the constitutional talks in London, the UPC, which
had far less to lose than the DP from this approach,

accepted the Kabaka's demand that Buganda's legislature rather than its citizens should elect Buganda's representatives to the national legislature. The opportunity for the DP to capitalize on internal dissent within Buganda was thus minimized.[17]

Following the constitutional talks, a further national election was scheduled for April 1962 to clear the way for full independence. Shortly before this election, Obote and the Kabaka Yekka announced their bolt from the blue: a UPC-KY alliance. With a block of 22 Buganda seats in a legislature totaling 91 members (including 9 elected by the legislature itself), this meant that even if the UPC lost some ground to the DP outside Buganda, the alliance would form the government. And even though alliance with the KY might be expected to lose the UPC some non-Ganda sympathizers, few would be likely to join a DP whose leader was a Muganda.

Yet the alliance between the UPC and KY appeared on the face of it far more improbable than one involving the DP and KY. The KY was monarchist, elitist and supported a capitalist economic system; the UPC was republican, and had considerable leanings toward an egalitarian social order and a socialist economy. All that separated KY and the DP, by contrast, was the former's ethnic exclusivity, and the fact that it, like the UPC, was solidly Protestant in its higher ranks (though in the UPC's case this was not reflected in any apparent policy biases.)

However, the DP's 1961 defiance of the Kabaka's boycott had marked it and its leader as disloyal to Buganda. Obote for his part was fully prepared to use all his conciliating skills to take advantage of this opportunity, allegedly even offering to give way as prime minister to a nominee of the Kabaka's. (It is intriguing to speculate on what might have happened if the Kabaka had taken him up on this offer.)[18] It was this personal element of animosity between the Kabaka and Kiwanuka that opened the way for Obote to assume power and lead Uganda to independence in October 1962.

From 1962 to 1964 Obote worked carefully to consolidate the position of the UPC, making use of the extensive patronage at his disposal to whittle away the DP opposition and to bring members of the KY directly into the UPC. This latter task was not impossible, since KY was divided between the hard-line traditionalists around the Kabaka and a number of more "modernizing" individuals whose ethnic sympathies were balanced by their desire to

234

pursue the same goals of social change that Obote seemed to want. What Obote's own views were during this period is hard to determine. Critics suggest that his only unyielding principle was to keep himself in power. Others, notably Gingyera-Pinycwa, have made a more convincing case that he was all along a covert socialist, unwilling to reveal his goals fully as yet because of the delicacy required to weld together a suitable instrument first.[19] Whatever the truth, he gave little evidence at this stage of holding any "transformationist" ideas, concentrating on "middle of the road" economic policies while he built up support for his party in Parliament.

By 1964 Obote's astute wooing of KY and DP members had given the UPC a clear majority in the legislature, although even more than before it was a rather loose coalition of high-status local notables with their own power bases and interests to defend.[20] One part of the deal between the UPC and KY had been to give the Kabaka the highest-ranking status in Uganda, and in October 1973 he had become Head of State in a parliamentary monarchical republic, with essentially the powers of a constitutional monarch. This status, however, did not stop his continuing a highly partisan effort to keep in Buganda two counties handed to Buganda in 1900 by the British but comprising members of the neighbouring Bunyoro kingdom. To improve its chances in a referendum within the "Lost Counties" scheduled for late 1964, the Buganda government busied itself settling Baganda on the two counties' land. This issue of the "Lost Counties" along with other continuing strains and the fact that Obote had obtained a UPC majority in parliament, led Obote to terminate the alliance with the KY in August 1964. Henceforth the Head of State was in tacit opposition to his Prime Minister, the moreso after the referendum (in which the government denied the franchise to the recent Ganda settlers) resulted in an overwhelming vote for the counties to return to Bunyoro.

Meanwhile, the instrument of power toward which Obote was being forced had shown its potential for upsetting the established order. In January 1964, following mutinies in Tanzania and Kenya, the Ugandan army also mutinied, demanding higher pay and rapid Africanization of the officer corps. The mutiny was put down when Obote called in 400 British soldiers, but in its aftermath the pay increases and the Africanization of the officer corps were conceded, and only a few ringleaders were punished.

Unlike Nyerere,who rebuilt the Tanzanian army from
scratch after his mutiny, or Kenyatta, who kept
British troops stationed in Kenya as a deterrent on
a near-permanent basis after 1964, Obote left the
army largely unchanged, but lavished more money and
equipment on it.[22]

Given the choices, this was not as foolish an
approach as it appeared. While his own Langi people were not prominent in the army's two battalions,
the neighbouring Acholi tribe furnished nearly a
third of the total strength, and northerners predominated both among the African officers and among
the other ranks. To the extent that Obote could be
seen as a northerner struggling against the privileges of the southern kingdoms, he could expect the
army to serve as a loyal instrument, as long as its
material wants were satisfied.[23]

In the rapid Africanization of the officer
corps, and expansion of the ranks that took place
from the mutiny to the time of the 1971 coup (from
independence to 1971 the total strength rose from
1,200 to 9,000) the personal appeal of officers to
their men became more important than in a situation
where long traditions of unquestioning obedience
had been instilled. Here the fact that a very large
portion of the northerners in the army were "Nubi",
pastoral people from West Nile and the Sudan who
were peripheral to Ugandan society, becomes significant.[24] Idi Amin came from this background, and
this, coupled with the fact that he had risen from
the ranks and had a persuasive blend of joviality
and menace in his personality, enabled him to win
the support of his men in a way matched by few
other officers.[25] Moreover, his limited education
and peasant roughness made it seem improbable that
he would develop ambitions to take over power from
the ruling civilian intelligentsia. This combination of qualities more than offset blots on his
record such as his implication in the murder of
three Kenyan cattle rustlers while on patrol shortly
before independence. Following the 1964 mutiny he
became the new Commanding Officer of the 1st Battal-
ion, one of the two ranking African officers in the
army. Since the other senior officer, Brig. Shabani
Opolot, had Baganda connections, Obote began to by-
pass him and work through Amin, particularly for
such undercover missions as supplying arms to Congolese rebels and the Anyanya guerillas in Southern
Sudan.

Then came the 1966 crisis, which left Obote
with supreme power, but dependent on the army to

maintain it. The crisis began in February 1966
when a Kabaka Yekka member of Parliament demanded
an inquiry into allegations that Amin, Obote and
other ministers had colluded with Congolese rebels
to smuggle gold and ivory. In Obote's absence
almost his entire party supported a motion demanding Amin's suspension and casting doubts on the
Prime Minister's integrity. It appears that many
southern members of the UPC saw this as an opportunity to replace Obote as leader, although it is not
clear who they would have put in his place, or how.
In any case, the Prime Minister forestalled them
when at a Cabinet meeting on February 22, he had
the police burst in and arrest five ministers,
including the UPC general secretary, Grace Ibingira.
Two days later Obote announced that in order to
forestall an alleged <u>coup</u> by the Kabaka and Obote's
UPC opponents, he himself was assuming all governmental powers. On February 26 he suspended the
1962 Constitution, thus removing the Kabaka from
any position in the central government. A few
weeks later he brought in a new constitution making himself president and head of the military, and
ending Buganda's claims to any degree of autonomy.
When the Buganda government responded by ordering
all central government personnel and property off
Buganda soil (in other words, seceding), and followed this by distributing arms to Ganda war veterans and peasants. Obote ordered the army under
Amin's command to attack the Kabaka's palace. Amin
obeyed with gusto, some hundreds of Baganda were
killed in two days' fighting, and the Kabaka fled
into exile, leaving the power of Buganda apparently
broken.[26]
    But the cost for Obote was to prove too high.
The anger and alienation of the Baganda might have
been accepted, despite their central position in
the state, if Obote could have built a new consensus from the rest of the country. But Obote's readiness to destroy constitutional restraints in order
to save himself undermined his position as a great
reconciler, even though he indicated a continuing
commitment to democratic forms by setting up an im-
partial commission to inquire into the original
charges against him.[27] And his party, which was
still the faction-ridden assemblage provided by the
1962 elections, offered little hope as a mobilizing
force for building a new consensus.
    The lengths to which he went in 1966 to seize
power doomed Obote. If in February 1966 he had
been content to arrest the five ministers on

trumped-up charges, and declared a state of emergency in order to detain them and any supporters,
he would probably have succeeded in intimidating
his opponents sufficiently to dissuade them from
further plotting, while at the same time leaving
the door open to conciliating some Baganda and
other southerners. Ousting the Kabaka from his
figurehead post was surely not necessary; there was
no way Britain would have sent in troops against a
Ugandan army obeying the Prime Minister's orders,
no matter how strongly the Kabaka as Uganda's
President might have appealed for it to do so. If
Buganda had still threatened secession, Obote could
have sounded far more like a tolerant man whose
patience was exhausted before sending in the troops,
and thus would likely have reaped far less hostility in Buganda and the other southern kingdoms. As
it was, the combination of intense Ganda hostility
and his own reputation for violating the constitutional rules pushed him heavily toward reliance on
the army.

After 1966, and even more after the abolition
of the other southern kingdoms' kings in 1967, a
reconciliation strategy based on balancing divergent
ethnic claims looked increasingly unpromising.
While other southerners as well as northerners were
generally glad to see the Ganda cut down, members
of the political and economic elites could not help
but be apprehensive about Obote's willingness to
break the rules that other leaders obeyed. All
southerners were concerned about northern dominance
of the security forces, while northerners knew that
their areas were still disadvantaged compared to
the south. To strengthen his own position, Obote's
ideal strategy would be one which led people away
from ethnic concerns completely.

Then too, Obote may have wanted to try to
achieve a more egalitarian and socialist society,
although whether he would risk his personal power
to seek this goal is questionable. Now, however,
with the Kabaka and other kings who could act as
foci of resistance to national integration removed
from the scene, and with most of his declared rivals
ousted from political office, Obote may have felt
the time was ripe to try to bring about a significant transformation of Ugandan society.

Whatever the motive, in 1969 Obote announced a
new set of economic policies which, if they became
the focus of Ugandan political debate, would move
the country's political alignments from an ethnic
to a class orientation. The "Common Man's Charter",

238

essentially worked out by Obote himself with little
consultation within the UPC, proclaimed that in
order to reduce the dangerous polarization between
a wealthy, privileged elite and the great mass of
farmers and wage-earners, much of the economy would
be put under the control of the state or co-
operatives.[28] Much of the charter was general rhetoric, with little analysis of the core problems
that would have to be overcome to provide a more
equitable distribution of wealth. Nevertheless, by
critically highlighting the growth of a privileged
elite, it provided a marked change in tone from the
established pattern of economic development.

However, in seeking to implement the Charter,
Obote faced almost insuperable problems, most of
which came back to the UPC as a tenuous coalition
of factions. The first problem was that the dominant figures in the UPC were the legislators, who
had for the most part won election in 1962 on the
strength of their local status. Extra-
Parliamentary cadres of militants who might have
animated local party branches had been lacking ever
since the 1964 conference had replaced a radical
secretary-general, who was trying to build up such
a party, with the more conservative Ibingira. This
purge, incidentally, secured the acquiescence, if
not the connivance, of Obote himself.[29] The party
as constituted in 1969 could certainly not be expected to help mobilize people in favour of Obote's
goals of greater social and economic equality; in
fact, it was likely, despite the detention of some
of his more conspicuous personal opponents, to offer
considerable resistance to such goals.

Although elections were promised for 1971, the
crop of new MP's who would enter the legislature
was not likely to be very different. An ingenious
system requiring candidates to put together a plu-
rality from four separate constituencies in different parts of the country was being introduced to
reduce or eliminate blatant ethnic appeals. However, it also had the side effect of vastly increasing the amount of wealth a candidate required to
finance a campaign, a factor which was beginning to
show by 1970.[30]

A further problem was that Obote himself was
not a leader possessed of great personal appeal.
While he was shrewd, calculating and had a talent
for reconciling diverse demands, he appeared somewhat aloof and lacked the magnetism of a Nkrumah,
a Touré or a Nyerere. Unlike these leaders, he
could not claim heroic stature in the fight against

colonial rule; decolonization had been thrust upon
a reluctant Uganda rather than being wrested by
Ugandans from the colonialists, and Obote himself
had not gained prominence until independence was
assured.

Even if the appeal to the "Common Man" to
better his lot through socialism could reach him,
it was questionable whether this appeal was strong
enough to override conflicting ethnic claims. In
Buganda, most notably, there was a long-standing
conflict between the chiefly oligarchy who had col-
lected rents on much of the land as a result of the
1900 Agreement, and the small farmers and tenants.
Unfortunately the latter tended to be the strongest
supporters of the Kabaka as Buganda's sacred head,
and as a result, after 1966 wanted nothing to do
with Obote. In the other southern kingdoms also,
perceptions of Obote as a northerner who had
abolished kings in 1967 overrode any potential class
appeal. Even in the north, concern over Obote's use
of his fellow Langi in the security services
aroused other ethnic groups' concerns, while his
socialism was equated with atheism, which made him un-
attractive to Catholics. In short, the potential
class appeal of the Charter was unable to overcome
cross-cutting commitments among Obote's potential
supporters, but it did succeed in arousing suspicion
among many in the elite groups who had hitherto
accepted him, and intensified the enmity of others.

This atmosphere of growing hostility took a violent turn in December 1969, when a would-be assassin
shot Obote in the face as he left the UPC conference
just after it had endorsed the Common Man's Charter.
Fortunately, Obote was not seriously injured, but
the action showed just how ready passions were to
erupt. The government quickly banned the DP and
other opposition groups, detained 20 people, and
after lengthy investigation sent five Ganda with
links to the Kabaka's family to trial. Eventually
they received life sentences for attempted murder
and conspiracy to commit murder.[31]

While Obote and his government acted with restraint in dealing with the assassination attempt,
he was taking some forceful steps to protect his
position. Alongside the army, he set up two further
paramilitary bodies, the Special Force within the
police, and the General Service, ostensibly bodyguards and intelligence officers but trained in
military techniques, and under the command of
Obote's cousin, Akena Adoko. Although the army by
1970 had grown to 6,700 men[32] while the other forces

were considerably smaller, many army officers saw
themselves as being shunted aside by this rival organization, which was comprised largely of Langi
from Obote's own home district.

Since the army was riven by the same ethnic and
other factions that divided the polity as a whole,
the small size of Obote's loyal security groups
might not have been important, except that they
served to spread a pervasive discontent throughout
the army ranks even among the generally pro-Obote
Acholi, who comprised at least a third of the army.
Meanwhile, unknown to Obote, Idi Amin was recruiting
his own loyal following in the form of Anyanya guerrillas from the Sudan; by the time of the coup,
these numbered some 500 or more, and played a vital
role in seizing the armoured regiment's barracks.[33]

Obote, for all his general caution, may have
been over-confident in dealing with Amin. In
September 1970 Obote tried to move Amin out of a
direct command by appointing two brigadiers beneath
him to control the army battalions and the fledgling
air force. Unfortunately, this did not destroy
Amin's popularity with the rank-and-file, nor did it
stop him from placing his own West Nile supporters
in key positions. Obote's most astonishing move,
however, came in January 1971. Just before he flew
off to the Commonwealth conference in Singapore, he
demanded that Amin provide a written explanation of
what had happened to $7 million of unaccounted army
funds, and how guns from armouries had found their
way into the hands of some of the numerous armed
gangs who infested Uganda. While he probably did
not tell Amin that some robbers had implicated him
in the murder of his second-in-command in early 1970,
it seems likely that Amin had heard that Obote was
also aware of his involvement in this killing.
Granted that Amin's popularity in the army was such
that Obote could probably not have arrested him
without starting an insurrection, it still seems in-
credible that he would place Amin in a very tight
spot without staying around to deal with Amin's
likely responses.

At this point, Obote's fatal weakness may have
been his moderation. While he could not risk publicly arresting and charging Amin, a more ruthless leader would surely have had him killed, just as Amin
had had Brig. Okoya killed. Obote, however, had the
worst of both worlds: he created many enemies
through the General Service's arrests and detentions,
but the detainees were fairly confident they would
remain alive to plot again. This pattern was to

change abruptly with Amin's successful coup on January 25, 1971.

Whether the coup was a defensive move by Amin to forestall his arrest or assassination by Obote's supporters, or a modification of an earlier plan by Amin to have Obote and several ministers assassinated on the latter's return from Singapore, will never be known. What is certain is that its success was largely due to the slowness and inadequacy of countermeasures by Obote's supporters, as well as a few security leaks at crucial points.[34] However, the fact that this particular coup's success was largely a matter of luck should not blind us to the very high probability that some further coup would have succeeded, even if Obote had managed to remove Amin from a position where he could act. Obote was just too isolated, had made too many enemies and too few allies, and had accumulated too much suspicion and distrust of his motives, to have much chance of building a sufficient base of support to withstand the continuing intrigues against him. Nor does it seem to me particularly significant that he was ousted after he had begun his "move to the left". Granted that the goals of the "Common Man's Charter" seemed vaguely menacing to the continued prosperity of many of his parliamentary colleagues, and thus helped intensify their desire to be rid of him, still they were so distrustful of his methods that the goals he had professed probably made very little difference. He had created his enemies by such actions as the February 1966 "constitutional coup" rather than by ideological argument, and few of his actions were of a kind that would win him a loyal following. The value of a leader who could manoeuver among the welter of Uganda's conflicting ethnic and class interests with only moderate use of force was not appreciated until after 1971.

IDI AMIN: POWER FOR POWER'S SAKE

Idi Amin's motives in seizing power seem to have been, in order of importance, his personal survival, a desire to prevent the down-grading of his West Nile people in relation to the Langi and Acholi, and a further desire to prevent the army from being overshadowed by the General Service Unit. Such motives did not provide any guidelines for government policy-making, apart from leading Amin to avoid concentrating power in any hands that could threaten him, making some effort to redistribute wealth toward West Nile, and increasing the army's already substantial share of national resources. In the absence of any coherent policies for economic development, social equity or political control and participation, Amin's government was guided by his instincts and prejudices, of which a shrewd sense of how to manipulate other individuals to ensure his own survival was uppermost. Beyond this "survival instinct" the most coherent themes to emerge from his regime were a strong assertion of black nationalism, and an almost equally strong tendency to humble any pretensions to superiority by an educated elite. Amin's own perception of the world seems to have been a near-Hobbesian state of nature, a "war of every man against every other man", moderated to a limited extent by loyalties arising from shared ethnic and religious ties, but basically resting upon an individual's skill in manoeuvering others to do his bidding.

There is a grim irony in Idi Amin's taking power from Milton Obote, even apart from the fact that Obote had protected and advanced Amin's career so that Amin's takeover became possible. Obote eliminated his rivals from power largely by means of sudden violations of the framework of rules by which others trustingly bound themselves. Yet he shrank from carrying his rule-breaking to its logical conclusion of killing off his rivals. Amin suffered no such inhibitions, any more than he allowed himself to be paralysed by seeing complexities in problems of statecraft. If someone was a threat to Amin, he was killed. The logic of winning by being more ruthless than anyone else had reached its ultimate conclusion.

Initially, however, Amin seemed to be trying to broaden his base of support. Whoever advised him at the beginning of his regime was skilled at public relations, particularly in dealing with the Western media and through them much of the rest of the world; the indecent haste with which the British Conservative government and Israel rushed to recognize him and to denigrate the nasty radical, Milton Obote, leaves a strong suspicion that rumours implicating these countries in the coup had some justification. Amin cheered Western investors by opposing the nationalization of foreign enterprises begun by Obote; he raised the Baganda's hopes by announcing that the Kabaka's body would be brought home for a proper burial; and he left a strong impression of pending reconciliation by releasing 55 political detainees, by inviting Obote's close associates to return to work, by saying that Obote himself was not a bad man,[35] and by appointing a Cabinet that consisted mostly of capable professional men, several of them senior civil servants from the Obote regime. Finally, unlike the secretive Obote, Amin was willing to talk readily and publicly to journalists and his colourful comments made good copy.

The dark side of his regime began to appear almost immediately, but reports about the killings and terror tended to be discounted in the international press because they came largely from refugee supporters of Obote. A large number of officers and men, particularly Acholi and Langi, were killed by Amin's West Nile and southern Sudanese troops within the first few days, including the army commander, Brig. Suleiman Hussein, who had tried to organize counter-coup measures. Obote's Minister of the Interior, Basil Bataringaya (a cross-over from the DP), who had headed the committee to try to stop the coup, was dismembered alive and his head put on display in Mbarara garrison.[36] But most of the killings in 1971 were within the army, and when word of them leaked out, were described as the result of clashes with "Obote's guerrillas", or with Tanzanian troops along the border. To fill the gaps in the officer corps, Amin promoted great numbers of semi-literate West Nile and Sudanese from other ranks, as well as new recruits from these areas. The sudden expansion of the army, coupled with Amin's insistence that the men rather than the officers were in control, destroyed what little discipline remained and led to the military being little more than coteries of armed thugs held together by the prospect of being able to plunder the state and private citizens. As more and more troops were drawn from West Nile or the Sudan, the army ceased even to be inhibited by personal ties to the civilian population, but could behave as indifferently toward civilian mores as if it were an alien army of conquest, which in a sense it was.

Nevertheless, for the first year and a half of his regime Amin could draw upon a good deal of popularity. As a simple but shrewd peasant warrior, he was a refreshing contrast to the sophisticated intellectuals of the previous regime, whose enjoyment of immense privileges widened the gulf between them and the "Common Man" in whose interests they professed to be working. To see someone with whom they could identify lording it over both the erstwhile Ugandan elite and over various foreign exploiters was a sight that gladdened the hearts of many ordinary

244

Ugandans. The populist, anti-elite strain in Amin's behaviour was instrumental in winning him widespread support, particularly before his actions began to affect many people outside the army.

One region in which Amin could scarcely fail to be acclaimed was Buganda, despite his personal role as Obote's agent in ousting the Kabaka. One of his first pronouncements, which temporarily consolidated Baganda support, was that the body of Mutesa II would be brought home from England, where he had died of alcohol poisoning in 1969, for a proper royal burial. This was duly done in March, with Amin proclaiming it an "Act of National Reconciliation".[37] (A sour note later was struck when 60 young Baganda who had volunteered as an honour guard were rounded up and killed by Amin's soldiers; they had apparently sought military training too eagerly for Amin's liking.)[38] But the move that would have won the Baganda permanently to him was one he refused to take: in October he firmly stated that there would be no restoration of the Kabakaship or any of the other kingdoms. From then on, the Baganda could no longer be counted as potential supporters of the regime.

The most significant action of Amin's career, and one which made him a hero throughout much of Africa was his mass expulsion of the Asians in 1972. The Asians, as we have seen, had firmly established themselves as an intermediate social stratum throughout Eastern and Southern Africa during the colonial era: they handled much of the retail trade and other small businesses, and held many professional and technical positions. While their control of the retail trade meant that they did business with most Africans, they held themselves aloof socially, almost never intermarrying and rarely giving Africans a chance to participate in their businesses as anything other than junior employees. Most African peasants were convinced that the Asian merchants cheated them both in buying their produce and selling them imported goods, and aspiring African businessmen were equally convinced that the Asians' control of trade blocked their entry.

When the East African territories were being readied for independence, the British government wanted to leave a bolt-hole for white settlers, and accordingly arranged that residents could opt for British nationality rather then that of the new state. One effect of this, of course, was that if a person opted for British rather than Ugandan nationality, his loyalty to Uganda was suspect; but the

Asians, under no illusions about their popularity and long-term prospects in East Africa regardless of their citizenship, took out British passports in large numbers. Then in 1968 Britain drastically tightened its immigration rules to deny entry to most of its passport holders of Asian origin, except on a rigid quota system. The quotas were such that it would take more than a decade for all the non-citizen Asians to be "repatriated" to Britain from Uganda and other African states.

By 1972 the Ugandan economy was encountering increasing difficulties, despite rising coffee prices, as government revenues fell and the army's demands increased.[39] Amin had already unnerved the Asians in 1971 when he had ordered a census of their numbers. Now in August 1972 he announced that all would have to go within three months. His inclusion of those who were Ugandan citizens drew angry protests of "racism" even from some courageous Ugandans, such as the vice-chancellor of Makerere University and the president of the National Union of Students, both of whom were subsequently murdered by Amin's troops.[40] Eventually Amin undertook to expel only the British passport holders, but then proceeded in practice to expel Asians who were Ugandan citizens as well.

The Asian exodus had two results: it opened up tremendous possibilities for building a new African bourgeois class, but at the same time it brought chaos to the trading economy. The properties of the departing Asians were supposed to be auctioned off, and the proceeds used for compensation. In practice, what seems to have happened was that most properties fell into the hands of Amin's troops and others linked to the government, many of whom had no idea of how to run businesses and simply helped themselves to the inventories before abandoning them. The collapse of much of the retail sector brought about severe shortages of staples such as sugar, milk and soap within the next few months, shortages which particularly affected the outlying areas. Amin's policies were beginning to affect the rural economy, even though for the first two years of his rule exports had actually increased.[42] Now, with scarcities of consumer goods, the incentive for farmers to produce crops for export was drying up, and gradually this vital source of foreign exchange decreased, thus perpetuating the spiral.

While ordinary rural-dwellers were suffering only economic deprivation from Amin's policies, the educated elite suffered more directly. In the first few months of Amin's rule, only a few civilians, such as Obote's Minister of the Interior, were butchered, although hundreds of soldiers died during this period. But gradually, as the soldiers realized they could kill civilians with impunity for such personal reasons as wanting to take over their houses, cars, or girlfriends, as well as for reasons of state security, the death toll mounted. Amin had quickly disbanded Obote's secret police, the General Service Unit, and set up two units under his own direct control, the Public Safety Unit, a group of bodyguards, and the 2,000-strong State Research Bureau, drawn almost entirely from Nubi and Kakwa tribes and operating in a manner similar to the Haitian Tonton Macoutes, complete with flamboyant shirts and sunglasses. "Graduates" from the State Research Bureau, which specialized in abductions, torture and mutilation of victims, were posted throughout the army, the civil service, and in embassies abroad to serve as an intelligence network for Amin. Most of their victims simply "disappeared"; Amin could thus deny they were dead, or blame their disappearance on "Obote's guerrillas" or "gangsters." It is quite probable that many "disappearances" were not a result of Amin's orders; the SRB, like the regular soldiers, was free enough from the fetters of discipline that its members could undertake private initiatives against individuals they happened to dislike or whose property they coveted.

Under these conditions, it is astonishing that government in Uganda did continue to function, seriously impaired by the shortages of materials and the loss of skilled personnel, to be sure, but nonetheless making do. While a large number of educated persons fled into exile, many more stayed, at least until they realized (if they learned in time) that their own lives were in danger. The agile young private secretary to Obote, Henry Kyemba, who managed to switch to Amin's government as head of the civil service and then as Minister of Health, fleeing only when he heard that his own murder was imminent, probably expressed a widespread view when he claimed that

> Any comment to Amin [on the arrests and killings of friends or staff] would risk our lives and the lives of our families. We therefore kept our heads down and got on with the routine business of government.[44]

With the extended family ties that character-
ized most of Ugandan society, the number of people
at risk through such a defection would often be
large. Nevertheless, an increasing stream of civil
servants, professional men and other skilled
persons left Uganda when the opportunity arose.

Within the army, his main instrument of power,
Amin successively whittled away potentially threatening elements. The Acholi and Langi, who had comprised more than a third of the armed forces at the
time of the coup, had been effectively eliminated by
the end of 1971. Following the abortive invasion
attempt by Obote supporters in September 1972, Amin
purged a number of Baganda officers whose education
and foreign training allegedly made them unpopular
with their less literate colleagues.[45] Even among
his own West Nile supporters, Amin found disaffection and responded by killing further officers,
including those whose Christian antecedents clashed
with his Muslim supporters' views, and also those
who had higher levels of formal education. By 1974
it was estimated that only some 2,000 of the pre-
coup army remained, and of the 10,000 new recruits,
some 4,000 were Sudanese ex-Anyanya rebels and
Zairois, while most of the remainder came from West
Nile, with 40% being Muslim.[46] Almost all posts of
strategic significance were occupied by West Nile
people, and increasingly by semi-literate officers
promoted from the ranks. Discipline had been further undermined by Amin's warning that troops should
not obey "false" orders from their officers.[47] Amin
was increasingly dependent on what amounted to a mercenary army, bound to him at least as much by the
rewards of pay, promotion, and access to loot as by
any sense of military duty or ethnic loyalty.

The breakdown of discipline was probably ad-
vantageous to Amin, since it meant that any officer
planning a coup against him could have no certainty
that his men would carry out his orders, nor could
he even be sure that they would not turn on him. It
had the further advantage that armed men, whose
actions were completely unpredictable, were certain
to terrify the civilian population out of any
demonstrations or other actions which might serve to
encourage opposition to Amin. The fact that it was
a Nubian army with few links to the population meant
that it could be far more brutal and ruthless than
an army whose members' own families were menaced.
All these factors facilitated Amin's holding on to
power, even though they did not create conditions
for popular support.

By the time Amin's seizure of 700 square miles of Tanzanian territory in October 1978 gave Julius Nyerere the pretext he needed to invade Uganda and topple Amin, Uganda's economy and social structures were in chaos. Coffee exports had declined by some 30% from 1972 to 1977, and cotton by about 50%, while copper exports had dropped from 20,000 tons in 1974 to 1,000 tons. Most of Uganda's industries, including East Africa's largest textile mill, had ceased to export at all, and were operating far below capacity, in large measure due to lack of spare parts and a breakdown in transport.[48] The extent of the social breakdown was indicated retrospectively by the fact that in 1981, two years after Tanzanian troops had liberated the country, armed bands of Amin's former soldiers were still roaming the countryside, and in major cities silence descended at nightfall, with people afraid to go out. Nor was the prospect of restoring civil society particularly encouraging. A series of internal coups saw three successive interim governments in these two years and in 1981, when elections returned Milton Obote to office, one of his former ministers organized a guerrilla army to oust him by force. The belief that might alone made right seemed entrenched for a long time to come.

It also seem unlikely that the system Amin built could have been overthrown without external intervention. His combination of informers and Nubian mercenaries seemed sufficient to frighten the civilian population out of making any serious challenge, and even if one of the several assassination attempts against Amin had succeeded, the Nubian mercenaries could probably have continued to control and loot the country. With Amin dead, they might have had difficulty in holding together, and in obtaining as much international support from Libya, the Soviet Union and Britain as they did, but there was little prospect of any more rational or orderly government emerging from a post-Amin period without outside help.

Could Idi Amin have taken Uganda in any different direction? The one point at which it seems possible that he might have avoided the downward spiral of terror and bloodshed was when he initially seized power. His first conciliatory gestures toward the Baganda, toward government officials and even toward members of the UPC, if they had been followed up, might have started to reduce the multitude of suspicions and tensions among the mosaic of ethnic and religious groups, although the process

would have been long and difficult. However, such
an argument neglects Amin's own power base in the
army. The "loyalty" of many of his West Nile supporters seems to have been largely mercenary; even
before the coup, he had promoted many of these supporters, and one reason for the enthusiastic round-
up and killing of many officers after the coup was
the rumour that men would be promoted to the rank
of the officer they had captured or killed.[49] As
military discipline broke down, the allure of material rewards became increasingly important as a means
by which Amin could retain some control over his
troops. To provide these rewards, however, required
channelling an increasing amount of the country's
revenues into the army, whereas to reconcile the
civilian populace would require at least some use of
government revenues for developmental purposes.
Given the limited revenues available, Amin's base of
support precluded a reconciliation approach.

Furthermore, any argument that Idi Amin might
have pursued a more conciliatory approach once he
had seized power assumes a personality very different from the army commander ready to kill and to
stage a coup to save his own skin. As he was advanced through the ranks, Amin constantly honed his
innate sense of suspicion toward others who might
threaten him. Without this sense of suspicion it
seems improbable that he could have survived for
long at the elevated levels to which he had risen.
Yet it is equally hard to imagine how a person so
distrustful of others, and so conscious of his own
educational inferiority and lack of sophistication,
could have made any genuine attempt to reconcile
members of the Ugandan elite. In short, his own
psychological make-up imposed as much of a barrier
to any reconciliation approach as did the country's
shortage of resources.

Nor could Amin have operated as a "robber
chief," looting the country for the benefit of his
supporters, without resorting to massive killing.
There were too many people in Uganda capable of organizing revolts against his regime for him to be a
less murderous despot; if his supporters had not
randomly and casually killed critics of the government, many political activists would likely have
risen in protest against the regime. Terror was an
integral part of Amin's system for retaining power.
Yet once he started killing, family links meant that
he inevitably created more enemies, and thus to ensure his own safety he had to kill even more. While
we will never know exactly how many people died at

the hands of Amin's killer squads, the total likely is well over a quarter of a million.

Any verdict on Milton Obote as a political leader will necessarily be equivocal. Basically he was a good and capable man struggling to achieve ambitious goals in a most difficult situation. His greatest success was his ability to reconcile the clashing ethnic interests that made up the state of Uganda. He did quite well at bringing together all Ugandans outside Buganda, and his "revolution" of 1966 did remove the foci of particularist sentiment in Buganda and the other Bantu kingdoms, the kings of these territories. He also showed a desire to improve the lot of ordinary Ugandans, although the "Common Man's Charter" gave little indication of the means by which Uganda might attain its goal of a more egalitarian society. However, his style contributed greatly to subverting his chances of attaining his goals, His deviousness and secretiveness contributed to a lack of trust which prevented him from making any successful mass appeal. More seriously, his penchant for drastic extra-constitutional actions, most notably in 1966, helped break down the restraints on political conduct, and thus paved the way for Idi Amin's complete destruction of the rule of law. Although it seems more likely that he misread the political situation than that he held an insatiable lust for unfettered power, the result was the same: his actions contributed to an atmosphere in which Amin could take over.

By his own lights, Idi Amin could be judged a successful leader, in that during his eight years in power he drove Ugandans a long way toward accepting his Hobbesian value system. However, by a more normal criterion of success, namely whether he succeeded in making the lives of his countrymen better in any way, he was a near-total disaster. The expulsion of the Asians, racist and cruel though it was, did have the potential benefit of clearing the way for Ugandan entrepreneurs to emerge. However, it is hard to find any other action by Amin which was not completely and unequivocally evil, or whose results brought any discernible benefit to the Ugandan body politic. Idi Amin has secured himself a place in history, but as a warning of just how easily a ruler can destroy the supports for civilized behaviour. He illustrates as clearly as any person in recent history how effective is the use of sheer terror in keeping a ruler in power, provided that he has no goal beyond extracting enough wealth from the state to maintain himself and supporters.

NOTES

1.   See G.F. Engholm and Ali Mazrui, "Violent
Constitutionalism in Uganda", Government and Opposi-
tion, 2, 4 (July-October 1967) pp. 585-99. However
Engholm and Mazrui note that under Obote, while
violence was often threatened, it rarely occurred.
2.   Notably Garth Glentworth and Ian Hancock,
"Obote and Amin: change and continuity in modern
Uganda politics," African Affairs, 72, (July 1973),
pp. 237-55; G.A. Gingyera-Pinycwa, Apolo Milton
Obote and His Times, (NOK, New York, 1978); Aidan
Southall, "General Amin and the coup: great man or
historical inevitability?", Journal of Modern
African Studies, 13, 1 (1975), pp. 85-105; and
Grace Ibingira, The Forging of an African Nation
(Viking, New York, 1973), and African Upheavals Since
Independence (Westview, Boulder, Colo., 1979).
3.   Donald Rothchild and Michael Rogin,
"Uganda", in Gwendolen Carter, (ed.), National Unity
and Regionalism in Eight African States (Cornell
University Press, 1966), p. 361. In 1965, the
Economic Commission for Africa estimated Uganda's
per capita GDP at $83, second only to Kenya in
Eastern Africa. See Economic Survey of Africa, Vol.
III (1971), pp. 15-16.
4.   United Nations, Economic Survey of Africa
Since 1950, 181, cited in Guy Benveniste and
William Moran, Handbook of African Economic Develop-
ment, (Praeger, New York, 1962), p. 114.
5.   Rothchild and Rogin, "Uganda", pp. 362-63.
6.   Lord Hailey, An African Survey, (Oxford
University Press, London, 1938), table opp. p. 1308.
7.   Peter M. Gukiina, Uganda: A Case Study in
African Political Development (University of Notre
Dame Press, 1972, Notre Dame, Ind., 1972), pp. 98-99.
8.   Ibid., p. 91.
9.   Rothchild and Rogin, "Uganda", pp. 351-52.
For this withdrawal by Buganda from nationalist
politics, see also R. Cranford Pratt, "Nationalism
in Uganda", Political Studies, IX, 2 (June 1961),
pp. 157-78; Cherry Gertzel, Party and Locality in
in Northern Uganda, 1945-1962 (Athlone Press,
London, 1974), pp. 34ff., 56ff.; and M.S.M. Kiwanuka,
"Nationality and Nationalism in Africa: The Uganda
Case", Canadian Journal of African Studies, IV, 2
(Spring, 1970), pp. 229-47.
10.   See Ali Mazrui, "Privilege and Protest as
Integrative Factors: The Case of Buganda's Status
in Uganda", in Robert Rothberg and Ali Mazrui (eds.)
Protest and Power in Black Africa (Oxford University

Press, New York, 1970), pp. 1072-87.

11. Gertzel, Party and Locality, pp. 47-48
12. Gingyera-Pinycwa, Obote, p. 221. Gingyera-
Pinycwa gives the most detailed account of Obote's
emergence during this pre-independence period.
13. Ibid., p. 222.
14. Ibid., pp. 2-3.
15. Gukiina, Uganda, pp. 104-05.
16. Gertzel, Party and Locality, p. 6.
17. See Gingyera-Pinycwa, Obote, p. 225.
18. Sir Frederick Mutesa, Desecration of My
Kingdom, (Constable, London, 1967), p. 160.
Ibingira, Forging of a Nation, pp. 201-05, minimizes
Obote's role in the UPC-KY deal, suggesting he went
along reluctantly.
19. Gingyera-Pinycwa, Obote, pp. 41-46.
Ibingira, by contrast, regards Obote's move to
socialist policies as essentially opportunistic.
20. For useful data on the UPC Parliamentar-
ians, see Robert O. Byrd, "A Portrait of Leadership
in a New Nation: The Case of Uganda", Queen's
Quarterly, 62, 4 (Winter 1963), pp. 521-36.
21. Gingyera-Pinycwa, Obote, pp. 240-41. See
also Judith Listowel, Amin (IUP Books, Dublin, 1973),
pp. 30-41.
22. David Martin, General Amin (Faber & Faber,
London, 1974), p. 21.
23. Ibingira, African Upheavals, pp. 82-87,
provides evidence of a deliberate bias toward northerners in recruitment to the army.
24. For discussion on the importance of this
Nubi core of the army, see Southall, "General Amin",
and Peter Woodward, "Ambiguous Amin", African Affairs, 77, (April 1978), pp. 153-64.
25. See especially Alexander Mitchell and
Russell Miller, "Amin: The Untold Story", Sunday
Times Magazine (London), October 29, 1972.
26. See Gukiina, Uganda, 126-32; also M. Crawford
Young, "The Obote Revolution", Africa Report, June
1966, pp. 8-14.
27. Note here the contrasting views of Engholm
and Mazrui, "Violent Constitutionalism", p. 595, and
Ibingira, African Upheavals, pp. 154-61, the former
stressing the impartiality of the enquiry, the latter noting severe curbs on both terms of reference
and witnesses' freedom.
28. The Charter is included as an appendix in
James H. Mittelman, Ideology and Politics in Uganda
Cornell University Press, Ithaca, 1975). See also
Selwyn Ryan, "Economic nationalism and socialism in
Uganda", Journal of Commonwealth Political Studies,

11, 2 (July 1973), pp. 140-58 , and Irving
Gershenberg, "Slouching Toward Socialism: Obote's
Uganda", African Studies Review, IV, 1 (April 1972),
pp. 79-95.

29.   A.B. Mujaju, "The Role of the UPC as a
Party of Government in Uganda", Canadian Journal of
African Studies, X, 3 (1976), pp. 458-61.

30.   Gingyera-Pinycwa, Obote, 73. For a more
detailed discussion of the proposed scheme, see
Norman W. Provizer, "The National Electoral Process
and State Building; Proposals for New Methods of
Election in Uganda", Comparative Politics, 9, 3
(April 1977), pp. 305-26.

31.   Africa Contemporary Record, 3 (1970-1971),
p. B190.

32.   Holger Bernt Hansen, Ethnicity and Military Rule in Uganda (Institute of African Studies,
Uppsala, 1977), p. 75.

33.   Martin, General Amin, pp. 25, 45.

34.   The most detailed reconstruction of the
actual moves and counter-moves by the Amin and Obote
forces is provided by ibid., pp. 31-61.

35.   Gingyera-Pinycwa, Obote, p. 244.

36.   Martin, General Amin, p. 47.

37.   Listowel, Amin, p. 84.

38.   Martin, General Amin, P. 139.

39.   Michael J. Schultheis, "The Ugandan
Economy and General Amin, 1971-75", Studies in Comparative International Development, 10, 3 (Fall
1975), pp. 11-22.

40.   Even Listowel's amazing apologetic for
Amin admits these murders. Amin., p. 151.

41.   Ibingira, African Upheavals, pp. 278-279.

42.   Schultheis, "Ugandan Economy", p. 16.

43.   See Henry Kyemba, A State of Blood: The
Inside Story of Idi Amin (Ace Publishers, New York,
1977), pp. 114-15.

44.   Ibid., p. 101 For a claim that people
resisted passively as well as they could in the
face of totally ruthless and unpredictable terror,
see the description by a nameless Ugandan written
from Kampala shortly before Amin's downfall, in
Africa Contemporary Record, XI (1978-79), pp. B421-
22.

45.   F.J. Ravenhill, "Military Rule in Uganda:
The Politics of Survival", African Studies Review,
17, 1 (1974), p. 242.

46.   Ibid., p. 241.

47.   Ibid., p. 242.

48.   See Ibingira, African Upheavals, p. 281,
for a list of the industries which had collapsed.

For a more general account of the breakdown see Aidan Southall, "Social Disorganization in Uganda: Before, During and After Amin", <u>Journal of Modern African Studies</u>, 18, 4 (1980), pp. 627-56.

      49.   Martin, <u>General Amin</u>, p. 47.

Chapter Eleven

ETHIOPIA: A REVOLUTION DESPITE ITSELF?

        The most thorough uprooting of old institutions
and their replacement by new ones in an African
state in the last half-century overthrew not a
regime imposed by outside forces, but the ancien
regime which could call upon the longest indigenous
historical tradition of any in sub-Saharan Africa.
The northern core area of Ethiopia can trace a continuing history back to the ancient Aksum state,
contemporary with Rome. In the fourth century A.D.
Aksum adopted Christianity, and the Ethiopian Church
from that time onward provides a unifying core for
the dominant groups in the Ethiopian state. In the
19th century Ethiopia extended its boundaries to
incorporate ethnic groups with only marginal affini-
ties to the core areas, and under Emperor Haile
Selassie's rule (1930-1974) the central government
increased its control over outlying areas. However,
the Amhara, although comprising only a quarter of
Ethiopia's population, continued to dominate the
entire state, but did not succeed in assimilating
other peoples into their culture. One source of
friction thus was the divergent cultural aspirations
of different ethnic groups.
        However, it was the class structure of Ethiopia
that set it apart from the post-colonial African
states. Unlike these states, which came to be controlled by a Western-educated elite developed under
colonial rule, Ethiopia's dominant class was its
hereditary nobility, with the Emperor at the peak
of the hierarchy. Under him, the great provincial
lords and the lesser nobles within the hierarchy
extracted, with the aid of religiously sanctioned
custom, most of the surplus production of the ordinary farmers. At the same time, they checked the
efforts of successive Emperors to centralize power
in their own hands. Most of the country's political

history, in fact, had consisted of the continuing
struggle between Emperors and their nobles over
how much power the Emperor should enjoy. The peasants, of course, had no role in this apart from
providing the crops that sustained the upper levels
of society. Occasionally they would thrust themselves onto the stage in protest against a particularly rapacious lord or against an action by the
central government which seemed to threaten their
limited hereditary rights, but for the most part
politics was the preserve of the hereditary upper
class.

Haile Selassie in his long rule did more to
change this system than any previous Emperor, by
introducing Western education and elements of Western bureaucratic structure and military organization.
These changes greatly strengthened his personal
power in relation to the provincial nobility, but at
the same time created an unanticipated new set of
challengers who eventually overthrew both the Emper-
or and the old social structure. We should not
overestimate Haile Selassie's power to make changes,
however. The fact that he was operating in a well-
established system of rival power brokers, and that
his own role was fairly well-defined by custom, put
limits on him that the rulers of new African states
did not have to face, and ensured that any changes
he tried to bring about would require patient and
skillful manoeuvring. Moreover, the changes that
he brought about had only a limited effect in the rural
areas where most Ethiopians lived. In most of the
country, the strength of customary and religious
backing for the status quo seemed to ensure that the
dominance of the nobility would be eroded only over
generations, if at all.

Then suddenly, in 1974, all of this feudal
structure collapsed. Urban strikes and an intervention by young military officers removed first the
Emperor's advisors and then the Emperor himself, and
then the new military regime wiped out many of the
provincial nobles and encouraged the peasants to
organize themselves and to control their own land
through cooperative associations. The peasants
seized on this opportunity, and within three years
most of the inegalitarian, hierarchical structures of
rural control dominated by the nobility had been replaced by egalitarian peasant associations which
established a considerable degree of autonomy from
central government authority.

How could such a complete change come about so
suddenly? Only two years before the revolution,

when hundreds of thousands of peasants were starving to death in the northern regions, their condi-
tioning was such that the full granaries of rich
landlords were left untouched.[1] How could such
attitudes toward an Emperor and toward a system
which had been imbued for generations be reversed
in a matter of months - or could they? Or if popular attitudes did not sustain the old regime, how
had Haile Selassie survive so long? And finally,
what were the possible paths along which the Revolution might have travelled, and what produced the
turning points which brought it to its present
course?

A FEUDAL EMPIRE

        Ethiopia was the last African state to be sub-
ordinated to a European power, and its period as a
colony was far briefer (and less profound in its
impact) than that of any other territory. Until
1935 it had been unique among African states in
that its indigenous ruler had been treated by
Europeans as the head of a sovereign state. In
late 1935, when Italy invaded Ethiopia, the Western
powers indicated that they took Ethiopia's claims
to sovereignty as seriously as those of any European state by offering almost the same combination
of polite moral condolences and total physical in-
action as they were later to offer Austria and
Czechoslovakia. By May 1941, with World War II well
underway, a joint British-Sudanese-Ethiopian force
had driven Mussolini's troops out of Ethiopia and
allowed Haile Selassie to re-enter Addis Ababa.
Ethiopia's one brief period of direct subordination
to an outside power was over, and in the period of
decolonization after World War II Ethiopia could
act as a voice on behalf of the colonized African
territories.
        The lack of any prolonged colonial exploita-
tion, coupled with the reluctance of the Emperor's
entourage to permit socially disruptive activities,
contributed to Ethiopia's low ranking on the conventional indicators of "development." A United
Nations study based on 1965 data showed that within
the Eastern African region (Ethiopia to Malawi)
Ethiopia's per capita Gross Domestic Product of
$59 placed it near the middle of the region, above
Burundi, Rwanda and Malawi at $46, but well below
Uganda ($83) and Kenya ($100). Ethiopia derived
some 65% of its GDP from agriculture, a higher

percentage than any other state in the region. Government revenues and expenditure, a useful indica- of the hold a government has over its society, were lower per capita than any other government's except Burundi and Rwanda.2 In education, Ethiopia's ratio of primary school pupils to total population, 1.68%, was lower than any other state except Somalia, and lower by a factor of 4 than the 6.87% average for the region.3 Similarly, in health care, Ethiopia's ratio of 0.34 hospital beds per 1,000 population was lower by a factor of 3 than the next lowest country in the region.4 Finally, Ethiopians' life expectancies at birth of 34 years in 1960 and 38 years in 1975 place the country second last and last for those years among African states by this general indicator of public health.5 Ethiopia under Haile Selassie, in brief, remained what it had been for much of its history, a poor, backward and somewhat isolated land.

Some of this isolation and backwardness, to be sure, was a direct result of Ethiopia's physical characteristics. The spectacular mountains that comprise the central heartland of the Empire facilitate regional and local isolation, and also aid a long tradition of fending off attempts by the central government to impose control over local areas. There have always been some unifying forces, particularly for the core areas; the Ethiopian Church served to provide a common bond among Amhara, Tigreans and even some Eritreans, while Amharic as a national language, even though it was associated with a dominant ethnic group, did possess features found in both northern and southern languages, and had been in use as a lingua franca for centuries.6 Then too, the Emperor himself served to some extent as a symbol of unity, the moreso as he sought to buttress his position with religious appeals. Nevertheless, despite these unifying factors, most of Ethiopia's history consisted of a struggle between successive Emperors' attempts to bring regions under some central control and the regions' attempts to establish their autonomy, if not break away completely. At the same time, cutting across these regional conflicts was an underlying class conflict, which while usually held in bounds by the force of custom and religion, would occasionally erupt into open struggle.

Since Ethiopia is a predominantly agricultural state, and since in its mountainous terrain arable land is at a premium, control over land was the crucial feature in determining who had power.

259

While the details of Ethiopia's land tenure system under the Empire were incredibly complex, two major systems predominated. In the north-central part of the country, the core area of the Empire, a system of hereditary peasant rights to the ownership of land was overlaid by the claims of the nobility to tribute from the land and from the peasants themselves. Every male in every family lineage had a hereditary claim (<u>rist</u>) to a portion of the land belonging to that lineage, regardless of where he lived or whether he worked it. Superimposed on these hereditary rights were the <u>gult</u> rights given to individuals as a gift from the Emperor for service,, and theoretically not inheritable. These were rights to a share of the peasants' produce in a <u>gult</u> holding as well as to compulsory labour by the peasant. Under this combination of <u>rist</u> and <u>gult</u> almost everyone owned some land, and there were infinite gradations of land-holding size and the wealth obtainable from the land, with no great gap between <u>gult</u>- and <u>rist</u>-holders. Small peasants as well as great nobles, in fact, perceived themselves as having rights which could be jeopardized by too powerful a central government, and consequently were prepared to work with the nobles against central government attempts at land reform.

In the south, the situation was different. These areas (comprising in the 1960s a third of Ethiopia's population) had not been added to the Empire until the late 19th century, and their people, the Galla or Oromo, had up to that time enjoyed their own system of land tenure. After the conquest the Emperor rewarded his soldiers by giving them large estates, far larger than an individual could farm for himself by hand. Since the soldiers were largely Amhara, and since the Ethiopian government did not recognize any hereditary right to land among the Oromo peasants, the effect was that of a foreign ruling class treating the peasantry as tenants on what used to be their own land. The costs of being a tenant were high; peasants had to pay between a third and a half of their crop as tribute, plus a 10% tithe, and provide free labour for the landlord's own land. Not surprisingly, there were frequent uprisings in these areas, although unlike the northerners, Oromo who resisted these exactions even by passive means could be sold into slavery.[8] To hold the local population down, the Emperor Menelik in the late 19th century set up a series of fortified garrison towns in the conquered provinces, which remained

Christian Amhara centres in Muslim or pagan hinter-
lands, and thus helped reinforce the distinction
between conquerors and conquered.[9]
    However, the degree to which the peasants were
exploited by the ruling class really was not that
different between north and south; the main difference was the extent to which the Christian church
in the north succeeded in making this order legitimate in the eyes of the peasants, rather than being
based purely on force. Even in the north, legitimacy had its limits; there were frequent peasant
revolts against excessive taxes, although interestingly, these revolts were generally led by dissident members of the nobility.[10] These revolts were
rebellions rather than revolutionary attempts to
change the fundamental structures of Ethiopian
society, and were necessarily limited to local objectives by the limited communications and horizons
of both the peasants and the provincial nobility.
Furthermore, there was some benefit even to the
peasants from the existence of the Ethiopian state;
without this system of ordered exploitation, as
agriculturalists they would have been subject to
more sporadic but far more destructive depredations
by armed marauders.[11]
    The central figure in the Ethiopian empire was
the Emperor. Once installed, an individual could
call upon the sanctity of his own imperial presence, a tradition going back to the time of
Solomon and the Queen of Sheba, and above all, the
blessing of the Ethiopian Church, as supra-rational
supports to his rule. He also enjoyed more concrete
sources of power, most notably his control over the
allocation of gult rights to the nobility, and thus
over the basic sources of wealth in Ethiopian society. An individual noble could be disciplined by
stripping him of his offices and thus of his wealth
and his ability to hold supporters, although if the
noble were attacked in a way that seemed to threat-
en the privileges of the nobility as a class, an
Emperor would encounter too much collective resistance to impose his will. The main limits to the
Emperor's power were, first, the fact that until
after World War II he was dependent for nearly all
the armed forces of the country upon the private
armies of the major nobles; second, the poor communications within Ethiopia; third, the fact that the
Emperor was not generally perceived as a defender
of the peasants against the nobility, but simply as
a more distant and potentially even more threatening exploiter; and fourth, the fact that outside the

261

ranks of the nobility it was almost impossible at least until the 1960s to find either the revenues or the individuals with the training and skills necessary to create alternative structures of power to challenge the nobility. The Emperor, in short, was confined by the existing system to a role which involved manipulating and brokering among the nobility, without being able to make fundamental changes in the structure of power.

The nobility and the Church, for their part, also needed the Emperor. Without his temporal power, the church's substantial wealth would be unprotected, while without his symbolic central role, it would be hard to see how the Ethiopian state would hold together, and without an Ethiopian state the nobles' fiefdoms would have been picked off by the colonial powers in the 19th century. While the nobles tried to restrain the Emperors's accumulation of power in order to protect their own, they (and the Church) could agree with the Emperor on one fundamental point: the ordinary people were to be excluded 'from power. Whatever their disagreements, none would suggest opening up the political process to mass participation.

HAILE SELASSIE: THE CENTRALIZATION OF CONTROL

During his half-century as the ruler of Ethiopia, Haile Selassie managed to create enough new social groups in Ethiopia to shift the balance of power substantially to the central government and against the landlords, but in doing so he created conditions that eventually led to his own downfall. Born in 1892, the son of a great lord and the great-great-grandson of a king, Ras (Prince) Tafari Makonnen became a provincial governor at age 14, and emerged at age 24 as Regent and heir apparent to the Empress Zauditu. In the following 14 years he honed his skills of intrigue, alliance-building, and the use of both threats and persuasion to consolidate his position, and when the Empress died in 1930, was crowned Emperor.

From 1930 onward, Haile Selassie combined traditional and innovative methods to consolidate his control. With a quarter century of practice already behind him, and endowed with immense energy, a shrewd sense of what would bring a particular individual to his side, and a prodigious ability to keep track of administrative details, he skillfully played off the various lords against one another,

and co-opted key ones through strategic appoint-
ments. His diminutive but regal presence was not
confined to Addis Ababa; throughout his career, he
was likely to make on-the-spot inspections of even
remote corners of his empire. He also brought in
a number of organizational innovations which
strengthened central government, such as creating a
central bank and currency in 1931, which gave the
central government more direct control over revenues.[12] The aftermath of the Italian invasion facilitated this centralization. After his restoration in 1941 the Emperor was able to get help from
the British and Americans in setting up a Customs
Department in 1943[13] which gave the central government further direct control over revenues. He also
brought provincial and local governors directly
under his jurisdiction,[14] and set up the Haile
Selassie I University in 1951, which provided a new
educated cadre of administrators directly beholden
to the emperor for their positions (even though
most were still drawn from the aristocracy).[15]
Most important of all, he established a central
army professionally trained and equipped by the
Americans.[16]
        While strengthening the central power, he at
the same time introduced a number of regulations
weakening the hold of the nobility in the pro-
inces.[17] While the nobility still held the governors' posts at all levels, they were forbidden to
raise their own military forces or operate their
own police units. They could not appoint, transfer
or dismiss subordinates on their own authority, and
they could not levy taxes or dues other than those
fixed by the central government. The peasants'
labour as part of their gult privileges was removed
in 1941, and three years later other customary
forms of tribute were outlawed. Their income was
henceforth to come from salaries paid by the central treasury, a move which left them decisively
subordinated to the central government. The main
function remaining to them was judging local disputes while their privileges now were confined to
retaining portions of the peasants' land tax and
being exempted from paying this tax themselves.
        However, this exemption from land tax illustra-
ted that while Haile Selassie could reduce by round-
about means the nobility's power to challenge him,
he could not bring about significant structural
changes by a direct frontal assault on the nobility's land wealth, their main source of power. In
1942, the government proposed to impose a land tax

based on the amount of individuals' land holdings, a
move which would have severely curtailed the wealth
of the nobility. In the northern provinces where
land was held communally, widespread resistance
eventually led to these provinces being exempted.
Elsewhere, the large landlords objected strenuously,
and they too were generally exempted or allowed to
pass their tax on to their tenants. Where they
could obtain neither of these loopholes, they refused to pay.[18] It was later estimated that if
land were taxed at the prescribed rates, instead of
bringing in only some $2.2 million in revenue, the
land tax could bring in between $15 million and $49
million.[19] An equally abortive attempt to get at
the nobility's wealth, this time by means of a tax
on an individual's gross income from the harvest,
occurred in 1967. This time the Chamber of Deputies, which because of the income requirements for
membership was essentially a landlords' body, "voted to nullify the tax insofar as feudal powers were
concerned but passed those measures which applied
against the peasants."[20] Once again the landlords
were also able to enlist support from smaller rist
landholders with the claim that their tenure was
threatened, and a rebellion in Gojjam province lasting over two years eventually led the government to
withdraw the tax measure. The episode made it abun-
dantly clear, especially to the younger, reform-
minded administrators, that the Emperor either could
not or would not force changes that the nobility and
the Church opposed.[21]
     While the nobility fought stubbornly against
any change in the burden of taxation, in several
areas they were quick to take advantage of opportunities for cash crop sales, either for the domestic
market or for export. Thus in the Awash Valley in
southeast Ethiopia, a Dutch company first set up a
sugar plantation, then a British firm began a cotton
plantation. At this point several local chiefs saw
the potential for enriching themselves, and established their own plantations, putting their own
pastoral peoples' grazing land under irrigation in
the process, so that the herds were forced onto less
fertile and more crowded pastures. When drought hit
the region in 1973, many of the pastoralists died of
starvation along with their herds.[22]
     In another area, in south-central Ethiopia, a
Swedish aid project began in 1967 to improve the
productivity of local farmers through fertilizers
and high-quality seeds. The local landowners soon
saw that these new techniques combined with

264

mechanization could offer a far better return than traditional tenancies, and evicted some two thousand tenants. Others let tenants stay, but raised their rents, and at the same time took over pasture land and access to water for their mechanized operations, thus reducing the small farmers' ability to use their oxen for ploughing. The overall effect was to widen the gap between tenants and land-owners,[23] and to lead the Swedes and other foreigners to demand major land reforms as the price of continuing aid.

Meanwhile, in Addis Ababa the Emperor's build-up of a central bureaucracy as a counter-weight to the provincial nobility was beginning to have a number of dangerous effects. First, it began to suggest to the nobility that their interests were not necessarily served by the Emperor and thus reduced their readiness to support him. Second, it created a group of influential men who lacked close ties to the rural areas, and consequently lacked a sense of what was possible and what was needed in the countryside. Third, the encouragement of secondary and post-secondary education created a growing body of individuals with high material aspirations. However, Ethiopia's restricted economy put limits on the number of well-paid jobs that could be provided, and consequently there were growing numbers of youths disillusioned with the imperial system. Fourth, in his attempts to build up the economy, Haile Selassie had encouraged large numbers of foreign industries and agri-businesses to establish themselves. Unfortunately, these did not provide many jobs, but they did produce economic dislocations, as noted above, and did encourage suspicion of foreigners. Fifth, the influx of formally educated, rationalist Ethiopians into the bureaucracy, coupled with the demands of foreign governments and international institutions for land reform, intensified the criticism of the landed nobility as a parasitic drag on "progress."

All these pressures in the urban sector intensified throughout the 1960s. Some impatient reformers had tried in 1960 during Haile Selassie's absence to stage a coup through the Imperial Bodyguard, but this had quickly been put down by conservative leaders of the regular army, and there was little evidence of popular support for this coup attempt save among students.[24] More and more it became apparent that reform through existing channels was impossible. The Emperor would not tamper with key powers of the provincial nobility because

he needed them, yet without a frontal assault on
this nobility, there was little hope of any change
toward a more equitable society, or one which allowed non-aristocratic talents to rise. One partial
channel for mobility, interestingly, lay in the
army, where a number of the younger officers had
been drawn from rural peasant backgrounds.[25] However, even here there was a blockage; the top positions stayed firmly in the hands of the nobility, or
at least those among the nobility whom Haile
Selassie thought were likely to be loyal.

Cross-cutting these essentially class conflicts
were other more severe ones based on ethnicity. In
their domination of Ethiopia, the Amhara tried to
force assimilation of other ethnic groups, making
Amharic the only national language and the
Christian church the only recognized religious body,
and generally ignoring the existence of other groups..
Yet neither the Amhara as an ethnic group nor the
church were readily penetrable; and there were many
forms of discrimination against those whose background was recognizably non-Amhara and non-Christian.

The result was predictable. Ethnic resentments
smouldered beneath the surface of much of Ethiopia,
and gathered force as communication increased in
the 1960s. The Oromo had always resented their subordination as a conquered people, and frequently
rose in rebellion. The Tigreans, though historical-
ly one of the main components of Ethiopia, resented
the Shoan ascendency and found their language
treated as badly as those of all other non-Amhara
speakers. From 1960 onward, with the advent of an
independent Republic of Somalia claiming to be the
government of all Somalis, the southeastern Ogaden
region became increasingly insecure. The most
serious threat of all to Ethiopian unity, however,
came from the Red Sea province of Eritrea, which had
been under a succession of non-Ethiopian rulers
until the Italians were driven out in 1941. After
nine years of wrangling, Britain handed over control
to Ethiopia in an arrangement that gave Eritrea
self-government in a kind of federation with
Ethiopia. The Ethiopian central government never
gave any sign of wanting this system to work, but
instead systematically worked to draw Eritrea under
the same system of tight central control that prevailed in all other areas.

The Ethiopians for a while found support for
this approach among part of the Eritrean population.
The highland part of Eritrea was peopled largely by
Christian Tigreans who inclined toward union with

266

Ethiopia in any case, and who were systematically favoured by the Ethiopian government. The lowland areas were largely peopled by Muslims who were equally systematically discriminated against by Ethiopia. In 1961 an Eritrean Liberation Front came into being, largely supported by Muslims at first, although over time it acquired some support from Christians who resented Amharic domination. A more radical offshoot, the Eritrean Peoples Liberation Front, broke away from the ELF in 1970, and after some fratricidal struggles, emerged as the dominant anti-Ethiopian force. Both movements were aided by the fact that under Italian colonialism, the power of the indigenous chiefs had been largely destroyed and an indigenous bourgeosie had developed to a far greater extent than in Ethiopia proper. Besides encouraging an "Eritrean" identity, this gave the Eritreans a sense of superiority over the "backward" Ethiopians, and thus sharpened their sense of grievance. For their part, the Ethiopians dared not make too many concessions to Eritrean particularism, since to permit regional autonomy here would open the floodgates throughout the Empire. Hence much of the Ethiopian army became increasingly bogged down in a brutal struggle to suppress the Eritrean nationalist movement, a struggle which by 1974 seemed to be growing ever more hopeless.

The stalemates that had been reached by 1974 showed how dangerous a brokerage style of leadership could become when the channels through which the broker had to work were strongly biased in favour of one set of participants. The nobility, buttressed by the church and the Amharic orientation of most of its members, was strongly enough entrenched that it could prevent any compromise that would assuage the rising frustration among the growing mass of non-noble intellectuals, urban workers and mobilized non-Amharas. If the nobility had been less strongly entrenched, or if they had been farsighted enough to open the doors to significant participation by the mobilized but excluded groups, there was the possibility that a new balance could have been struck in which the Emperor or his successor would have relied much more heavily upon the new groups in the political arena. But to work out such a compromise, it was essential that all groups be included in the bargaining, and there was little sign that this would happen under Haile Selassie.

Right up to 1974, even though it was clear that to resolve the ethnic and class stalemates there needed to be a major shift in strength away from the

nobility, the situation did not seem explosive. It
seemed generally agreed that a shift would come to
break the blockages, but that this would not be
until after Haile Selassie's death, an event which
despite his celebrating his eightieth birthday in
1972 seemed an indeterminate distance away.[26]

The major question was what kind of change would
come after Haile Selassie's death. It seemed unlikely that the changes would be revolutionary, that
the nobility would be swept away or that the peasants would be able to assert themselves in any significant way. The nobility were just too strongly
entrenched to be swept aside. They owned most land,
urban as well as rural; their educated sons filled
many bureaucratic posts; and they owned much of the
growing industrial and agri-business sectors. The
peasants, by contrast, were psychologically too accustomed to obedience and clientage roles to be able
to organize themselves to challenge the nobility's
control in the provinces. Their behaviour, it was
generally thought, was based not just on their perception of self-interest within a nobility-controlled
set of institutions, but was also reinforced by the
legitimacy of both the Emperor and the Church. A
major change might lighten their burden of taxes,
but could hardly be expected to overturn the existing order.

The real question that seemed most significant
was how far the nobility would have to open up opportunities for new members of the bourgeoisie. The
nobility could count on a substantial body of support
among the peasantry, particularly in the north and
central regions, and in the same areas they also
benefitted from the power of the Church with its
170,000 clergy[27] and huge land holdings. They also
enjoyed control over many top-level government posts
through their educational advantages. Against these
assets had to be weighed the suspicion with which
they were regarded as a group by many of the younger
"meritocratic" civil servants drawn from humbler
backgrounds, particularly in light of their unremit-
ting opposition to any equitable taxation system.
Their tendency to focus on regional and local problems, and to quarrel among themselves on these bases,
was also a weakness, though not a serious one, since
they usually managed to unite in defence of their
class privileges.

The new bourgeoisie, those high-level civil
servants, businessmen, and military officers who were
not of the nobility, was in a weaker position, although its strength was growing. Its economic base

was still weak, since many of the economic opportunities that such a group might normally fill were pre-empted by foreign businesses. Its civil service component was technocratic, and while both capable and frustrated, was likely to be out of touch with the realities of ordinary rural life. The military had the potential to play a significant role, but they were pre-occupied with Eritrea and later, with the Somali problem. Most serious of all, no component of this class - civil servants, businessmen, military officers - had a basis for rural acceptance comparable to that of the nobility.

What seemed likely, therefore, was a continuing autocracy dominated by the nobility, but giving somewhat greater scope to the new bourgeoisie. Without the central figure of the Emperor, the centrifugal tendencies in the empire would likely have greater effect, and might be met by some degree of regional devolution, and possibly even by concessions on language policy and official attitudes toward various regions. Yet as long as continuing adherence to the central government offered benefits to dominant provincial groups, there was no reason to expect the empire to break up.

Still, one had to remember that despite the Church and the symbolism of the Emperor, the basic attachments to established structures in Ethiopia were mercenary. People did not stay loyal to the Emperor or to their local lord out of some suprarational commitment, but simply on the basis that he had the power to help or harm them. If the lord no longer possessed this power, there was no stigma or sanction for abandoning him.[28] If by some unforeseeable event the structures of power were destroyed, people would not retain their loyalty to these structures, or rebuild them. They could just as easily switch their support to any other type of structure.

In 1974 the Empire's political structure still looked strong and imposing. Few suspected it was like a painted wooden building that had been riddled by termites, so that at each point where the soldiers or civilians pushed their demands it crumbled in front of them, until the whole edifice lay in ruins. Yet so strong was the belief in the solidity of the system that few even realized it was collapsing until most key features had fallen. Most initial demands were extremely modest, such as requests for a more equitable taxing system or for more representative institutions. But as more and more hitherto silent elements felt emboldened to put forward their demands, it became very clear that a radical restructuring of the whole society would be needed to accomodate them.

But what would this radical restructuring include? In a situation where most people had felt too inhibited to even think about sweeping changes, let alone to organize public demands for them, there was an almost infinite range of proposals. However, a great advantage lay with the radical groups who had created an underground opposition to the Emperor. They could quickly present plausible and comprehensive goals capable of rallying support even though these goals had been unthinkable only a few months earlier. Radical movements quickly emerged among the urban workers, the students, and within the military, all pressing for thorough structural changes, but all mutually suspicious of each other.

A second factor proved to be even more crucial in settling who actually could grasp the levers of government. With several groups each presenting programmes of considerable popular appeal, the group that could control force and use it most effectively would be able to push its rivals aside and obtain popular acquiescence. The military clearly had a potential advantage over civilian groups here if some person or group could direct it, and in the radical younger officers who were to form the Co-ordinating Committee or Dergue, it had such a group.

THE CREEPING REVOLUTION

The Ethiopian Revolution went through four stages. First, it saw demands become increasingly sweeping and radical, as the limits imposed by the old regime collapsed. Second, it went through a struggle for power among different radical groups, particularly the army officers against students and other civilian groups, with the differences between them being not so much over the future shape of Ethiopian society as over who should hold power. Third, in the course of their struggle for power, the different groups tried to outbid each other for popular support, with the culmination of this escalation being the sweeping land reform of 1975. Fourth, as the eventual winners of the struggle for control of the central government, the military radicals, consolidated their power, and Major Mengistu eliminated his personal rivals, he found himself

270

forced to live with the new structures created in
the heat of the struggle. Specifically, the land
reform and the creation of an armed peasantry created a barrier to the regime backsliding toward any
large-scale rural land-holding, whether by a revived
nobility or by state collective farms.

Several background factors set the stage for
the "creeping coup" of 1974. The failure of the
attempted land reform in 1967-69 made it clear to
both civilians and military officers who wanted
change that this could not be brought about under
the existing order.29 Then in the early 1970s when
drought struck northern Ethiopia along with the rest
of northern Africa, Haile Selassie's government
tried to conceal the situation rather than alleviat-
ing it, with the result that some 200,000 people
starved to death.30 A major contributing factor in
this was the tremendous growth in export crops at
the expense of domestic food supplies, a policy encouraged by the government.31 While the police had
no trouble keeping the starving peasants from caus-
ing trouble, nothing could stop many younger intellectuals from being repelled by the callousness of
the regime. The Emperor's liking for displaying
the majesty of his rule through conspicuous display -
the sumptuous thrones, golden plates, the fleet
of limousines - suddenly seemed less an affirmation
of the glory of Imperial Ethiopia than a gross display of contempt for human suffering.

In the towns the shortage of food helped fuel
a severe inflation, and this was compounded by the
widespread unemployment both among the unskilled
illiterates who had come in from the countryside and
also among the school leavers for whom Ethiopia's
narrow industrial structure could offer few opportunities. The drought even affected the food and
water supplies of the armed forces, who were already
unhappy over the dangers of the Eritrean campaign.

On January 12, 1974, the rank and file of a
small garrison in southeast Ethiopia rebelled
against their officers over poor food and a shortage
of drinking water.32 The Emperor decided not to
punish the mutineers. Word of both the mutiny and
the Emperor's action flashed throughout the army and
police barracks around the country, and a month
later the NCOs at a key air base near Addis Ababa
also rebelled. They were soon followed by the en-
listed men and NCOs of the Second Division at Asmara,
who began broadcasting their complaints over the
radio station. Meanwhile, students and university
professors and high school teachers had demonstrated

against proposed changes in the educational system, and they were quickly joined by other groups protesting against specific grievances, from taxi drivers' complaints about a 50% increase in gasoline prices to the urban poor protesting against food price increases. The Emperor hastily changed prime ministers, and promised dramatically to make the prime minister responsible to Parliament. However, this seemed merely to whet peoples' appetites, and from March to May group after group both in Addis Ababa and the countryside demonstrated, protested or struck on behalf of long-suppressed demands. At the end of April, the regime attempted to restore the old order. The army arrested 19 notoriously corrupt government officials, but at the same time the government began cracking down on strikes and the newly-formed unions. Then on June 28 some deputies tried to have those officials held by the military released. The military's response was unexpected. A secret Co-ordinating Committee, later to be known as the Dergue, announced that the armed forces would no longer automatically obey the prime minister, and while they proclaimed "unswerving loyalty" to the Emperor, began systematically to arrest all those around him. By August the newspapers began carrying stories about the Emperor's abuses of power, and on September 12, with all his close associates already jailed, the Emperor was taken from his palace and placed under house arrest, although the Dergue did not formally proclaim the end of the monarchy until March 1975.

The direction of the revolution - and in fact whether it really was a revolution - was still not at all clear when the Emperor was deposed. The junior "radical" officers who comprised the core of the Dergue were no doubt emboldened by the lack of resistance to their actions, but there was still considerable controversy over what to do next. Students and trade unionists in Addis Ababa began demanding that the military give way to a civilian "Peoples' Government", and this view won some support within sections of the armed forces. However, a majority of the Dergue decided to maintain the organization as a ruling council and enforced their decision by arresting the trade union leaders and the military dissidents. But they still had to work out policies toward the political prisoners they had taken and toward Eritrea.

The most prominent member of the Dergue was General Aman Michael Andom, a widely-popular war hero of Eritrean and upper-class origins, whose

demands for restructuring the 120-man Dergue into a
smaller body were regarded by other members as a
sign of personal ambition. He felt strongly that
the Eritrean conflict should be resolved by a peaceful settlement, even by negotiating with the Eritrean Liberation Front. He equally strongly
opposed executing the political prisoners, both on
principle and because many were his personal friends.
When a majority of the Dergue overruled him on both
issues, he tried to rally the army rank and file,
but was blocked from reaching them, and then retired
to his home on November 15. On November 23, he was
killed at his home in a gun battle with troops sent
to arrest him. The same night, 57 political prisoners were taken to the central prison and executed.
The "hard liners," led by Major Mengistu Haile
Mariam, had won a first round.

The next few months saw an equally irrevocable,
and more genuinely revolutionary step. After proclaiming in January that the goal of the revolution
was "Ethiopian socialism," the Dergue gave substance
to this in March 1975 with a simple but drastic solution to the rural land problem: it declared all the
land nationalized, tenancy abolished, and farmers
given "possessory rights" over land they were working up to a maximum of ten hectares. To ensure that
land was redistributed in accordance with these
rules, and that land tenancy and tributes were eradi-
cated, the government sent out into the countryside
some 40,000 teachers and students. These in turn
organized peasant associations, which were confined
to former smallholders and tenants, and were given
powers to settle land disputes, establish service
co-operatives, and set up local militias.[33] The
associations spread quickly. By the end of the sum-
mer of 1975, the Ministry of Land Reform claimed
there were some 18,000 of them, with 4.5 million
members,[34] while by 1977 there were perhaps some
25,000, with some 7 million members,[35] of whom some
300,000 comprised an armed militia.

Despite the government's subsequent use of the
peasant associations' militia to conscript thousands
of young men for use as ill-trained cannon fodder in
Eritrea, the associations seem to have retained their
popularity among peasants. In mid-1979, the government moved to replace them by "producer co-operatives"
which would concentrate on economic activities rather
than embracing the wide range of political and judi-
cial functions of the peasant associations,[36] but it
is unclear how much effect this has had in curbing
the peasants' newly-won control over their own lives.

Between the peasants' increased literacy and their armed militia, any government would have a struggle to impose centrally-controlled collectivization in the near future.

Meanwhile in the urban areas the conflict between students and unionists demanding civilian rule, and an army determined to keep power in its own hands, grew increasingly bitter. The most militant civilian organization, the Ethiopian Peoples Revolutionary Party, gained prominence in 1976 for its harsh verbal attacks on the military regime. By September, when its members had largely gone underground, its attacks became physical, and though it just missed assassinating Major Mengistu September 23, it did succeed in killing several hundred persons with links to the Dergue and to the civilian Political Bureau the Dergue had set up. The Dergue then launched its own counter-terror and within a few months had killed several thousand EPRP supporters, leaving that organization shattered. In the process, the Dergue itself split, with the then chairman, General Teferi Banti, urging reconciliation with the EPRP. On February 3, 1977, this difference of opinion within the Dergue was resolved when a shoot-out at a Dergue meeting left Teferi Banti and six of his supporters dead, against a single Mengistu supporter. With most of his major rivals now eliminated, (the last real threat, Lt.-Col. Atnafu Abate, was finally executed in November 1977), Mengistu now emerged as the strongman of the revolution.

The Political Bureau still had to be dealt with, since its intellectuals now thought the time was ripe for them to supplant the military men. The latter's response was predictable; the Political Bureau members were now hunted down and killed or jailed just as the EPRP had been earlier. By the end of 1977, all civilian groups had been terrorized into acceptance of the military regime's control, to the point where they were unlikely to offer open challenges to the military.

REVOLUTIONARY ON THE THRONE

Within the military regime, Comrade Chairman Mengistu Haile Mariam occupied the gold and red velvet armchair atop the dais formerly used by Emperor Haile Selassie.[37] Described by diplomats as "head and shoulders above those around him in determination, intelligence, and total commitment to his

vision of what he wants for Ethiopia,"38 Mengistu
spent the years after the "Red Terror" securing his
personal position with the aid of some 10,000 Cuban
troops, hundreds of Russian and Cuban technical
advisors, and a security force organized by the
East Germans. However, despite this heavy reliance
on the Communist bloc, and the fact that it was
Cuban troops who enabled him first to beat back a
Somali threat in 1978 and then to contain the
Eritrean nationalists, Mengistu showed few signs of
subordinating his own goals to those of the Russians and their allies. For example, he had managed up to 1981 to resist the Russians' attempts to
build a political party which might be beyond his
personal control.39
     Despite its bloodshed and the appearance of
being first and foremost an attempt by Mengistu to
win power for his personal satisfaction, the military regime did produce lasting changes in Ethiopia.
The land reform is something that any government,
no matter how determined to bring all Ethiopia under
centralized control, would find very hard to undo.
An almost equally revolutionary step has been the
massive literacy programme, involving some seven
million adults, or nearly half the adult popula-
tion.40 Medical care and provision of water supplies to rural areas have also been dramatically
improved. Against this, however, have to be set
some heavy costs. The loss of some 40,000 educated
Ethiopians who fled into exile, the deaths of some
5,000 to 10,000 youths supposed to have been involved in the EPRP, the disappearance of 10,000 to
40,000 people into the political prisons (the
regime does not inform anyone of who is being held
in jail) the allegations that the government prac-
ticed genocide against the Somali nomads in the
Ogaden through systematic poisoning of their
wells,41 and the help received from foreign troops
to put down radical nationalist movements in the
Ogaden and Eritrea, all left the regime looking
like a hybrid between Stalinist Russia and Mobutu's
Zaire. It was not surprising that many radicals
felt this was a "revolution betrayed."42
     Perhaps a fairer summary, however, would be
that this was a successful revolution despite itself. First of all, the fact that the Emperor was
overthrown at all was due, I suggest, to his initial
hesitancy when the January 1974 mutiny took place.
If he had dealt with that mutiny as summarily as he
had always dealt with similar uprisings earlier in
his rule, it seems unlikely that the next mutinies

would have occurred as soon as they did, or that he would have been afraid to use the army to quell the civilian disturbances. As it was, the fact that each protest "got away with it" emboldened the next, until the entire army and the urban population were aroused against the regime. Even as late as June 1974, Haile Selassie might have retrieved the situation if he had followed the counsel of some of the nobility and used the loyal troops of the Imperial Bodyguard to attack and destroy the Dergue at its headquarters in the Fourth Division. Instead, he vetoed this plan, and "sat as if in a stupor" while his close associates were arrested, including, two months later, the officers of the Imperial Bodyguard.[43]

Why did Haile Selassie behave as he did? One possibility is simply that old age (he was 82) and weariness had finally dulled his reactions to the point that he could not comprehend clearly what he had to do to ensure his survival. Another explanation that complements this is that he had come to believe his own legend so fully that he could not conceive of junior officers actually molesting him or defying his orders. This explanation gains credence from the fact that members of the aristocracy who were named in July as being wanted by the military on charges of misusing their positions came voluntarily to the Fourth Division headquarters to submit to incarceration. Whether this was out of a conviction that their superior status would protect them against any harm by the junior officers and NCOs, a belief that the Dergue was a passing phenomenon which would collapse quickly, a confidence that they would be found innocent of wrongdoing by any tribunal, or some other reason, there can be few cases of a ruling class submitting so readily to their own destruction.[44] With such self-confidence in their own invulnerability, it was understandable that both the Emperor and the nobility would be unable to comprehend the need for drastic countermeasures to retrieve the situation. At the same time, skillfully negotiated compromises that might have assuaged most of the expressed discontents of both the military and the civilians were equally out of the question; the nobility were not accustomed to negotiating with those of inferior status.

Once the Emperor was removed, there was still a wide range of possible directions the military could have taken. Most critically, the land reform could have been a much less thoroughgoing one, with a reduction in tributes, some requirement that

arable land be used, or perhaps that the largest
estates be redistributed among tenants, but without
such a complete redistribution and certainly without
setting up peasant associations to enforce the reform.   There is no evidence to suggest that any of
the officers envisioned from the start the dramatic
change that in fact took place. What seems to have
happened was that the radicals among the military
and the radical civilians who were trying to outbid
them for support escalated the extent of the reform
until the military finally came up with their sweeping solution in March 1975.[45] The most striking
feature in all this is that there did not seem to
be any intense demand from the peasants for such a
drastic reform; the impetus seems to have come from
the top down, even though the peasants took up the
goal with enthusiasm once it was presented to them.
    Once the land reform decree was proclaimed,
both the military and their civilian antagonists
had their own reasons for ensuring that it was carried into reality. With the bulk of the army tied
up in Eritrea, a rural police force too closely
tied to the ousted landlords to be trusted, and
limited ability to move troops around the mountainous countryside, the Dergue had to find some structures through which it could control the countryside, and the burgeoning peasant associations
seemed to be the only possible instrument of control.
The students and other opponents of the military,
for their part, saw the associations as a potential
weapon against the Dergue. In fact, from the time
they were initially sent into the countryside to
organize the peasants, many students stressed to
the latter that they should run their organizations
as they saw fit regardless of what the government
wished them to do, a doctrine which the peasants
took to heart.[46]
    As for Major Mengistu's emergence as the leader
of the Dergue, what was decisive was not so much the
content of his beliefs as his ruthlessness in securing his own position. The killing of General Aman
and of the nobles in November 1974 and the "Red
Terror" which decimated the EPRP and then the
Dergue's Political Bureau "allies," the shoot-out
between Mengistu's supporters and General Teferi's
faction, and the executions of Col. Atnafu and other
"radical" rivals all seem to have had far less to do
with the content of the rival groups' political
beliefs than with their temperaments. Mengistu, to
put it simply, was ready to kill others more quickly
than they were ready to kill him. To be sure, this

277

ruthlessness may in part be attributable to the fact that he had a more definite idea of what he wanted to do than did his rivals, and thus could act with more certainty, but I do not see any necessary connection between the degree of radicalism per se in his ideas and the readiness to take drastic steps to implement these ideas.

Mengistu, however, was more than just a ruthless power-seeker, or he would never have presided over the kind of transformation of Ethiopia that he in fact accomplished. Even though the timing and scope of the Dergue's land reform programme were largely pushed on him by circumstances, it seems fairly clear that the over-all result it produced, and in particular the breaking of the Amharic nobility, was in accord with his overall view of what Ethiopia needed. Certainly the ruthlessness and cunning were essential parts of his ability to emerge in control of the levers of power, but he seems much more akin to Sékou Touré in his determination to achieve change, than to Idi Amin's pure drive for personal survival.

The degree of popular support he enjoys is very hard to judge. Probably his lower-class and non-Amharic origins (he generally has been identified with the Galla) enhanced his heroic image as the leader who changed Ethiopia by destroying the old social order. Perhaps too, his determination to keep Eritrea and the Ogaden helped give him standing both as a heroic warrior and as an Ethiopian nationalist. On the other hand, the secrecy of the Dergue's deliberations and its collective nature limit the extent to which he can claim personal credit for its actions. Also, the fact that he was caught up in a repressive spiral first against the EPRP and then against the Political Bureau, have undoubtedly alienated some potential supporters. Finally, given Ethiopians' longstanding suspicions of foreigners, his heavy reliance on the Russians and Cubans has probably done his popular standing no good.

Yet even though Mengistu probably does not command widespread popular support, his initiatives have brought major changes to Ethiopia, and the greatest of these changes, the land reform, must be ranked as an improvement. Even if he has in many respects "betrayed" the revolution, both by his slaughter of civilian radicals and by establishing his personal autocracy, still the land reform and the concomitant destruction of the old nobility mark as thoroughgoing a change as any other new group in

Africa has accomplished. While he may not have
originally intended to shape the reform in the way
it evolved, he did support its taking this shape,
and in particular he gave the peasant associations
encouragement at the crucial moment of their birth.
In these respects his credentials as a revolutionary leader are well-established.

NOTES

1. David and Marina Ottaway, Revolution in
Ethiopia (Holmes and Meier, New York, 1978), p. 32.
2. United Nations Economic Commission for
Africa, Economic Survey of Africa, Vol. III (1971),
pp. 15-16.
3. Ibid., pp. 46-47.
4. Ibid., p. 48
5. World Bank, World Development Indicators,
(World Bank, Washington, D.C., 1978), Table 17. We
should note that this table includes only countries
with populations of one million or more.
6. Donald Levine, "The Roots of Ethiopia's
Nationhood", Africa Report, May 1971, pp. 12-15.
7. John Markakis and Nega Ayele, Class and
Revolution in Ethiopia (Spokesman, Nottingham, 1978),
p. 24.
8. Gene Ellis, "The Feudal Paradigm as a
Hindrance to Understanding Ethiopia", Journal of
Modern African Studies, 14, 2 (June 1976), p. 283.
9. Patrick Gilkes, The Dying Lion: Feudalism
and Modernization in Ethiopia (Julian Friedmann,
London, 1975), p. 14. For a discussion of the depth
of Oromo bitterness, see P.T.W. Baxter, "Ethiopia's
Unacknowledged Problem: The Oromo", African Affairs,
LXXVII (1978), pp. 283-96.
10. Gilkes, p. 15.
11. Frederick C. Gamst, "Peasantries and
Elites Without Urbanism: The Civilization of
Ethiopia", Comparative Studies in Society and History, 12, 4 (October 1970), p. 386.
12. Peter Schwab, Haile Selassie: Ethiopia's
Lion of Judah (Nelson-Hall, Chicago, 1979), p. 54.
13. Ibid., p. 82.
14. Ibid., p. 83.
15. Ibid., p. 86.
16. Ibid., pp. 91-92.
17. Markakis and Ayele, Class and Revolution,
p. 36.
18. Schwab, Haile Selassie, pp. 78-79.
19. Ibid., p. 82.
20. Ibid., p. 129

21. See ibid., pp. 125-35, for a full discussion of this uprising. However, Addis Hiwet, Ethiopia: From Autocracy to Revolution (Merlin Books, London, 1975), pp. 100-101, gives the very different interpretation that this was a genuine peasant uprising against the central government's attempt to force peasants into market relationships.

22. For a detailed discussion of the invasion of corporate farming and its effects, see Lars Bondestam, "People and Capitalism in the North-east Lowlands of Ethiopia", Journal of Modern African Studies, 12, 3 (1974), pp. 423-39.

23. John M. Cohen, "Green Revolution in Ethiopia" in James Scarritt (ed.), Analyzing Political Change in Africa, (Westview Press, Boulder, Colo., 1980), pp. 114-15.

24. See Christopher Clapham, Haile-Selassie's Government (Longmans, London, 1969), pp. 24-25; also his "The Ethiopian Coup d'Etat of December 1960", Journal of Modern African Studies, 6 (December 1968), pp. 495-507.

25. See Ottaway, Revolution in Ethiopia, pp. 135-36; Observer, "Revolution in Ethiopia", Monthly Review, 29 (July/August 1977), p. 52.

26. See, for example, Clapham, Haile-Selassie's Government, p. 26.

27. Gilkes, Dying Lion, p. 62.

28. For example, Clapham comments: "The relationship between Haile-Selassie and his officials is chiefly one of power rather than personal feeling, and in this author's judgement a completely powerless Haile-Selassie would be attended only by a few of his present entourage." Haile-Selassie's Government, pp. 96-97.

29. See Schwab, Haile Selassie, pp. 125-35.

30. Peter Koehn, "Ethiopia: famine, food production and changes in the legal order", African Studies Review, 22 (April 1979), pp. 51-57.

31. Ibid., pp. 52-54.

32. I have taken most of the details on events during the revolution from the Ottaways' book.

33. Koehn, "Famine", pp. 57-60.

34. Ottaways, Revolution in Ethiopia, p. 76.

35. Ibid., p. 181. However, Colin Legum, in Africa Contemporary Record, XI (1978-79), B238, says there were 7 million families in the association, which would mean most rural Ethiopians were members.

36. See Africa Contemporary Record, XII, (1979-1980), p. B204.

37. See Victoria Brittain, "Ethiopia Eludes Moscow in a Savile Row Suit", Guardian Weekly,

March 22, 1981, p. 8.

38. Ibid.

39. Ibid; also "Imperial colonel", The Economist, November 28, 1981, p. 34. For a suggestion that Mengistu wanted to create a party, but was incapable of doing so, see Edmund J. Keller, "The Revolutionary Transformation of Ethiopia's Twentieth-Century Bureaucratic Empire", Journal of Modern African Studies 19, 2 (1981), p. 332.

40. Brittain, "Ethiopia Eludes Moscow".

41. See Africa Contemporary Record, XII, (1979-1980), p. B199.

42. See, for example, Michael Chege, "The Revolution Betrayed: Ethiopia 1974-79", Journal of Modern African Studies, 17, 3 (September 1979), pp. 359-80; also Markakis and Ayele, Class and Revolution.

43. Ottaways, Revolution in Ethiopia, p. 54.

44. Ibid.

45. Marina Ottaway, "Democracy and new democracy: the ideological debate in the Ethiopian revolution", African Studies Review, 21, 1 (April 1978), pp. 19-31.

46. See Marina Ottaway, "Land Reform in Ethiopia, 1974-1977", African Studies Review, 20, 3 (1977), esp. pp. 84-85. That it is not entirely fanciful to think that peasants given this initial encouragement to organize can transform their attitude from one of dependence upon a "superior" social class to one of self-reliance is suggested by a study of Peruvian Indians in similar circumstances when the Velasco government encouraged them to form co-operatives. See Cynthia McClintock, Peasant Cooperatives and Political Change in Peru (Princeton University Press, Princeton, N.J, 1981).

Chapter Twelve

CONCLUSIONS

One hundred years ago, the leaders of most
African polities were sharply constrained from exercising any significant degree of political leadership. A king of Ashanti or of Buganda, not to
mention lesser chiefs, was limited in what he could
do not just by the ubiquitous constraints of external power or of resource limitations, but also by a
wide range of domestic structures and values. His
choices were circumscribed by the need to win the
approval of designated elders and other notables,
and even more important, by the need to act within
rules of conduct that were known and accepted by
all. A serious deviation from these accepted patterns of conduct could result in his subjects desert-
ing him. There were, to be sure, leaders such as
Shaka and Samory who built up new states through
their ability to inspire support, but short of
building one's own state, a leader had to act within a fairly confining framework of institutions.
        The political leaders we examined faced a much
more fluid situation, with the newness of their
states' institutions creating both tremendous problems and tremendous opportunities. The crumbling of
old structures and attitudes and the rise of new
expectations under the impact of the industrialized
world's military power, economic demands and mass
communications left them with little certainty even
about who considered themselves to be their subjects,
let alone about what patterns of conduct those subjects regarded as acceptable. Furthermore, they
were severely frustrated by the limits imposed by
their countries' lack of physical and human resources, and by the range of economic and other
pressures applied to them by the industrialized
states.
        On the other hand, they faced few barriers to

introducing new patterns of conduct from older,
widely-supported sets of values. The fact that the
new states were generally composed of disparate
peoples with few, if any, bonds to restrain their
conduct toward each other, the fact that in many
states new men came to power with little background
in the traditions of its wise exercise, and the fact
that since independence the path to power has often
opened most readily to individuals who excel in cunning and ruthlessness rather than in more statesman-
like qualities such as breadth of vision or concern
with justice and equity, all allowed leaders to act
in ways that would have been unthinkable a century
ago.

Most important of all, however, is the extent
to which a modern ruler can monopolize both mass
communications and the expensive and complex technology of coercion. The sophisticated weaponry available to a leader to control his people gives a fearsome new point to the three-centuries-old warning of
Thomas Hobbes that when there are no rules binding
on all, "clubs are trumps".

An important recent study[1] argues that the
weakness of institutions in most African states has
produced a situation in which the ruler is largely
able to shape the rules of conduct to suit his own
convenience, a system which the authors term "personal rule." These rulers are not totally un-
restrained, even apart from the limits imposed by
external powers and lack of resources; most have
simply accepted a role as chief broker among a
number of powerful barons, as we saw in the cases of
Leopold Senghor and Haile Selassie. However, some
rulers have managed to overcome any limits imposed
by lesser actors in the polity, whether by historic
chance or by force of personality, by their prophetic
vision or by sheer use of terror to eliminate rivals;
and these individuals have had a very clear-cut
opportunity to put their own distinctive mark on
their polities. Jackson and Rosberg classify these
dominating rulers into three types, the prophet, the
autocrat and the tyrant,[2] and distinguish them along
two dimensions: the extent to which they are committed to a goal beyond their own survival, and the
extent to which this goal calls for the transformation of the lives of the polity's citizens.

These types of ruler can be partially linked to
the "accommodation" and "transformation" strategies
for development discussed earlier.[3] The accomodation
strategy, in which the ruler sought mainly to keep
order while domestic or foreign entrepreneurs sought

profits (of which the ruler might take a cut), was the only one open to the tyrant, the autocrat, or for that matter, to the prince or broker. The fact that it did not need to inspire people to change their behaviour or attitudes made it ideal for leaders who lacked the facility of instilling their vision of a better world in others. It did carry two risks, to be sure: a failure to generate enough economic activity to improve peoples' living standards would lead to generalized discontent, while the growth of inequalities would stimulate either the poorer sectors or the intelligentsia acting on behalf of the poor to attack the regime's inequities or its "sell-out" to foreigners. For a tyrant such as Idi Amin, who rightly feared the rise of indigenous wealthy individuals and whose erratic behaviour scared away many foreign investors, the accommodation strategy was unlikely to work, though it was hard to see any alternative strategy that promised better results. However, for a prudent autocrat such as Houphouet-Boigny or a broker such as Senghor, with no burning desire to transform his countrymen's lives, the accomodation strategy could offer the hope of a reasonably secure existence, provided there were some capitalists willing to be accommodated.

The transformation strategy, by contrast, called for a prophet's vision to inspire the changes in peoples' attitudes necessary to attain his goals. It was a riskier strategy because it faced attack from two sides. The privileged groups which had been dispossessed would inevitably oppose it, but there was also a strong probability that its supporters would turn against it if their expectations outran the regime's ability to achieve its goals. While far more than an accommodationist, the leader preaching transformation could live on the credit of a promised better future, at some point his people would start to demand at least partial payment. These demands would start sooner if, as we saw with Nkrumah and even to a degree with Nyerere, people became disillusioned as they saw the leader's subordinates departing from the goals he professed to be pursuing.

We also saw earlier that both of these strategies had mixed results,[4] and in the case studies I indicated those specific factors which enabled some leaders to succeed in achieving their goals while others failed. Two factors were particularly important.

LEADERSHIP'S VITAL INGREDIENTS: POWER AND TRUST

In looking at what caused leaders to succeed or
fail, one crucial factor was how they used the power
that accrued to them in the role of leader. I am
using the term "power" here to cover all cases
where a leader produces an intended change in the
behaviour of a subject whether by coercion, where
the subject makes the change against his will, or
by leadership, where the subject sees that the
change is beneficial to him and makes it voluntarily.[5] Some use of power is clearly necessary for
a leader's own survival, as well as to produce
changes, as witness the fate of leaders who failed
to use power at critical times. Milton Obote
failed to stir the UPC notables to active support
for the Common Man's Charter in 1969, and then
failed to use coercive power against his army commander before his trip to Singapore in 1971. Haile
Selassie failed to use either coercion or persuasion
to end the first stirrings of army rebellion in
1974. Leopold Senghor chose not to build a party
independent of the marabouts in the 1950s, and
thereafter was blocked from any reshaping of
Senegalese society by the marabouts' control over
the countryside. By contrast, Houphouet-Boigny and
Nyerere each used power to bring substantial changes
to their countries, the former through such actions
as protecting French investors and directing
Ivorian capital into such economically-enriching
activities as oil-palm plantations and improved
harbours, the latter through curbing civil service
privileges, bringing public control of major enterprises, and forcing the villagization of most of
Tanzania's population. Major Mengistu also used
his power to break permanently the grip of Ethiopia's
landlords, and to allow the peasants to develop
their own associations.

Yet the use of power could also destroy both
the polity and the power-holder. Idi Amin illustrates well the danger of absolute power corrupting
absolutely, while Sékou Touré and Kwame Nkrumah both
failed to reach their goals in large measure because
of the ways they used power. Touré's early turn to
coercion alienated many of the urban and rural
workers whose active participation his revolution
needed if it were to achieve the goals of successful
state-run industrialization and self-sufficient
agriculture. Nkrumah's failure stemmed in part
from his readiness to crush opposition movements by
force, which by driving them underground, contributed

to the fearful isolation in which he operated during his last years in office.

My main argument has been that coercive power is self-defeating in the long run, that leadership or power by persuasion is superior. There are two major reasons for this. First, changes produced by leadership rather than by force necessarily involve followers changing their attitudes, rather than merely giving the superficial compliance that marks forced change. Over generations, of course, a change initially produced by force can become internalized - witness the general acceptance of Communist Party values by the people of the Soviet Union - but the process is a good deal less certain than that of change by persuasion. Second, a system based on leadership tends to remain more open and thus more readily able to correct its short-comings. A leader who relies on persuading his people to support his goals must of necessity be alert for signs that they are no longer responding favourably, and to adjust his appeal accordingly, whereas a leader who has become accustomed to forcing his wishes on his people will be far less responsive. A case in point is the contrast between Julius Nyerere's attempt to replace private village stores with co-operatives, which was dropped after a few months of peaceful protest, and Sékou Touré's similar attempt to replace the women's markets with co-ops, which was only dropped after a mass protest by thousands of market women and the killing of several of them by Touré's security forces. It may be that the leader knows what is best for his people, and that in the long run history will vindicate his use of force - Nyerere's forced villagization programme may be such a case - but the price he will pay in fear, distrust and loss of tolerance is a stiff one. Conversely, the leader who changes his goals in response to public pressure may be capitulating to ignorance or ingrained conservatism, but he has at least kept the channels of communication open so that he may try again to persuade on another day.

For the leader who seeks widespread changes in people's behaviour, such as are necessary to improve agricultural or industrial productivity, coercion is ultimately self-defeating. Even if the leader has cadres of dedicated supporters who can enforce outward obedience to the leader's goals, there is no way they can overcome the quiet, passive resistance of unhappy workers or farmers, as Guinea's experience clearly shows. Intensifying repression will simply increase this passive resistance, while if the leader eases the repression he is likely to be faced with even more open resistance, to the point of rebellion or guerrilla warfare. Furthermore, the assumption that the leader can find dedicated cadres to impose his vision on the entire polity is doubtful in Africa; few regimes, with the possible exception of Mozambique's FRELIMO, have been forced through struggle to develop sufficient commitment to offset the tendency to self-seeking and the claims of family, clan, tribe or religion. A regime whose own cadres cannot live up to its professions can hardly expect to win even limited popular backing.

A purely coercive regime whose leader seeks only his own survival, such as those of Idi Amin or Jean-Bedel Bokassa, can endure popular passive resistance for a considerable time. However, since such a ruler's supporters are invariably bound to him by mercenary ties, he must keep the economy functioning at a high enough level to provide pay-offs for these supporters. Amin and other dictators could live for some time off the accumulated resources from previous governments, but their regimes' behaviour was gradually destroying the economic bases they needed in order to survive.

Despite these great advantages for leadership, there are tremendous pressures in all African states favouring a coercive approach. The first of these pressures is a universal one, and is particularly a problem for the leader who strongly desires a goal he knows is best for his people. Such a leader can easily view resistance to his goals as evidence of obtuseness, ignorance or even deliberate sabotage by "enemies of the revolution." This attitude was apparent not only in Sékou Touré, but even in Julius Nyerere in his desire to save peasants from the "living death" of rural isolation. The role of leader furnishes the instruments to compel obedience, and thus to achieve the satisfaction of seeing his goals implemented.

This rationale for using coercion is reinforced by a factor more specific to the African situation, the weakness of restraining institutions. In a system of personal rule, where the leader can bend the rules to suit his own desires, there is little chance of courts, civil libertarians or other external influences stopping the leader's use of coercion. Furthermore, in such a system the leader himself may well have risen to the top, and certainly has managed to stay there, not by scrupulous obedience to rules of law, but by possessing more cunning and drive to dominate than do potential rivals.

A further pressure toward coercion is also widespread in Africa whether a leader has a clear goal beyond survival or not. Partly because of the weakness of institutional restraints on challengers, and partly because of the difficulty of achieving improvements in the lives or ordinary Africans, most African leaders are somewhat insecure. This insecurity creates a constant pressure not to be tolerant, not to take risks, but to deal with real or imagined threats firmly. Again, the end result is that persuasion is quickly abandoned in favour of force.

Against these pressures there are few external forces that can induce a leader to rely on the slower and less obviously effective techniques of persuasion. The strength of other key individuals in the polity may force the leader to try persuasion rather than coercion on them, but this has no bearing on whether he will use it as a general approach. The populace. can passively resist even the most tyrannical ruler, but whether he will interpret this as a signal to try persuasion or simply to step up the amount of coercion depends on his own personality.

Yet a number of leaders have resisted the temptation to turn to force against their people. The counter-weight to this pressure to use coercion seems to be a cluster of attitudes held by the leader toward his people. A leader who trusts other people, has faith that they are reasonable and can understand what he is trying to do, has confidence in the route he has chosen to his goals and in his own powers of persuasion, and feels reasonably secure in his position, generally is willing to follow the slow path of persuasion and example. Conversely, the leader who is suspicious and fearful of possible rivals, who feels uncertain about his legitimacy as a ruler, or his ability to persuade people of the rightness of his ideas, or who doubts that people can be brought to understand and accept his goals through persuasion, is likely to turn quickly to coercion. Nyerere and Houphouet-Boigny, both very clear on what they wanted, nevertheless usually managed to refrain from coercion because they could justifiably rely upon their own power of persuasion and their peoples' responsiveness to this persuasion. Milton Obote, though far less secure in his position, and with large sections of Uganda questioning his very legitimacy as a ruler, also showed a considerable confidence in his ability to win his way by persuasion. On the other hand, Nkrumah, full of uncertainty about how to achieve his goals, and knowing that much of Ghana's "Establishment" questioned his right to lead them, was much more susceptible to the temptation of force, especially as the challenges mounted after independence. Sékou Touré and Major Mengistu Haile Mariam knew what they wanted to achieve, but doubted the commitment of many of their more educated contemporaries to their goals, and had gained power and held it through being thoroughly suspicious of, and ruthless toward, potential rivals. Idi Amin, of course, had no clear goals to pursue, but as he rose to successively more exposed positions he became progressively more wary and ready to safeguard himself by any means available. These insecure and suspicious leaders fulfilled their own worst fears, since people who were not persuaded to join in pursuing their goals tended to hesitate and thus become "enemies of the revolution."

From the foregoing, it seems clear that the main restraint on African political leaders' use of coercion to achieve their ends is not the institutional checks that have evolved in older political systems, but the internalized check that came from their faith that they could attain their ends through leadership. How far was this optimism on the part of some leaders justified? Were leaders who relied on persuasion more likely to survive than those who tended to coercion? Did they provide more well-being for their people in gross economic terms, in the distribution of wealth, or in providing a relatively secure and peaceful environment? Since there is a considerable amount of subjective judgment in determining which leaders exercised leadership, as well as in determining some of these levels of well-being,[6] I will confine this brief analysis to the nine leaders we have examined in some detail, rather than trying to expand it to cover all post-independence African leaders. Table 12.1 summarizes the achievements of the leaders who relied more upon persuasion and those who relied more upon force.

Over all, the leaders relying on persuasion were more likely to survive than their more coercion-inclined counterparts, although Obote's reluctance to use force may have contributed to his overthrow, and Touré and Amin certainly showed that against domestic threats, force could offer considerable protection. There is, of course, the question of whether leaders turned to force because they felt their survival threatened, but in the cases we considered, with the

289

Table 12:1: Persuasive versus coercive leaders: a comparison of their survival and successes.

Leader (years in power)	Strategy (accommodation or transformation)	Well-being of population		Security
		GNP growth per capita	Change in life expectancy	
Persuasive				
Houphouet-Boigny (1960-)	Accom.	2.4%	10 years	High
Senghor (1960-1980)	Accom.	-0.2%	6	High
Nyerere (1961-)	Trans.	2.3%	10	High
Obote (1962-1971)	Accom./Trans.	1.6%	5	Low
Coercive				
Nkrumah (1957-1966)	Trans.	0.6%	5	Medium
Touré (1958-)	Trans.	0.3%	9	Low
Amin (1971-1979)	--	-0.4%	....	Low
Haile Selassie (1930-1974)	Accom.	2.4%	4	Medium
Mengistu (1975-)	Transf.	....	2	Low

Sources: GNP and life expectancy data from World Bank, World Development Reports to 1981; data for leaders still in power are for 1960-1979, and for Amin, I have taken the estimate of growth in GDP for 1970-1978. For Nkrumah, I calculated GNP growth rate from the IMF's International Financial Statistics data for 1957-1966, and for both Nkrumah and Obote, I calculated changes in life expectancies from United Nations, Demographic Yearbook Historical Supplement (1979). I have estimated "security" as it affected the average citizen according to two criteria: freedom from random violence, including both individual and collective assaults, and freedom from arbitrary treatment at the hands of state functionaries, including illegal taxation, imprisonment without trial, torture and execution.

exception of Nkrumah it appears that those who relied on force did so because of a basic predisposition to use it rather than as the result of specific perceived threats.

The persuasive leaders also seem to have made life better for their countrymen than did the rulers who relied on force. Senegal's economy performed poorly, and Obote was never able to curb either Uganda's gangsterism or its ethnic conflicts, but otherwise the performances of these leaders were generally good. Among the coercive leaders, Haile Selassie managed to induce an economic boom in Ethiopia in the 1960s, although its distribution left a great deal to be desired, and Nkrumah ran a regime that had a good deal of success in containing threats to personal security and in encouraging national integration, but otherwise the records of these leaders were undistinguished. These data, in summary, suggest that leadership does benefit both ruler and subjects. A further indicator of the benefits of persuasion is Ruth Collier's finding that regimes that absorbed opponents into their ranks were much more resistant to military coups than were those that suppressed their opponents by force.[7]

POPULAR SUPPORT FOR A LEADER

So far, we have considered leaders' abilities to persuade in very abstract, general terms. But what specific appeals did they address to their people, or what was there about them that made people willing to do what they wanted?

For all the first-generation independence leaders in this study, with the partial exception of Obote, the most effective aspect of their appeal was the fact that they had led the challenge to the colonial power and had ended colonial rule. Starting with few resources, they had to rely on leadership to draw their first followers to them, and as their movements grew, they acquired an aura of authority that enabled them to continue to guide their followers without resort to force. The fact that they were challenging colonial regimes which were widely disliked, but which had largely ceased to apply severe sanctions against such challenges, helped ensure that they would not have to use drastic means to attain their goals.

Haile Selassie, of course, does not fit this pattern; such leadership as he showed came from the fact that he enjoyed all the prestige that surrounded the ancient Ethiopian monarchy, including its sacral qualities. In this his situation was more like that of the Kabaka of Buganda or the Nigerian Emirs than of the secular rulers who emerged in the other African states.

As for the remaining two leaders, Amin and Mengistu, although both had some potential for leadership, both the manner of their coming to power and the ways in which they exercised control once in power made it improbable that they could change to more persuasive approaches. Mengistu did have some appeal through being identified with the Oromo, through having shown that the Emperor's regime could be overthrown, and through redistributing land to the peasants, but he never did try to draw upon these "heroic" acts to win people by persuasion. As for Amin, though he could charm individuals in specific situations, and though his expulsion of the Asians won great popular acclaim, he never seriously tried to avoid using force.

However, heroic acts in the independence struggle were not enough to sustain a leader indefinitely, as Nkrumah, Sylvanus Olympio of Togo, Modibo Keita of Mali and several others learned to their cost. Continuing material payoffs appeared useful in strengthening the bond created by early heroism or even in substituting for it, as the success of Amadou Ahidjo of Cameroun suggests. It is true that two of the leaders we have looked at, Senghor and Touré, survived despite a marked lack of economic prosperity in their states, but they are unusual; in fact, of the 14 African states listed by the World Bank as having a growth rate of 1.0% or less from 1960 to 1976, Senegal and Guinea are the only two which did not experience at least one forcible change of government.[8] Prosperity by itself did not guarantee survival; but its absence seems to have made survival very difficult.

However, prosperity seems to have simply reduced peoples' incentive to seek actively to remove a leader; what we need to find here are attributes which would induce people to actively support him. One personal quality seemed important here: the extent to which the leader appeared to have the interests of his people at heart. A leader could enrich himself, provided that he did not do it at the expense of ordinary people; it was when he seemed to be amassing personal wealth while ignoring ordinary peoples' needs that he would lose support. Even the Emperor Haile Selassie alienated many of his people when during the severe drought in the early 1970s he appeared indifferent to the starvation of thousands of peasants. Conversely, the perception of Léopold Senghor as a "good man," even though his policies produced few benefits for most Senegalese, was sufficient in combination with his early stature as the "man of the people" and as the years went by, the fact of his having been leader since the beginning of political activity, to maintain his acceptability.

This need for a leader to be perceived as acting in the best interests of his people should be used, I think, to temper Mazrui's argument that there is a "monarchical tendency" in Africa.[9] Mazrui's assertion that Africans seem to want leaders who make a conspicuous display of wealth, personalize authority, and accept glorification in sacral terms applies, I suggest, only to those leaders who have at the same time provided material benefits to their people. When people are left worse off, all the leader's monuments and attempts to wrap himself in traditional symbols of glory - as Nkrumah came to model himself more and more on the role of a great chief[10] - have no effect in making his rule more acceptable.

No leader can reach all of his people directly; he must necessarily rely upon subordinates to help carry his message to ordinary people, and even more to perform the day-to-day actions necessary to implement his vision. In fact, the more comprehensive the changes he is trying to bring to his country, the more he needs committed cadres who have the ability to understand and execute his wishes, and the commitment to do so. Several problems arise here, both from the leader's personality and from the imperatives that play on his subordinates.

Many leaders, such as Nkrumah and Touré, were too suspicious of others to be good team leaders. This meant that it was difficult for them to find lieutenants who could cover their weak areas, although for several years Nkrumah leaned heavily on Gbedemah for organizational tasks. Even a relatively trusting leader like Senghor eventually broke with the lieutenant who complemented his weaknesses, Mamadou Dia, although later he seemed to establish a similar relationship with his successor Diouf. The basic problem was that in the uncertain insitutional framework of most new states, it was hard for a leader to be sure that his subordinate would not try to usurp his place, as Dia did with Senghor.

A more general problem was the fact that bureaucrats, army officers, and party officials all had their own "power imperatives," the need to establish their own significance and to safeguard their interests. We noted in Tanzania that when Nyerere tried to encourage popular participation in planning, his goal was undercut by bureaucratic experts who knew better than ordinary peasants what needed to be done, and therefore made sure that their views prevailed.[11] Similar problems of bureaucrats pursuing their own ends could be found in all states. Where the leader himself relied on coercion, it probably made little difference to the ordinary man whether he was forced to act in ways he did not choose in order to comply with the leader's vision or in order to comply with the whim of some bureaucrat anxious to demonstrate his own power. But where the leader wanted to introduce new attitudes among the people, as in Tanzania, Uganda under Obote, and to a lesser extent in Ghana and Guinea, the use of force by subordinates could easily undermine his intention of winning voluntary acceptance of his goals.

There were various ways a leader could try to protect his goals against such sabotage. To some extent his own persuasiveness and personal example could inspire his subordinates as well as ordinary people, although failure to achieve his goals could destroy his persuasive power, and so, ironically, could success. As a leader succeeded in making his society more affluent, and bringing more sectors under control of its nationals, he increased both the power of bureaucrats and the temptations to which they were exposed. The proliferation of state controls and the consequent opportunities for bureaucrats to act in arbitary or corrupt ways in Ghana, Guinea and Tanzania underlines this point.

Persuasion had some chance of success when backed by mechanisms for checking bureaucratic power-seeking. In the long run, any mechanisms had to be underpinned by a popular attitude that abuses of authority would not be tolerated.[12] This could work if organizations could develop whose self-interest pushed them toward imposing such restraints. The peasant associations in Ethiopia showed some signs of exercising such a check on the central government, and in Tanzania Nyerere encouraged TANU to take such a role in relation to the government bureaucracy. The problem which could not be easily resolved here was how to keep the party itself from becoming a further centrally-controlled organization, with minimal grassroots input. The best that seemed attainable was to have the government bureaucracy and the party bureaucracy each checking to ensure that the other did not abuse its power. A similar but even more serious problem was how to prevent the military using its weapons to replace the government. Again, a combination of the leader's persuasiveness and his control over key posts, along with attempts to check the military through other forces such as a popular milita, seemed promising, but the experience of Ghana and Mali, where the military's resentment of a militia contributed to its staging a coup, indicates that such checks were not fully effective.

To maintain support then, a leader had to be seen to be working in the interests of his people, and to keep his subordinates also working for these goals. His ability to persuade and inspire had to affect a wide range of individuals with distinct interests of their own, and often with little awe of a man whom they had known at close range over many years. This problem of appearing only life-sized would be particularly acute for the second-generation leader who took over from a legendary "Father of his Country," whether through a coup d'état or by being designated as a successor.

WHAT PROSPECTS FOR LEADERSHIP?

Since independence, the hope for African leaders to instill new values and impose new patterns of behaviour has diminished greatly. In the period of decolonization, when most people were seeking major changes under leaders of their own, they could be guided to accept any of a broad range of new values. However, since that time, the existing state boundaries and the presence of central governments have come to be taken as fixed and immutable parts of a traditional heritage.[13] More generally, people have adapted themselves to whatever pattern of behaviour their governments have established. In those numerous cases where coercive regimes have retained power, the popular response has been one of withdrawal or resignation, with most people regarding the central government warily as something to be avoided. In other cases, the central government is regarded less as a threat than as a benefactor, although still beyond control. In a very few states, there is some feeling that the central government is responsive to people's needs, that it can work with

people to provide for their well-being. In short,
in all states new patterns of interaction between
leaders and people are evolving, whether through
the leader's conscious choice or simply as a consequence of his actions.

For those leaders who have sought change
through persuasion, opportunities have been closed
off in several ways. All leaders suffered to some
extent as the shared goal of independence gave way
to divisions over what policies should be pursued
for economic and political development, and as the
hope that leaders could attain popular goals was
eroded by economic hardship, by disillusionment with
elites' self-seeking and corruption, and by the
readiness of many leaders to turn to forms of coercion as bad or worse than those of colonial rule.
Then too, the nagging questions which underlay the
industrialized world's discontent with its leaders
in the early 1980s - whether the existing recession
was merely a harbinger of a coming "Age of Scarcity,"
whether the environmental damage caused by industrialization was becoming unsustainable, and whether
the pursuit of material abundance did in fact
improve human happiness[14] - may have seemed totally
irrelevant to ordinary Africans, but were beginning
to undermine the confidence of some African leaders
in the desirability of their long-term developmental
goals.

Both the accommodation and the transformation
strategies had been sufficiently entrenched in
specific states by the 1980s that a peaceful change
of direction seemed improbable. The accommodation
states that had integrated themselves more or less
successfully into the periphery of the capitalist
system had built up privileged groups of traders,
managers, politicians and skilled workers who would
be most unlikely to be persuaded by any leader to
make the sacrifices required if their state was to
change course. Similarly, the transformation
states which had survived for a decade or more had
built up their own cadres of committed activists
who would equally forcibly resist any change. In
short, it would take a violent revolution to bring
about a major change of strategy for most states.
Persuasion alone could only be expected to bring
modest incremental changes, since neither accommodation nor transformation strategies could demonstrate
convincing superiority over the other; and even to
bring incremental changes a leader would have to
work harder than had his predecessors in the 1950s
and 1960s, to build up the trust and hope necessary

to provide him with popular support.

The states whose present leaders have relied heavily upon coercion face the most difficult problems in the years ahead. A leader such as Touré or Mengistu cannot afford to relax his grip for fear that enemies he has made will take their revenge. The problem of a successor is a particularly difficult one for such a leader, since he can hardly allow a potential challenger to build up strength while he still rules. Any designated successor needs to be a nonentity who poses no threat to him; but such an individual would have a difficult time surviving in a coercive system. The other possibilities are for a great deal of intrigue and in-fighting at the time of the leader's death, or for his earlier removal by armed overthrow, both of which make it likely that the new leader's main skill will be in the use of force. The prospect of continuing instability at the top and reliance on coercion is reinforced by the likelihood that the population has become habituated to seeing the political process as an elite struggle in which they can have no possible part. A coercive regime, in other words, institutionalizes a pattern of popular withdrawal and alienation, of distrust between government and people, and of continuing governmental coercion. Even a regime which produced general revulsion, such as Idi Amin's, seems to have so conditioned people to violence that a successor regime has to use a great deal of force merely in order to survive, a problem which seemed to beset Obote in mid-1982.

A leader who relied on persuasion had a better chance of building tolerant stability, but he too faced problems. Like Obote in 1971, he might be overthrown by a more ruthless subordinate. If he sought to pass power to a designated successor, as Senghor did in 1980, there would usually be the problem that the successor could not build up the personal authority enjoyed by the retiring leader.

However, this could be an advantage. To ensure an orderly succession, an aging leader could encourage adherence to constitutional or other regularized procedures for choosing a successor, and to the extent that these procedures allowed the politically effective sections of the society to make their preferences known, this institutionalization of the selection process could both produce an acceptable leader and begin the process of putting restraints on him. Successor leaders such as Daniel Arap Moi in Kenya and Dr. Quett Masire in Botswana had to remain conscious of the fact that they had been chosen as

leaders through processes operated by colleagues
equal in stature to themselves, an awareness which
helped encourage them to work within generally
accepted limits.

Even apart from facilitating a smooth transition to a new generation of leaders, building effective institutions could be considered a vital part of
successful political leadership. In the years immediately after independence, when people had not yet
developed a set of basic shared values and commitment to their new state, African leaders had the
opportunity and the responsiblity to inspire and
guide their people in developing these commitments.
But to the extent that they succeeded in creating
new commitments, the leaders could then reduce their
own role to a brokerage one of resolving disputes
within this broad framework. Good leadership in a
sense renders itself superfluous, since in inducing
people to join with him to pursue shared goals, the
leader also persuades them to take a share of the
responsibility for determing the goals and the means
to their attainment. As people become more confident in exercising this responsbility, they no
longer need the leader to provide them with comprehensive goals, but only to facilitate finding equitable means of attaining them.

Some leaders, such as Nkrumah, Touré, Haile
Selassie and Mengistu, were clearly too concerned
for their own positions to allow grassroots organizations, even those they had created, to exercise any
real responsibility. Whether from insecurity or from
a sense of supreme confidence that they knew what
was best for their people, they preferred to compel
people to look to them, the leaders, for all answers.
The inevitable result was that the leader tended to
lose touch with what the people wanted, so that ultimately he lost his power to lead.

However, some leaders, notably Nyerere but also
to a lesser extent Senghor, Obote and eventually
even Houphouet-Boigny, made some effort to establish
institutions that would allow their people to share
in shaping the polity, and in doing so would check
even the leader himself. Though tentative and
limited, such actions as providing elections and
intra-party policy discussions gave people some
sense that they could affect their own destinies,
and that their leader might respond to their wishes.
By keeping alive this belief that leader and people
still shared common interests and goals, these
leaders kept alive the possibility that they and
their successors could continue to exercise leadership

We have seen that persuasion, despite its frustrations and risks, is more effective than coercion in producing well-being for the people of a country. Furthermore, by encouraging their participation in political life, it builds institutions which can work to check abuses by future rulers. A leader who wants to be remembered by history for having a long-term beneficial effect on his country would be well advised, whatever the development policies he seeks, to bring his people with him by persuasion.

NOTES

1.   Robert H. Jackson and Carl Rosberg, Personal Rule in Black Africa: Prince, Autocrat, Prophet, Tyrant (University of California Press, Berkeley, Los Angeles and London, 1982).
2.   Ibid., pp. 73-82.
3.   See above, pp. 59-67.
4.   See above, pp. 67-69.
5.   Cf. James MacGregor Burns, Leadership (Harper and Row, New York, 1978), pp. 12-22.
6.   Some attempts have been made to provide objective criteria for measuring such phenomena as political instability, but even when it is possible to establish reasonably clear-cut, measurable and relevant criteria, there are still serious problems in obtaining accurate data. For one of the best such attempts and a discussion of its limitations, see Donald Morrison, R.C. Mitchell, John N. Paden and Hugh M. Stevenson, Black Africa: A Comparative Handbook, (The Free Press, New York, 1972), pp. 122-31.
7.   "Parties, coups and authoritarian rule: patterns of political change in tropical Africa", Comparative Political Studies, 11, 1 (April 1978), pp. 73-74.
8.   Growth rates taken from World Bank, World Development Indicators (1978), Table 1.
9.   Ali Mazrui, "The monarchical tendency in African political culture: British Journal of Sociology, 18, 3 (1967), pp. 231-50.
10.   See David Apter, Ghana in Transition, (Atheneum, New York, 1963), pp. 365-66.
11.   See above, pp. 183-84.
12.   As, for example, Tanzanian factory workers checked the behaviour of their managers. See above, p. 183.
13.   Cf. Aristide Zolberg's observation of

several years ago that political parties by the mid-1960s had already become part of "tradition." Creating Political Order: The Party-States of West Africa (Rand McNally, Chicago, 1966), pp. 144-45.

14.   Out of the huge literature on these topics, I will only note two of the most important: William Ophuls, Ecology and the Politics of Scarcity (W.H. Freeman, San Francisco, 1977), and Fred Hirsch, Social Limits to Growth (Harvard University Press, Cambridge, Mass., 1976).

SELECT BIBLIOGRAPHY

Since I have indicated through footnotes most
of the important sources on leadership in the specific countries examined, I am confining this bibliography to works of a general or theoretical nature
on leadership, and works providing general information about African countries.

Barber, James D. The Presidential Character
    Prentice-Hall, Englewood Cliffs, N.J., 1972
Burns, James MacGregor. Leadership. Harper and Row,
    New York, 1978
_____. "Wellsprings of Political Leadership",
    American Political Science Review, LXXI, 1
    (March 1977), pp. 266-75
Cartwright, John R. "Some Constraints Upon African
    Political Leadership", Canadian Journal of
    African Studies, XI, 3 (1977), pp. 435-53
Collier, Ruth B. "Parties, coups and authoritarian
    rule: patterns of political change in tropical
    Africa", Comparative Political Studies, 11, 1
    (April 1978), pp. 62-93
Cox, Robert W. "Leadership in Perspective: a
    comment", International Organization, 28, 1
    (Winter 1974), pp. 141-44
Damachi, Ukandi G. Leadership Ideology in Africa:
    Attitudes Toward Socio-Economic Development.
    Praeger, New York, 1976
Dettman, P.R. "Leaders and Structures in Third World
    Politics", Comparative Politics, 6, 2 (January
    1974), pp. 245-69
Edinger, Lewis J. "Comparative Analysis of Political
    Leadership", Comparative Politics, 7, 2 (Janu-
    ary 1975), pp. 253-70
Ekeh, Peter P. "Colonialism and the Two Publics in
    Africa: A Theoretical Statement", Comparative
    Studies in Society and History, 17, 1 (January
    1975), pp. 91-112
Friedland, William. "For a sociological concept of
    charisma", Social Forces, XLIII, 1 (1964-65),
    pp. 18-26
Halal, W.E. "Toward a General Theory of Leadership",
    Human Relations, 27, 4 (1974), pp. 401-16
Ilchman, Warren F. and Uphoff, Norman T. The Politi-
    cal Economy of Change. University of California
    Press, Berkeley, 1969
Jackson, Robert H. and Rosberg, Carl, Personal Rule
    in Black Africa: Prince, Autocrat, Prophet,
    Tyrant. University of California Press, Berke-
    ley, 1982

Kipnis, David. The Powerholders. University of
    Chicago Press, Chicago, 1976
Kofele-Kale, Ndiva. "The Problem of Instrumental
    Leadership in Contemporary African Political
    Systems", Journal of Asian and African Studies,
    XIII, 1-2 (January & April, 1978), pp. 80-95
Laitin, David and Lustick, Ian. "Leadership: A Com-
    parative Perspective", International Organiza-
    tion, 28, 1 (Winter 1974), pp. 89-117
Levine, Charles H. "Leadership: Problems, Prospects
    and Implications of Research Programs Aimed at
    Linking Empirical and Normative Modeling",
    Policy Studies Journal, 5, 1 (Autumn 1976),
    pp. 34-41
Levine, Victor T. "Changing Leadership Styles and
    Political Images: Some Preliminary Notes",
    Journal of Modern African Studies, 15, 4 (1977),
    pp. 631-38
_____. "African Patrimonial Regimes in Comparative
    Perspective", Journal of Modern African Studies,
    18, 4 (1980), pp. 657-73
Mazrui, Ali, "The Monarchical Tendency in African
    Political Culture", British Journal of Socio-
    logy, 18, 3 (September 1967), pp. 231-50
McClelland, David C. "The Two Faces of Power",
    Journal of International Affairs, 24, 1 (1970),
    pp. 29-47
Meeker, Joseph W. The Comedy of Survival: Studies
    in Literary Ecology. Scribner, New York, 1974
Nwosu, H.N., "Strategies of state-building: African
    experience reconsidered", Civilisations, XXVIII,
    1/2 (1978), pp. 31-51
Paige, Glenn (ed.), Political Leadership: Readings
    for a New Field. Free Press, New York, 1972
Pennock, J. Roland. "Political Development, Political
    Systems and Political Goods", World Politics,
    18, 3 (April 1966), pp. 415-34
Roth, Guenther. "Personal Rulership, Patrimonialism
    and Empire Building in the New States", World
    Politics, 20, 2 (January 1968), pp. 194-206
Rothchild, Donald and Curry, Robert. Scarcity, Choice
    and Public Policy in Middle Africa. University
    of California Press, Berkeley, 1978
Rustow, Dankwart (ed.), Philosophers and Kings:
    Studies in Leadership. Braziller, New York, 1970
Searing, D.D. "Models and images of man and society
    in leadership theory", Journal of Politics, 31,
    1 (February 1969), pp. 3-31
Stodgill, Ralph M. (ed.), Handbook of Leadership: A
    Survey of Theory and Research. Free Press, New
    York, 1974

Tsurutani, Taketsugu. The Politics of National Devel-
    opment: Political Leadership in Transitional
    Societies. Chandler, New York, 1973
    _____. "Political Leadership: Some Tentative
    Thoughts from Early Meiji Japan", Journal of
    Political and Military Sociology, 1, 2 (1973),
    pp. 201-14
Tucker, Robert C. Politics and Leadership. Univer-
    sity of Missouri Press, Columbia, Mo., 1981
    _____. "Personality and Political Leadership", Poli-
    tical Science Quarterly, 92, 3 (Fall 1977)
    pp. 383-93
Welsh, W.A. "Methodological Problems in the Study of
    Political Leadership in Latin America", Latin
    American Research Review, 5, 3 (Fall 1970),
    pp. 3-33
Wiatr, Jerzy J. "Political Elites and Political
    Leadership", Indian Journal of Politics, 7, 2
    (1973), pp. 137-49
Wriggins, W. Howard. The Ruler's Imperative. Colum-
    bia University Press, New York, 1969

Guinea 206; exodus
from Uganda 247-8;
purges in Ethiopia 275
education: effects 10-12;
Ivory Coast 100, 111;
Senegal 147; Tanzania
156; Guinea 201; Ugan-
da 229; Ethiopia 259,
275
elections: Ghana 74, 75,
80, 81; Ivory Coast 100-
1, 114; Senegal 132,
144-5; Tanzania 166,
169, 175, 180, 182;
Guinea 197, 198-9;
Uganda 233, 234, 239
see also referendum
equality 8; and transfor-
mation strategy 65;
goal in Tanzania 170-4,
183; goal in Guinea 21
Eritrea 259, 266-7, 272,
273, 275
Ethiopian Church 256, 261,
262; unifying force
259; opposes reform 264
Ethiopian Peoples Revolu-
tionary Party (EPRP)
274
ethnic conflict 15-6; as
constraint on leader
28; Ghana 81; lack of
in Tanzania 156-7;
Guinea 200, 210, 213;
Uganda 226, 231-2, 238-
9, 240; Ethiopia 266-7

farmers 12, 30, 41-2, 61;
Ghana 88-90; Ivory
Coast 112-3; Senegal
129, 143; Tanzania 158-
9, 162, 178, 182-3; see
also agriculture, pea-
nuts, peasants
force see coercion
foreign investment 55;
constraint on leader 32;
Ghana experience 75, 78,
85, 86, 90; Ivory Coast
104, 105, 109; Uganda
243

France: policy toward
French West Africa 137;
plots against Guinea
206-7 see also de Gaulle
French presence: Ivory
Coast 97, 99, 101, 104,
111; Senegal 131, 135-
6, 137, 147-8; removed
from Guinea 199, 202
French West African Fed-
eration: French under-
mine 107, 137-8
Fula 69, 198, 200, 210;
alleged plot against
Touré 207-8

Gbedemah, Komla 81, 90,
293
Ghana: economic strate-
gies 59, 66, 75-6;
resources 27, 60, 72,
73; attitudes 71-3,
82; aids Guinea 200
goals for leaders 33,
160, 161, 168, 211,
283
Gueye Lamine 132, 133,
134, 136, 138, 139,
212
Guinea 30, 50, 107, 108,
109, 136, 137, 193ff;
development strategy
59; social indicators
67-9; relations with
Western investors 198,
209

Haile Selassie, Emperor
38, 220, 256, 262ff;
as broker 257, 283;
conflicts with nobili-
ty 256-7; style of
control, 262-3; deposed
272; why fell 275-6
Houphouet-Boigny, Felix
36, 43, 45, 97ff, 212;
goals 34-5, 102, 104;
basis of support 37,
102, 119
ideology 33; in Guinea
220-1; irrelevance in

Uganda 242; in Ethiopian revolution 277
independence, negotiated 51; unifying force in Ghana 84-5; illegitimate in French colonies 119
indigenization 35, 120; Houphouet-Boigny opposes 112; Senegal 131, 137, 141-2; Guinea 202
industrialization: as development strategy 59, 76, 85, 216
investissement humain 203-5
Ivory Coast: economy 13, 14, 59, 60, 96ff; growth rates 104; attracts other Africans 117; lacks participation 114-5, 120; opposition to federation 107; conflict with Guinea 207

Kabaka, Sir Frederick Mutesa II 230, 235, 245; removed as Head of State 237
Kabaka Yekka 233-5, 237
Kambona, Oscar 164-5
Kawawa, Rashidi 164, 168
killing of opponents: Ghana 82; Guinea 207-8, 210; Uganda 246, 247; Ethiopia 273, 275

land reform, Ethiopia: blocked 265, 271; revolution and 273, 275, 276-7
land tenure: colonial threat in Tanganyika 159; Ethiopia 259-61, 264-5
Langi 232, 240; killed by Amin's men 244, 248

leader: defined 20; types 49, 283, 295; external constraints on, 23-32, 51-2, 282-3, 297-8; attitudes and values 2, 5, 13, 33-6, 76, 214, 288-9; styles 38-9; qualities for success 29, 37-8, 62, 292-3; use of power 23, 54, 57, 285-92
leadership 22, 298; defined 21; heroic stature 19-20, 84, 101-2; needed for transformation strategy 65-6
Leadership Code 170
Mali Federation: independence 108; break-up 138-9
marabouts 130-1, 143; political power 135, 142, 146-7
Mengistu Haile Mariam, Maj. 5, 270, 273ff
Murids 130, 134
Muslim brotherhoods 129-31

national integration: effect of accommodation and transformation strategies 67-9
nationalist movements 45-9, 101, 165; goals 43-4, 45; ease of coming to power 49-51; Ghana 73-5, 83-5; Ivory Coast 99-104, 118-20; Senegal 133-5, 148-9; Tanzania, 158-61; Guinea 196-8, 212-8; Uganda 230, 231
Nkrumah, Kwame 1, 38, 44, 50, 52, 71ff, 222; political appeal 74, 80, 102; turn to coercion 75; loss of support 79, 87-8; motives for economic

296; compared with
accomodation 67-9;
failure in Ghana 83,
84, 91; obstacles in
Guinea 193, 211, 216-
8; Obote shift to
238-9